SOCIAL ENTREPRENEURSHIP

Social Entrepreneurship: Theory and Practice is about the creative ways in which social entrepreneurs solve pressing and insurmountable social problems. Theories of social change are presented to help demystify the "magic" of making an immense, yet durable and irreversible social impact. Utilizing case studies drawn from various fields and all over the world, the authors document how social entrepreneurs foster bottom-up change that empowers people and societies. They also review the specific personality traits of social entrepreneurs and introduce the new kind of leadership they represent. This book will be valuable to undergraduate, graduate, and postgraduate students while remaining accessible to nonacademic readers thanks to its clear language, illustrative case studies, and guidelines on how to become a successful social entrepreneur.

Ryszard Praszkier, Ph.D., is a researcher at the University of Warsaw Complex Systems Research Center. His main field of interest involves the mechanisms of profound peaceful transitions, including social-change processes facilitated by social entrepreneurs, with a special focus on the role and properties of social networks supporting durable social change. Dr. Praszkier has authored several academic publications in that field. For more than fifteen years, he has worked for Ashoka: Innovators for the Public, an international association that promotes social entrepreneurship in more than seventy countries.

Andrzej Nowak, Ph.D., is a professor and lecturer at the Warsaw School of Social Sciences and Humanities (where he is the cofounder of the Institute of Social Psychology of the Internet and Communication), Florida Atlantic University, University of Warsaw (where he is the cofounder of the Institute for Social Studies and a founding director of the Complex Systems Research Center), and Columbia University in New York. Dr. Nowak has written and contributed to a number of foundational theoretical books, monographs, and articles in the fields of social psychology, dynamical social impact, social networks, and the dynamics of societal transition.

Social Entrepreneurship

THEORY AND PRACTICE

Ryszard Praszkier
University of Warsaw and Ashoka

Andrzej Nowak
Warsaw School of Social Sciences and Humanities

CAMBRIDGE
UNIVERSITY PRESS

727126742

CAMBRIDGE UNIVERSITY PRESS
Cambridge, New York, Melbourne, Madrid, Cape Town,
Singapore, São Paulo, Delhi, Mexico City

Cambridge University Press
32 Avenue of the Americas, New York, NY 10013-2473, USA

www.cambridge.org
Information on this title: www.cambridge.org/9780521149785

© Ryszard Praszkier and Andrzej Nowak 2012

First published 2012
Reprinted 2012

A catalog record for this publication is available from the British Library.

Library of Congress Cataloging in Publication Data

Praszkier, Ryszard, 1945–
Social entrepreneurship : theory and practice / Ryszard Praszkier, Andrzej Nowak.
  p. cm.
Includes bibliographical references and index.
ISBN 978-0-521-76731-6 (hardback)
1. Social entrepreneurship. I. Nowak, Andrzej (Andrzej Krzysztof) II. Title.
HD60.P727 2011
361.7´65068 – dc23   2011021238

ISBN 978-0-521-76731-6 Hardback
ISBN 978-0-521-14978-5 Paperback

CONTENTS

v

LIST OF FIGURES

LIST OF PHOTOS

PREFACE

We usually assume that big social changes require huge resources and investments. There are, however, situations in which large-scale, systemic, and durable social changes have been introduced by individuals who initially have no resources other than their social passion, creativity, and entrepreneurial frame of mind; we can say that, in a way, they create "something out of nothing." Those individuals are called social entrepreneurs, and this book is devoted to portraying and analyzing the specific "magic" of their approach.

Indeed, there is something intriguing about the phenomenon of social entrepreneurship and those who practice it. These unique individuals usually address, mostly with great success, seemingly unsolvable social problems, and in so doing, not only manage to motivate the key players and influence people's mindsets, but also generate a huge impact on the social landscape. They often trigger a bottom-up process, a sort of chain of change, involving and empowering society as a whole.

Peter Drucker (Gendron, 1966, p. 37) captured this social-value creation process in these words: "The social entrepreneur changes the performance capacity of society," meaning that the impact of social entrepreneurship exceeds by far the entrepreneurs' specific areas of interest (e.g., disabilities, education, women's issues, or the environment) by empowering societies to enhance their overall performance.

It is hence understandable that there is an increasing interest in the field of social entrepreneurship among academics and social activists (Leadbeater, 1997; Gentile, 2002; Steyaert & Hjorth, 2006) as well as among many in the private sector (Brinckerhoff, 2000; Martin, 2007). According to Mair, Robinson, and Hockerts (2006, p. 1), "in the past decade 'social entrepreneurship' has made a popular name for itself on the global scene as a 'new phenomenon' that is reshaping the way we think about social-value creation." Also, Kramer (2005) says that in recent years, the term "social entrepreneur" has sparked the interest of major foundations and private funders, spreading rapidly throughout the nonprofit sector.

Who are they? What is actually so remarkable about their approach? How do they do it? They seem different from all the other related groups: social activists, corporate social responsibility managers, and professional innovators (Bornstein & Davis, 2010). How do we identify this difference? These probing questions – and the thought-provoking answers to them – are the core motivations for writing this book. Perhaps the best point of departure is to recount the fascinating story of one passionate and multi-talented individual who, more than three hundred years ago, was determined to alter the status quo; in so doing, he brought genuine, far-reaching change to American society.

When the United States of America was still a collection of thirteen colonies, there was a young man who couldn't accept the reality that books were a rarity in the "New World" and that reading skills were nearly nonexistent. He was convinced of the power of widespread literacy to bring people together and as a result to be a significant force for social change. When he was as young as fifteen and working at his brother's printing house, he was writing letters to the editor of a local newspaper; because of his young age, however, they were never published. Undaunted, his strong drive to communicate with the public led him to pose as a middle-aged widow, using a pseudonym for a signature; those letters were published, and enthusiastic responses from readers ensued in the form of lively discussions and the further sharing and dissemination of ideas. The impact on society was tangible and confirmed his belief in the value of writing, reading, discussing, and sharing.

Eventually, his masquerade was exposed, and he was forced to leave his job. Without any viable means of support, he moved to the new city of Philadelphia. He could not let go of his profound conviction that communicating through writing was the most powerful vehicle for effecting change, and he was determined to do something big and meaningful to implement this idea.

However, confronted with the reality that there was not, as he had hoped, widespread interest in the pursuit of ideas and intellectual ferment, he came to the conclusion that his first challenge had to be finding a way to increase literacy, to instill in the population a love for books, and – most importantly – to stimulate intellectual activities. Finally, in 1727 at the age of 21, he founded the Junto (defined by Merriam-Webster as "a group of persons joined for a common purpose"), which was devoted to self-improvement, serving the public good, and intellectual inquiry. They purchased from England books and other reading materials, which at the time were rare commodities. He inspired the members of the Junto to establish a free lending library – the first in America. Democratic in nature, and created by and for the community of subscribers, with the books chosen because they would be mutually beneficial to the shareholder members, this completely new idea revolutionized the act of reading and sparked a significant movement around discussing books. Within a few years' time, the charter of the Library Company of Philadelphia was established. To this day, it is known as a world-class research library specializing in American history and culture from the seventeenth through the nineteenth centuries. By leading Junto, this young, shall we say, social entrepreneur had triggered the process and eventual growth of intellectual development, which ultimately had a significant impact on a wider swath of society in Philadelphia. He eventually expanded Junto to all the other colonies by organizing the American Philosophical Society (still active and vibrant).[1] Obviously, the institution of the lending library has also survived.

This remarkable man was none other than Founding Father, author, publisher, inventor, scientist, political leader, signer of the Declaration of Independence, elder statesman, philosopher, and perhaps America's first "Renaissance man" Benjamin Franklin. So significant and wide ranging were his many contributions to society that Franklin can be considered a true force of nature. He was, for example, a natural innovator: He created the lightning rod, a new version of glass harmonica ("armonica"), the "Franklin stove," and bifocal glasses; he was also instrumental in improving the lighting of city streets. It is important to note that his fascination with innovations had a strong social component: he wrote that his scientific works were to be used for the improvement of human life.

For example, he coined and initiated the idea of "pay it forward" – the legal concept that a good turn be repaid by performing a good turn to others; through this legal innovation, payment could be channeled to a third party that might in turn use it to meet some social need. In addition, through Junto he established volunteer fire brigades, the first public hospital, and police departments, and he introduced paved streets. He was also the founder of the University of Pennsylvania.

Indeed, his social passion and myriad innovations contributed immensely to the human cultural capital (a term that would be coined three centuries later). The Junto club, together with the subscription library,

[1] See http://www.amphilsoc.org/.

comprised several layers of social innovation: according to Mumford (2002), the first layer was the direct and cumulative effect of the innovation; at a deeper level, the initial pooling of books within the club served as an informal demonstration of how, with the application of creative thinking, enterprises could be mutually reinforced. This model, if expanded, could generate social innovations and cultural capital in American society.

Whereas Franklin's narrative is extraordinary, owing especially to the scope of his contributions to American culture and to the political circumstances of the time, many other social entrepreneurs deserve our consideration. For example, the winner of the 2006 Nobel Peace Prize, Mohammad Yunus, proved that in Bangladesh, one of the poorest countries in the world, social innovations can transform lives even in communities where hopes for a better life are quite modest if not nonexistent. Mohammad Yunus and his Grameen Bank, with the tagline "banking for the poor," offers micro credits to poor women in the form of revolving loans, which enable them to launch their own small business ventures. Conceived in 1976, the program has resulted in a global proliferation of similar enterprises in rural areas, changing the lives of millions and spreading the microfinance system throughout the world and ultimately empowering the poorest of the poor.

We can point to numerous such cutting-edge social innovations, and we observe that behind nearly every one of them usually stand visionary individuals whose passion, commitment, innovativeness, and entrepreneurial spirit lead them to devise and spread solutions to seemingly insurmountable social problems (Bornstein, 2004). In so doing, they often trigger a ripple effect, a phenomenon that seems to distinguish them from other great leaders and innovators, including social activists, business entrepreneurs, and professional innovators. Grasping this difference is the fundamental challenge of this book.

One of the reasons behind the popularity of social entrepreneurship is that there's something inherently interesting and appealing about entrepreneurs and the stories of why and how they do what they do; after all, these extraordinary people come up with brilliant ideas and against all odds succeed at creating new solutions that improve people's lives (Martin & Osberg, 2007).

The fascination with the stories of social entrepreneurs who are finding solutions for seemingly unsolvable problems seems absolutely natural: there is probably no better way to demonstrate the nuts and bolts of this phenomenon than through following the concrete paths of their process – their thinking, probing, learning by failures, finding new solutions, and spreading what worked – often against all odds, not the least of which is dealing with the rigidity of the existing structures they face. Nicholls & Cho (2008) point out that in the literature on social entrepreneurship the main focus is on specific examples of innovative praxis, often underpinned by profiles of "hero" social entrepreneurs. Perhaps this is to be expected, thanks to the immense diversity of those stories. They differ (1) by field (women's issues, renewable sources of energy, environmental protection, working for peace, rural development, combating trafficking, and education, to name a few); (2) by location (saving the endangered culture of high Himalaya mountain settlements, rural community development in post-communist countries, instituting education for girls in the nomadic Maasai tribes in Tanzania, bringing modern technology to children in the Brazilian *favelas*, protecting the rainforest in British Columbia, combating child trafficking in Asia, and more); and (3) by social entrepreneurs' status and cultural backgrounds (educated or uneducated, financially comfortable or extremely poor, able-bodied or physically challenged, age, and gender). Those stories also differ in the available resources and methods used in the concrete circumstances they faced. This diversity both adds to and detracts from the possibility of succeeding in our venture.

On the plus side, these cases are compelling, colorful, often close to "magic" as they reveal how, in seemingly hopeless situations and starting with nothing, those special individuals find brilliant solutions – solutions that begin with the process of creating "something out of nothing," and that "something" gradually revolutionizes the whole field. The negative side, however, is that a distant and neutral position in analyzing these remarkable cases can pose a significant challenge. This challenge is another reason for writing this book. It represents the attempt to create a solid theoretical background; to identify the key factors that render the change lasting and irreversible; to identify the specific personality traits that facilitate the process; to grasp the dynamics of social change initiated by social entrepreneurs; and finally, to provide a roadmap for others who might want to become social entrepreneurs.

We thought that the solution would be the combination of the conceptual path with the case studies, the theory with practice – and that is the rationale behind the title of this book. The idea for writing it came to us when we became convinced that in this diverse and complex field we had identified some invariable principles. The blend of the authors' practical and theoretical experiences was a crucial factor in the discovery of those invariable principles common to social entrepreneurs.

It is worth mentioning that all the cases described in this book are based on in-person and in-depth interviews evaluating candidates for acceptance

as Fellows by Ashoka: Innovators for the Public; the interviews were conducted by one of the authors, Ryszard Praszkier (for the description of those
interviews, see Chapter 3). The criteria for selecting cases for this book are
mostly based on those personal interviews, and we are glad to present social
entrepreneurs from Africa, the Americas, Asia, and Europe. Unfortunately,
the criteria didn't allow the inclusion of the equally meritorious contributions of many other outstanding social entrepreneurs.

FOR WHOM IS THIS BOOK INTENDED?

First, the intention is to fill a market gap by providing a suitable textbook for
graduate and postgraduate students, as well as for undergraduate seniors
who are especially interested in social entrepreneurship and social-change
theories and practice. As an academic textbook, it is also intended for social
scientists; for researchers in psychology, sociology, and the social and political sciences; and for students and professionals in management, business,
and public administration. Moreover, it will serve as a basic textbook for
use in courses on social entrepreneurship and social change offered in MBA
programs and business schools. The multiple inspirations from the case
studies, as well as from the analyses of social change, are equally applica-
ble to the social-service and business sectors, both of which can be serious
launch pads for effecting social change. For the latter case – the business
sector that is socially conscious – it is thought to be a canonical textbook
for training in corporate social responsibility. Finally, the social sector will
benefit from useful information on the methodology of introducing social
change.

   The book takes the reader from the classical definitions of social
entrepreneurship through a framework of five pivotal dimensions shaped
into a syndromic concept of this phenomenon, followed by a summary of the
various academic and theoretical approaches to social change: sociological,
psychological, Hellenistic philosophy, complexity theory, social networks,
and social capital theories. Then the research is presented. This confirms
that social entrepreneurs facilitate durable, irreversible, bottom-up social-
change processes, which prompts us to ask several questions: How do they
do it? What personality traits are inevitable for fostering these sorts of
change processes? What kind of leadership is involved? The book concludes
with a new, dynamical delineation of social entrepreneurship, followed by
some reflections on manifestations of this phenomenon in the past as well as
predictions for the future. Finally, in a few appendices (following the title's

promise to cover both theory and practice), the focus is on the practical side.

Section I introduces the phenomenon of social entrepreneurship by presenting two cases that provide a sense of the social entrepreneur's reality. Chapter 1 presents the existing definitions of social entrepreneurship. Chapter 2 introduces its critical dimensions. Chapter 3 contemplates the practical aspects of identifying and distinguishing social entrepreneurs from other social activists.

Section II describes the dynamics of social change. Chapter 4 provides an overview of social-change theories. Chapter 5 introduces complexity theory and the dynamical systems approach in relation to social change. Chapter 6 recounts the social-emergence theory.

Section III focuses on the social capital built by social entrepreneurs. A closer view of the concept of social capital and social networks is provided in Chapters 7 and 8. In Chapter 9, we explore the personality traits that facilitate the process of building social capital.

Section IV explores the unique kind of leadership demonstrated by social entrepreneurs. In Chapter 10, basing our presentation on the dynamical systems theory, a new description of social entrepreneurship emerges; as a consequence, we introduce the new kind of leadership that is beginning to materialize (Chapter 11). In Chapter 12, the reader will get to witness this kind of leadership in practice, displaying the innovative ways social entrepreneurs address insurmountable and intractable social problems and conflict situations.

The Epilogue presents examples of social entrepreneurship from the past and mentions some possible future trends. The Conclusion recaps what has been accomplished in this book. Some recommendations on how to become a social entrepreneur are presented in Appendix 1. Appendices 2 and 3 illustrate the applications of the criteria for social entrepreneurship in practice.

ACKNOWLEDGMENTS

First and foremost, we want to express our deepest gratitude to social entrepreneurs, who are the core source of knowledge for this book. Listening to their reflections, exchanging ideas with them, site-visiting their programs, and absorbing/internalizing their style of thinking and the elegant way they solve problems – all of this, and more, were indispensable to achieving this work.

This book has benefited greatly from the inspiration of William Drayton, Ashoka founder and CEO, who probably doesn't even realize how meaningful his comments were during professional discourses and how much they sowed the ideas used herein.

Discussions with many other Ashoka staff and board members and friends have been helpful in shaping some of the ideas. We especially want to thank William Carter, Celia Cruz, Carol Grodzins, Roger Harrison, Paul Herman, Ewa Konczal, Shawn MacDonald, Lucy Perkins, Beverly Schwartz, Diana Wells, and many other friends.

The fruitful discussions with the academic group from the Complex Systems Research Center[1] helped us to sharpen some ideas. In this regard, we especially acknowledge the contribution of Agata Zablocka-Bursa, who coauthored some of the questionnaires cited in this book and whose field research confirmed some of the conjectures about networks.

It is a pleasure to thank friends who have been critically important advisers throughout this endeavor. In particular, we note the invaluable mentorship of Dr. Zbigniew "Bish" Turlej, a physicist and business analyst whose healthy skepticism kept us on track and in particular helped us avoid confusion in describing the functioning of social networks and

---

[1] See http://www.complexsystems.edu.pl.

the telecommunication systems. We also thank Shawn MacDonald, Paul Herman, and David Brée for their thoughtful comments and feedback.

Our work was supported by the Future and Emerging Technologies Program FP7-COSI-ICT, EU Commission, Project QLectives, grant No. 231200.

Finally, our profound thanks to the editor, Maxine Gold, to whom we owe a debt of gratitude for her editorial skills and her significant comments and suggestions, which have added immeasurably to the final shape of this publication.

SECTION I

SOCIAL ENTREPRENEURSHIP

INTRODUCTION

There are certain kinds of people who garner enormous satisfaction from successfully taking on a "mission impossible" and, by so doing, actually manage to change the world, sometimes in surprising ways. Such individuals are rare, and when we become aware of them and their astonishing achievements, we observe that they cannot easily be pigeonholed or defined by their own circumstances. That is to say, they are the products of rural as well as urban areas; of developing as well as developed countries; of large cities as well as remote areas; they may be Gurkhas from the Himalayan Mountains or Maasais from East Africa. They may be well-known figures, such as Mohammad Yunus, recipient of the 2006 Nobel Peace Prize, or anonymous, unrecognized teachers from small villages.

The question then becomes: If they are such a diverse group, what characteristics do they have in common that allow us to identify them under one unifying rubric? Which of these shared attributes distinguish them from other social activists? These are the underlying questions that inform the book.

In this section, we will introduce the concepts of social entrepreneurship. As a departure point, we will present two cases that illustrate how one single social entrepreneur's individual passion, commitment, creativity, and entrepreneurial spirit can change an entire country or field of endeavor.

Munir Hasan, Bangladesh: Enhancing the value of mathematics in Bangladesh and bringing youth to International Mathematical Olympiads

Munir Hasan, a Bangladeshi who had always dreamed of turning his country – a place where the general population is not known for possessing

PICTURE 1. Mathematics Festival, Q&A session with the teachers

a significant mastery of the field of mathematics – into a nation of world-class, advanced mathematicians who, under his leadership, would eventually represent the country at the International Mathematical Olympiads.[1] This idea came to Munir Hasan when he was a young university employee. He began his research by talking to those he identified as key players – teachers, parents, students, school authorities – and met with significant resistance. None of his interlocutors saw the value in improving and/or championing the teaching of mathematics. This lack of interest was not limited to the educational community but was echoed in the publishing houses, which refused to produce math textbooks, citing their lack of profitability. Facing the dual failure of his attempts to motivate people by approaching them directly, and of the top-down governmental programs, Munir Hasan continued to grapple with the challenge of how to generate an interest in mathematics, a subject that virtually nobody wanted to study.

Munir Hasan's innovative solution took a U-turn from his original approach, which was forcing the study of mathematics on less-than-willing students and teachers. Instead, he decided to treat the issue as if it were a team sport. He instituted mathematics festivals, known as the Bangladesh Mathematics Olympiad, where students would enjoy competing in regional and

[1] See http://www.ashoka.org/mhasan

PICTURE 2. The joy of the Mathematics Festival

national contests. On the day before the actual challenge, students would meet, play, and sing. The following day, they would freely discuss math problems with teachers – a completely new development in the postcolonial authoritarian school system. The festive atmosphere motivated students, teachers, and the local governments, who saw an excellent opportunity for coverage by the media. These developments, in a feedback loop, engaged parents and school principals as well as potential donors to educational programs.

The idea soon caught on throughout the country, as other schools also wanted to have their own festivals. Munir Hasan then turned his attention to the general public and convinced some leading daily newspapers to publish clever mathematical riddles, which triggered enormous interest. In a few months, the riddles section grew large enough to earn its own stand-alone insert.

In a few years, Bangladesh became saturated with interest in mathematics, as increasing numbers of schools and communities started to push for participation in math olympiads on all educational levels; moreover, teachers of other subjects (for example biology) launched their own discipline-specific festivals and olympiad movements. The math textbook business was now booming because of the growing market demand, and math riddles became a regular feature in the print media. Munir also initiated a teachers'

PICTURE 3. Munir Hasan at the Mathematics Festival

organization, so that school teachers, through a self-help movement, could develop their math-teaching skills to much higher standards. Similarly, a university student volunteering organization was helping with the ground operations of festivals and olympiads.

These new developments eventually transformed the entire educational system, and finally, Munir Hasan realized his dream: Bangladesh had become a participant in the International Mathematics Olympiad.[2] In fact, two Bangladeshi students brought home bronze medals from the 2009 International Mathematics Olympiad held in Bremen, Germany.

Steve Bigari, USA: Empowering disadvantaged citizens to successfully pursue their professional careers

The Colorado Springs, Colorado, McDonald's enterprises were facing a serious problem – a high rate of absenteeism among newly hired low-income workers, owing to their difficulties dealing with the considerable obstacles in their personal lives. This state of affairs usually engendered a constant – and costly – cycle of staff turnover and, for the jobless workers and their families, the economic strains of recurring unemployment; such instability often affected the children, who were prone to becoming school dropouts

[2] See http://www.matholympiad.org.bd

and to pursuing drug- and crime-ridden lives. Understandably, attempts to convince employers to retain low-income workers were met with negative responses: "What? I have received too many calls from this guy saying that he is not coming to work because his car has broken down or his kid is sick!" For the employers, this scenario and others like it occurred so frequently that such reactions became the norm and were treated as routine.

Observing this recurrent pattern, Steve Bigari,[3] a highly valued and promising franchisee at McDonald's, resolved to change it in a way that both the employers and the workers would benefit. He refused to accept the notion that because low-income workers have such scant resources and poor coping skills, they see no other way out but to simply leave their workplace, the dire consequences of which he observed firsthand. On the other hand, as a manager he was acutely aware of how much money was being wasted on constantly acquiring and training new staff.

Initially, he met with stiff opposition among his friends and colleagues. "Steve, give up," they would say. It always has been like that; low-income workers will always drop out, and nothing you do will change that." Undaunted, he took it on himself to research the problem and to reverse it by making a U-turn at the initial high-potential-conflict situation. He totally modified the way the workers were handled when they called in and reported problems. When someone called in saying she/he could not report to work because of car issues, for example, the call was transferred to the top manager. The latter, seeing the situation as a great opportunity to turn things around, would tell the employee that he was going to send someone right away to help fix the problem; as a bonus, the employee would be taught how to deal with such a problem in the future. Similarly, when someone called in sick, Steve Bigari turned this into a positive learning opportunity, having devised a network of local nongovernmental organizations "social-emergency systems" to train people to handle such situations. He also made deals with car repair shops, arranging discounts for low-income workers. The major change, however, was in the radical reversal of the way the manager responded to the calls.

The results of these sharp shifts in behavior were two-pronged: first, the workers easily adopted the new coping techniques, and the absentee rate rapidly decreased; second, the long-term retention of staff resulted in increased profits for the firm. The win-win strategy motivated others in the organization to pursue this approach. A more far-reaching result was that many of those who were, as Steve Bigari put it, "one crisis away

---

[3] See http://www.ashoka.org/fellow/3170

PICTURE 4. Steve Bigari

from dropping out," became valued managers and advanced rapidly. The relatively small amount of positive reinforcement provided at the beginning of their employment, plus minimal training, were enough to spur on these employees to study and advance professionally. In the end, they became the company's most loyal and dedicated staff members.

As a manager, Steve Bigari was able to demonstrate the positive financial results of such an approach and encouraged many other firms in the U.S. to duplicate this system. With employers taking a lead role in addressing the problems that contribute to workers' vulnerability, the cycle of persistent poverty was broken. They helped employees to achieve personal stability and to develop the skills they needed to get a foothold on the ladder to the middle class. Steve Bigari initiated a totally new approach by turning failures, which previously were arguments for firing the employees, into opportunities for learning and growth.

This valuable entrepreneur has since founded a nonprofit organization, America's Family,[4] and has created an innovative plan to provide health care

_____

[4] See http://www.amfol.com/

PICTURE 5. Training session at America's Family

coverage to low-wage workers. He persuaded Community Health Centers, a provider of high-cost emergency care, to create the Healthy Workforce program, with an emphasis on disease prevention and health education. To pay for the program, he instituted a payroll-deduction/employer-match system. In this way, employees gained access to affordable health care, while Community Health Centers gained a new source of revenue. Furthermore, because the Community Health Centers program emphasizes prevention and health maintenance, it dramatically lowers workers' dependence on costly emergency services.

Through their work with Steve and his organization, hundreds of workers are able to obtain computers, affordable child care and housing, reliable transportation, and online access to education. Clients of America's Family can purchase low-cost computers through a payroll-deduction program; they receive their computers by paying 50 percent of the cost and get free Internet service as a bonus. America's Family recently partnered with citizen groups and a government housing provider to create a 100-unit hotel that provides its clients with low-cost transitional housing. America's Family also works with car dealers and banks to help employees establish credit and qualify for loans, and trains employees to manage these loans through an online course on personal finance. By 2006, 100 percent of the 1,200 clients of America's Family had access to affordable housing, child care, cars, and e-mail. Many have progressed from subsidized to private health insurance. After a year under the America's Family program, the profits in four companies increased by $300,000. Turnover rates were 63 percent lower after one year and an additional 29 percent lower after two years. America's Family has already expanded from Colorado Springs, Colorado, to Dallas, Texas, and is now launching programs in Denver, Colorado.

These inspiring and fascinating stories of social entrepreneurs and many others like them lead one to wonder how these individuals manage to achieve such remarkable results. What are the methods and the traits that distinguish these change agents from other outstanding social leaders? What terms can best describe their unique approach?

In the next three chapters, we will address these questions. In Chapter 1, we will present a review of the existing definitions of social entrepreneurship, showing how they can be applied to the cases of Munir Hasan and Steve Bigari. In Chapter 2, drawing from those definitions, we will introduce the concept of five pivotal dimensions of social entrepreneurship. Chapter 3 will contemplate the practical aspects of identifying and distinguishing what makes a social entrepreneur.

1

Defining Social Entrepreneurship: An Overview

One of the classical definitions of social entrepreneurship and the social entrepreneur is provided by Dees (1998), who says that social entrepreneurs play the role of change agents in the social sector by:

- adopting a mission to create and sustain social value (not just private value)
- recognizing and relentlessly pursuing new opportunities to serve that mission
- engaging in a process of continuous innovation, adaptation, and learning
- acting boldly without being limited by resources currently at hand,
- exhibiting a heightened sense of accountability to the constituencies served and for the outcomes created

When we consider the cases of Munir Hasan and Steve Bigari, there can be no doubt that both acted as change agents; that they were committed to a social mission and they relentlessly were searching for, recognizing, and pursuing new opportunities to serve that mission; that they were engaged in a process of continuous learning (often prompted by failures) and innovation; and that they acted boldly against all odds, with limited resources (especially in Munir's case).

Still keeping in mind these two cases, let's explore some other definitions. Martin and Osberg (2007) see social entrepreneurs as those who:

- target underserved, neglected, or highly disadvantaged populations (Munir targeted the educational system; Steve targeted low-income workers.)
- aim at large-scale, transformational benefits that accrue either to a significant segment of society or to society at large (Munir changed

the whole educational system related to teaching mathematics, as well as the related societal mindsets; Steve coordinated the career paths and life cycles of low-income workers with the interests of employers.)

Most definitions of social entrepreneurs emphasize the innovative character of their initiative (Alvord et al., 2004). Munir changed mindsets through festivals, whereas Steve totally reversed the way low-income workers were treated and used their failures and problems as learning opportunities.

Finally, we see that Munir and Steve also meet Bornstein's (1998) characterizations of social entrepreneurs. He states that social entrepreneurs:

- open new possibilities by introducing innovative ideas
- combine visions with down-to-earth realism
- are creative and highly ethical problem solvers
- exhibit a total commitment to their ideas of social change

THE ASHOKA DEFINITION

Ashoka: Innovators for the Public, a citizen-sector organization, identifies and supports leading social entrepreneurs who are considered to be engines of social change and role models for the citizen sector, and helps them to achieve maximum social impact.[1] Ashoka's Founding CEO, William (Bill) Drayton, is credited with having coined the term "social entrepreneurship" (Hsu, 2005; Sen, 2007). Moreover, the special role of Bill Drayton and his organization has been widely noted in the media.

In 2005, Drayton was named by *US News & World Report* as one of "America's 25 Best Leaders," and in 2009 the Center for the Advancement of Social Entrepreneurship (CASE) honored him with the CASE Leadership in Social Entrepreneurship Award.[2] An article in the October 16, 2009, edition of the *Washington Post* titled "A Nobel Prize For Leadership?" states, "In our era, the father of social entrepreneurship is Bill Drayton, who began Ashoka 30 years ago. Drayton merits the new Nobel leadership award."[3]

Bornstein (2004) considers the Ashoka definition of social entrepreneurship the most comprehensive; according to Ashoka (2000), social entrepreneurs can produce small changes in the short term that reverberate through existing systems, ultimately effecting significant change in the

---

[1] See http://www.ashoka.org.
[2] See http://www.caseatduke.org/events/leadershipaward/07winner/index.html.
[3] October 18, 2009. Available at http://www.washingtonpost.com/wp-dyn/content/article/2009/10/16/AR2009101603977.html.

longer term. The selection criteria for Ashoka fellows, according to Drayton (2002, 2005) and Hammonds (2005) are:

- having a new idea for solving a critical social problem
- being creative
- having an entrepreneurial personality
- envisioning the broad social impact of the idea
- possessing an unquestionable ethical fiber[4]

Ashoka elects its fellows through a rigorous, multistage process, as described in the brochure "Selecting Leading Social Entrepreneurs" (2007); these procedures have proved to be highly effective.[5]

All of the previously listed traits manifested simultaneously rarely can be found in one person. "It doesn't happen that often. There is only 1 social entrepreneur for every 10 million of the rest of us, according to calculations of Ashoka . . . Ashoka founder Bill Drayton bases his calculations on nearly 30 years' worth of seeking out the elusive combination of vision and passion that social entrepreneurs put into practice."[6]

The estimate of "1 in 10 million per year" may, however, be misleading: Obviously, there are many, many more excellent social innovators. In fact, Ashoka's mission is "everyone a change maker," reflecting the conviction that everyone can (and should) become a social innovator. The calculus stated here refers strictly to Ashoka's specific selection criteria, which prompt a short-listing of the outstanding social innovators. For example, many have new ideas and are creative and entrepreneurial, but they are satisfied with a small-scale impact and are not willing to expand to another level, which is one of the criteria set forth by Ashoka (see more on the selection process in Chapter 3).

It may also be helpful to enhance the definition with some of Bill Drayton's explanatory statements:

> "The core defining element is that they simply cannot come to rest . . . until their dream has become a new pattern across all of society," he says. "This is very different from everyone else: the scholar or the artist expresses an idea, and they're happy. The manager . . . make[s] the company work. The social worker, the professional help people . . . make their

---

[4] See Ashoka selection criteria explained: http://www.ashoka.org/support/criteria.

[5] See the results of measuring effectiveness at Ashoka: http://www.ashoka.org/impact/effectiveness.

[6] *Christian Science Monitor*, September 7, 2009. Retrieved 30 November 2010 from http://www.csmonitor.com/2009/0907/p02s05-lign.html.

lives better. None of that would remotely satisfy the social entrepreneur. *Their job is to change the system."*[7] (Praszkier and Nowak italics)

For the purposes of this book, we have adopted the Ashoka definition for social entrepreneurs and social entrepreneurship.

SOME REFLECTIONS ON THE DEFINITIONS

The multitude of definitions of social entrepreneurship is a testament to the growing interest in the subject. The emerging excitement surrounding this phenomenon is evident in the large number of definitions that are currently in use (Mair et al., 2006). However, this diversity reveals that "perhaps the largest obstacle in creating a conceptual framework for the entrepreneurship field has been its definition" (Shane & Venkataraman, 2000, p. 218).

The ways of articulating the wide range of features that characterize social entrepreneurship depend in large part on the perspective of the defining discipline: Some might relate to the inherent quality of innovation, some to the promise of social change, some to crucial personality characteristics, and still others to solving social problems. On the one hand, it is probably a positive dynamic that the act of defining social entrepreneurship has become an interdisciplinary exercise incorporating the fields of sociology, psychology, business, organizational development, social politics, and more; on the other hand, such multiplicity creates a challenge for developing a more unified framework. Nichols and Cho (2008), for example, are concerned that the main focus rests on specific examples of innovative praxis, often underpinned by profiles of "hero" social entrepreneurs. They indicate that such an approach has yet to offer much in the way of serious theoretical discourse, especially noting the lack of any sociological interpretation of this phenomenon. They see social entrepreneurship as still in the process of self-definition, being a young, evolving and undertheorized area of practice and research; Nichols & Cho conclude that the time has come to explore and develop a range of foundational concepts of social entrepreneurship.

The concept of social entrepreneurship means different things to different people: Some refer to social entrepreneurship as not-for-profit initiatives in search of alternative funding strategies, or management schemes to create social value, whereas others understand it as the socially responsible practice of commercial businesses engaged in cross-sector partnerships, and

---

[7] ibid.

still others see it as a means to alleviate social problems and effect social transformation (Mair & Martı, 2006).

The challenge for the next chapter is to grasp the kernel of all those definitions in a way that reveals the richness of their various components and categories.

CHAPTER HIGHLIGHTS

- Social entrepreneurs are among us, although they are rare; they are exceptionally successful in solving social problems, combining passion and visionary thinking with down-to-earth planning and strategizing; they merge social passion and business acumen.
- There are also many more social activists, innovators, and change makers who do not necessarily fit the narrow definition of social entrepreneurship; this is a growing movement, reflecting the human trend to take responsibility into one's own hands and change what is needed.
- The definition of social entrepreneurship implies that its practitioners come up with new ideas for solving pressing social problems and replacing old, ineffectual ones; they are creative and purposeful, determined to spread their ideas beyond their immediate circle; moreover, they are highly ethical.
- The concept of social entrepreneurship was coined by William (Bill) Drayton, the founder and CEO of the international association Ashoka: Innovators for the Public; this association, in existence since 1980, identifies, selects, and empowers social entrepreneurs from nearly seventy countries.

2

Dimensions of Social Entrepreneurship

The multiplicity of existing definitions and the variety of their components underscore a pressing need for sketching out a more comprehensive conceptual framework. In their efforts to arrive at a synthesis, several experts point to key components, such as: social and entrepreneurial qualities (Meir & Martı, 2006); entrepreneurs, ideas, opportunities, and organizations (Light, 2008); and sociality, innovation, and market orientation (Nichols & Cho, 2008).

This array of existing delineations indeed reveals that the concept of social entrepreneurship spans several diverse dimensions, each of which derives from different conceptual categories, resulting in the conclusion that there are undoubtedly several indispensable and pivotal dimensions involved. This assessment is also confirmed by the cases presented here, as well as by the practical experience of others in the field.

Take, for instance, social engagement and passion – factors that comprise a kind of social compass by which, in the course of their work, social entrepreneurs navigate obstacles, austerities, and, yes, even temptations. A solid social passion is definitely one of the requisite dimensions.

Another indispensable component is the element of innovation. Social entrepreneurs usually deal with extreme challenges in areas where traditional solutions have failed; they understand the need to find the right key that unlocks the door to new solutions. And "the right key" must be imbued with the kind of innovation and creativity that will forge a new path, a heretofore untraveled road.

However, for our purposes, innovation also needs to be sustainable for the long term. For example, one big, spectacular, amazing event could create a short-term impact, which, if not sustained, will result in a relapse. Thus, our key must not only fit the lock, but also be able to *keep* it open long enough to trigger a durable ripple effect, so that change can survive and expand.

At this point the question arises: How can we attract key players, motivate partners and stakeholders, and design a system out of mutually reinforcing elements? How can we make the capacity for innovation expand, grow, and influence the entire field? Here is where the unquestionable need for entrepreneurship – the next central component – enters the picture.

It is clear that only individuals with some specific personality characteristics are capable of pursuing and achieving these goals: They must be motivated to fulfill a social mission and to address critical and insurmountable social issues. Furthermore, they must be able to generate innovative solutions, foster a sustainable change process, and cause the idea to thrive and expand. This makes the personality another crucial component.

Finally, we have identified five pivotal dimensions that form the skeleton around which the concept of social entrepreneurship seems to be constructed:[1]

- social mission
- social innovation
- social change
- entrepreneurial spirit
- personality

The following is a closer look at these dimensions.

SOCIAL MISSION

Many authors emphasize that social mission is central to the social entrepreneur (Dees, 1998; Drayton, 2002; Bornstein, 2004; Roberts & Woods, 2005; Nichols, 2008). Actually, the notion of social mission can be found everywhere, in all circumstances – there seem to be no limits. Sometimes it surfaces in a traditional context, where nobody expects a new social approach to materialize. Such was the case with the aforementioned Mathematics Olympiads in Bangladesh: Everybody was more or less satisfied with the situation until Munir Hasan appeared with his vision for a "Mathematical Bangladesh." Similarly, at the Denver McDonald's, the relentless turnover of low-income workers was an obvious and unchangeable factor

---

[1] A methodological caveat: Those five dimensions are nonexclusive and form a sort of *syndromatic concept*, a term coined by S. Nowak (1985), indicating the coexistence and mutual interdependency of the elements of the definition.

for everybody, until Steve Bigari made retaining staff a social mission. In a Maasai nomadic, tribal, and male-dominated community, unexpectedly, a small girl, Ndinini Sikar from Tanzania, was determined to open up avenues for the education of Maasai girls and created a huge stir. In the Czech Republic, under the Communist regime, one could find a young teacher, Helena Balabánová, suddenly challenging the nightmarish education of Roma children.[2] In Pakistan, Arif Khan's social mission was to bring economic development to underserved communities living in remote mountainous areas of the country through raising traditional handicrafts produced by women in the region to a marketable level.[3] In Germany, where the energy production and distribution systems are well established and organized, Ursula Sladek is passionate about the idea of creating a new energy-cycle paradigm by shifting all aspects of energy management and production to the communities (for Ursula Sladek, see the Epilogue); such a move, she thinks, will foster energy-saving habits and also build new renewable energy sources.[4] The challenge of counteracting the expansion of fast-food consumption is taken up by Carlo Petrini, a native of Italy, who created Slow Food, an eco-gastronomic organization for preserving local food traditions and promoting good, clean, and enjoyable food.[5]

Case histories like these are legion, as social entrepreneurs are inevitably drawn by a powerful calling to tackle social issues, and in so doing they continuously see new opportunities and forge new pathways.

Alvord et al. (2004) define the challenge of solving social issues as the sustainable alleviation of the constellation of health, education, economic development, political, and cultural problems associated with long-term poverty.

Analyzing the literature and the scope of problems covered by social entrepreneurs, we propose a representative list of social topics at the heart of which there is a social problem that needs to be addressed:

- aging
- chemical dependency
- children with special needs
- disabilities
- discrimination against minorities
- education
- information and communication technologies (ICT) exclusion
- energy production and distribution

---

[2] http://www.ashoka.org/fellow/2895.   [3] http://www.ashoka.org/akhan.
[4] http://www.ashoka.org/usladek.   [5] http://www.ashoka.org/cpetrini.

- environment
- health
- homelessness
- peace and conflict resolution
- poverty
- rural community development sanitation
- street children
- sustainable energy
- trafficking of women and children
- unemployment
- women's equality

Obviously, the applicability of these issues will depend on differences in culture; moreover, over time, new problems may emerge while others may become irrelevant.

SOCIAL INNOVATION

The social entrepreneur generally enters the scene at the point when a situation seems protracted and intractable – in a word, insurmountable. These situations invariably call for a new approach, a new idea, a new strategy. And most authors (Dees, 1998; Drayton, 2002; Alvord et al., 2004; Bornstein, 2004; Roberts & Woods, 2005; Roper & Cheney, 2005; Martin & Osberg, 2007) indicate that innovation is the sine qua non of social entrepreneurship.

As we have seen, Munir Hasan transformed the dull and scary image of mathematics into lively, colorful festivals; Steve Bigari reversed the way low-income workers were treated and at the same time created educational opportunities for them.

Kramer (2005) says that inherent in the definition of the social entrepreneur is the ability to find a new way of doing things.

Probably the most insightful definition of social innovation is provided by Mulgan et al. (2008); simply put: "New ideas that work." They go on to say: "This differentiates innovation from improvement, which implies only incremental change; and from creativity and invention, which are vital to innovation but miss on the hard work of implementation and diffusion that makes promising ideas useful. Social innovation refers to new ideas that work in meeting social goals."

New ideas that work: Munir Hasan and Steve Bigari did not come upon their new ideas for the pure joy of discovery; rather, it was a demonstration of their unique and creative response to some extreme and, as we have said many times, seemingly intractable situations. Moreover, those ideas not only just "clicked," but also became levers in the long run, influencing their respective societies and effecting a durable impact.

This way of understanding social innovation dovetails with other definitions, such as that of Mumford (2002), who defines it as the generation and implementation of new ideas about how people should organize interpersonal activities, or social interactions, to meet one or more common goals.[6]

SOCIAL CHANGE

We decided that it was critical to separate the element of social innovation from that of social change, with the understanding that the former is the spark and the latter is its long-term and far-reaching consequence.

Change is recognized as an essential and indispensible factor for social entrepreneurship by many authors – Drucker (1985), Dees (1998), Roberts and Woods (2005), and Martin and Osberg (2007).

Furthermore, the secondary *consequences of change* can be more important than the initial change; moreover, the *consequences of consequences* often can play a crucial role in the way change proliferates over time (Rogers, 2003). There are numerous examples of promising change initiatives that eventually fizzle out; in fact, only approximately 20 percent of change attempts manage to survive (Senge, 1999). Moreover, in some cases, short-term or top-down change efforts can backfire if they are not based on a thorough, in-depth analysis of far-reaching consequences. For example, attempts from an external source to energize lethargic communities by organizing feel-good events may, in the short run, achieve a modicum of positive results. In the long run, however, such initiatives are bound to fail, leaving in their wake many frustrated people feeling abandoned, because there is nobody left to organize more events for them. For example, before one of the social entrepreneurs launched his program, some top-down projects were introduced, such as a series of lectures given by outside experts; however, this approach was perceived by the community as "preachy" and patronizing (see Kaz Jaworski's case opening Section 2).

---

[6] It is worth mentioning that the international organization Ashoka: Innovators for the Public adopts the notion of *New Ideas* as a new solution or approach to a social problem – one that will change the pattern in a field, be it human rights, the environment, or any other – as the basic criterion ("knock-out test") for selecting fellowship recipients for its program for social entrepreneurs; see http://www.ashoka.org/support/criteria.

Let's trace the chain of change that runs through the previously mentioned cases:

> Munir Hasan's social innovation was the concept of the mathematics festivals. The change sequence that followed, however, was more far-reaching, much deeper, and even more durable.

The dissemination in the press of information about the festivals and the publication of mathematical riddles attracted the attention of the Bangladeshi population in general to mathematics and changed their attitudes toward mathematics. This new interest also influenced teachers' attitudes, as they understood that mathematics could be a highway to their own promotion and advancement. The school authorities at all levels (local, provincial, and governmental) became strongly involved and supportive.

Open question-and-answer sessions also had a great impact on the teachers' attitudes, transforming their relationships with students from the rigid, postcolonial style to a more open, interactive approach.

The idea of the mathematics festivals spread to all school levels, including the primary grades, enhancing the schools' visibility. The concept of the festivals was also adopted by the teachers of other subjects, so that it became a more widespread factor in the field of education.

As a result, an independent teachers' organization has been launched, aimed at training and promoting the new teaching methods, with an emphasis on openness and partnership with students. Instructors learn modern methods of teaching mathematics while modernizing the educational system at the same time. The effect snowballs, as their colleagues are easily encouraged to follow their example. Out of this, another movement has developed independently: University students are now volunteering to become deeply involved in promoting the idea of "Mathematical Bangladesh."

Steve Bigari initiated a totally new approach by turning individual work-related failures, which previously constituted grounds for firing employees, into opportunities for learning and growth. By doing so, he brought dignity to low-income workers and increased their motivation to grow and be committed to their work. This initiative opened a new path to learning and advancement.

As a result, the workers easily adopted the coping techniques he introduced, and the absentee rate soon plummeted; the long-term retention of staff resulted in increased profits for the firm and motivated managers to pursue this approach.

A more far-reaching result was that many of those who were deemed "one crisis away from dropping out" became valued managers for the company and advanced rapidly. This approach created a radical shift in overall attitudes: The low-income workers perceived themselves as valued members of the working community; their self-esteem grew immensely, as did the motivation to learn and grow. The managers adopted a respectful way of treating low-income workers, which resulted in supportive and cooperative working relationships.

As this approach produces profit, it easily spreads to other corporations dealing with problems of high staff turnover among low-income workers. To facilitate this multiplier effect, Steve Bigari has founded a social venture, America's Family. Following the success at McDonald's, he created an innovative plan to offer affordable health care to low-wage workers, which included preventive care and health maintenance, thus dramatically lowering dependence on costly emergency services.

America's Family also provides low-income workers and their families with easy access to computers and online educational sites, affordable child care and housing, and reliable transportation. The organization also works with car dealers and banks to help employees establish credit and qualify for loans, and trains employees to manage these loans through an online course on personal finance. This new dignity-based paradigm for the employer-employee relationship is currently spreading to other companies and cities. The following quote is a perfect commentary on the special nature of the social entrepreneur: "There is an ambition among social entrepreneurs to achieve on a scale that most nonprofits never even imagine – not just to serve a local constituency, nor even to build a national organization, but to create lasting changes in behavior across an entire nation or even around the world, improving the lives of millions of people" (Kramer, 2005, p. 6).

One of the conclusions we can draw from these two narratives is that as meaningful change spreads and proliferates, it creates a kind of ripple effect. Drayton (2002, p. 123) has captured the essence of that process: "[I]nnovation usually comes in waves. A big, pattern-change innovation triggers years of follow-on change as the innovation is adapted to more and more social and economic sub-sectors and spreads geographically."

ENTREPRENEURIAL SPIRIT

An individual's level of entrepreneurial spirit is seen as an important component of social entrepreneurship (see Bornstein, 2004; Meir & Martı 2006; Nichols & Cho, 2008), especially when perceived as the engine propelling much of the growth of the business sector and as a driving force behind the rapid expansion of the social sector (Austin et al., 2006). Drayton (2004) also mentions an explosive emergence of social entrepreneurship over the past two decades.

The term "entrepreneurship" was coined by a French economist, J. B. Say (Drucker, 1985; Dees, 1998; Martin and Osberg, 2007), who more than 200 years ago said that the entrepreneur shifts economic resources out of the area of lower productivity and into the area of higher productivity and greater yield. The word "entrepreneur" has obvious French roots (*entreprendre*), meaning "to take into one's own hands," from which we can infer that an entrepreneur is someone who "undertakes a significant project or activity."

Another contributor to the meaning of this phenomenon was, more than a century ago, Joseph Schumpeter (Livesay, 1982; Drucker, 1985; Dees, 1998). Schumpeter (1994) understood the role of the entrepreneur as someone who fosters a process of "creative destruction," achieved by reforming or revolutionizing accepted patterns. Drucker (1985, pp. 27–28) defines the role of an entrepreneur as someone who "always searches for change, responds to it, and exploits it as an opportunity."

Entrepreneurship may be viewed as the creation of new organizations (Gartner, 1998; Thornton, 1999; Light, 2008). Currently, however, it is seen as a process of doing something new and something different, and relating to the implementation of novelty for the purpose of creating wealth for the individual and adding value to society (Kao, 2006).

Probably the definition proposed in a publication of the Ashoka organization (*Selecting Leading Social Entrepreneurs*, 2007)[7] provides the most comprehensive description: Entrepreneurs are leaders who see opportunities for change and innovation and devote themselves entirely to making that change happen. These leaders often have little interest in anything beyond their mission, and they are willing to spend the next ten to fifteen years to create a historic development. This total absorption is critical to transforming a new idea into reality.

However, Ashoka warns that there are thousands of creative people who have the ability to lead, to administer, or to "get things done"; few of these, however, will ever change the basic patterns of society as a whole, and hence, they do not meet the criteria of entrepreneurship, which include persistence in achieving an impact on the whole field, at the national level or beyond.

In Munir Hasan's and Steve Bigari's cases, we can see an example of the aforementioned Schumpeter's "creative destruction," as both of these individuals substantially "destroyed or deconstructed" old patterns. Both demonstrated total commitment to their mission and devoted themselves to

---

[7] See also http://www.ashoka.org/support/criteria.

making the change happen. Both were doing "something new and something different" for the purpose of creating better education or wealth for the individual and adding value to society. And both would definitely meet the definition of the word "entrepreneurship" by taking matters into their own hands.

PERSONALITY: CREATIVITY AND ENTREPRENEURIAL SKILLS

The most prevalent use of the term "social entrepreneurship" focuses on the role of the risk-taking individual who, against all odds, creates social change. "Social entrepreneurship is not so much about pattern-breaking change, but about pattern-breaking individuals" (Light, 2006, pp. 47–48). Also Bornstein (2004), Drayton (2005), and Martin and Osberg (2007) see specific personality traits as an important component of the definition of a social entrepreneur.

Most of the definitions of social entrepreneurship imply two major personality traits: creativity and entrepreneurial skills (Bornstein, 2004; *Selecting Leading Social Entrepreneurs*, 2007). We believe that these two characteristics function as independent variables. In Chapter 9 we will analyze other hypothetical personality traits.

Other authors share the conviction that creativity is an indispensible component of social entrepreneurship. Kramer (2005, p. 5) says that inherent in the definition of a social entrepreneur is the idea of finding a new way of doing things – viewing the world through a different lens and working to change the attitudes and behavior of others. This emphasis on a novel approach differs from the methodology of ordinary nonprofit and nongovernmental organizations, which usually work within existing approaches and conventions. Martin and Osberg (2007, p. 33) say that the "entrepreneur thinks creatively and develops a new solution that dramatically breaks with the existing one. The entrepreneur doesn't try to optimize the current system with minor adjustments, but instead finds a wholly new way of approaching the problem."

Ashoka (*Selecting Leading Social Entrepreneurs*, 2007) distinguishes two kinds of creativity: visionary/goal setting and day-to-day/problem solving. Social entrepreneurs are sometimes also called "social innovators," as in Boschee (2008). The stress on creativity is obvious: Social entrepreneurs usually address issues that were considered unsolvable, as others tried traditional methods and failed. The challenge to solve insurmountable problems forces a new, innovative approach, as we have observed in the cases of Munir Hasan and Steve Bigari.

The other commonly acknowledged personality characteristic is the entrepreneurial approach. Some authors (Leadbeater, 1997; Brinckerhoff, 2000) mention that being entrepreneurial means constantly looking for new ways to add value to existing solutions by taking underutilized, discarded resources and spotting ways of using them to pursue the mission; being willing to take responsible risks; weighing the social and financial returns on each investment, and, first and foremost, sustaining the mission itself, understanding that without money there is no possibility of fulfilling the mission.

According to Ashoka,[8] being entrepreneurial means searching for and identifying the root problem, interpreting the challenges, seeing opportunities for change and innovation, and finally being totally devoted to making that change happen. In Ashoka's view, entrepreneurs seem to be possessed by their ideas, even though they maintain a balance between being passionate visionaries and being detached and realistic, so that they are "concerned with the practical implementation of their vision above all else."

Ashoka (*Selecting Leading Social Entrepreneurs*, 2007) also provides some clues for recognizing the entrepreneurial trait, which manifests itself in the person's interest in the practical implementation or "how-to" of the project at hand: *How* will they transform an idea into society's new norm? *How* will the pieces fit together? *How* will they deal with the many challenges they will certainly encounter?

Both Munir Hasan and Steve Bigari exemplified this entrepreneurial approach: They were totally committed to, and fixated on, their respective visions; they identified the basic problems, implemented a long-term strategy, mobilized human resources, found ways to motivate key players, launched self-perpetuating mechanisms, and, most importantly, kept working until they were satisfied that the change process had taken place on a larger scale.

A closer look at creativity and entrepreneurial qualities will be presented in Chapter 9.

THE FIRST TAKE ON THE DIFFERENCE BETWEEN SOCIAL ENTREPRENEURS AND OTHER EFFECTIVE LEADERS

The aforementioned five-dimensional definition of social entrepreneurship (social mission, social innovation, social change, entrepreneurial skills, and personality) means that social entrepreneurs would be positioned

---

[8] http://www.ashoka.org/support/criteria and http://www.ashoka.org/social_entrepreneur.

somewhere in the 5-D space, significantly advanced on all five axes. However, there are authentic leaders who do not fall under the definition of social entrepreneur. The five-dimensional model provides a framework for conceptualizing the difference:

> Other great leaders are far advanced in some, but not all, of the five dimensions. For example, many highly successful social activists may master routine procedures, an important factor in attempting to meet various social, environmental, or educational needs, but they do not necessarily generate innovative solutions. Conversely, there are the innovative, creative inventors, but not necessarily entrepreneurial enough to realize their imaginative visions. And, finally, it goes without saying that not every great entrepreneur chooses to involve herself/himself in social issues.

In other words, meeting the definition of social entrepreneur requires all five dimensions; *only this rare amalgam of qualities makes a social entrepreneur.* With such a high bar to attain, one can understand why Ashoka: Innovators for the Public declares that on average, only one in ten million social entrepreneurs, meeting all those criteria, appears on the scene annually.[9]

Later on, we will be returning to the challenge of understanding the difference between social entrepreneurs and other social leaders. Finally, in Chapter 10 we will present the dynamical definition of social entrepreneurship, seeing if and how it differentiates social entrepreneurs from the rest of the population.

The next chapter will reflect on the practical implications and difficulties of identifying social entrepreneurs.

CHAPTER HIGHLIGHTS

- The classical definitions of social entrepreneurship cut through fields and concepts, indicating that the phenomenon exists in several dimensions.
- Five pivotal dimensions of social entrepreneurship are identified: social mission, social innovation, social change, entrepreneurial skills, and personality.

---

[9] See *Christian Science Monitor*, September 7, 2009. Retrieved 30 November 2010, from: http://www.csmonitor.com/2009/0907/p02s05-lign.html.

- How social entrepreneurs differ from other socially engaged leaders is one of the leitmotifs of this book. At first glance, based on this chapter, it appears that social entrepreneurs are advanced in all five dimensions, whereas other leaders (social activists, professional innovators, and socially responsible business people) may excel only in some.

3

Identifying Social Entrepreneurs in Practice

The previous two chapters provided a conceptual understanding of the phenomenon of social entrepreneurship. However, the question still remains of how to move from theory to practice when attempting to identify an authentic social entrepreneur.

There are several situations that demand an unambiguous answer to the question of whether an individual is truly a social entrepreneur. In fact, such a question is of paramount importance when selecting candidates for social entrepreneur fellowships to work with social organizations. Ashoka, Innovators for the Public (established in 1980),[1] Echoing Green (established in 1987),[2] Schwab Foundation for Social Entrepreneurship (established in 1998),[3] The Skoll Foundation (established in 1999),[4] and the Draper Richards Foundation (established in 2002)[5] are such organizations.

This chapter is based on practical experience. A coauthor of this book, Ryszard Praszkier, has been involved in this process with Ashoka, Innovators for the Public since the mid-1990s. He thus has experienced the highs of identifying new social entrepreneurs as well as the lows of nagging doubts, ambiguity, uncertainty, and the responsibility inherent in making the "right" decision.

The first challenge is to find fellowship candidates; as was mentioned previously, social entrepreneurship comprise a highly diverse group in terms

---

[1] For the search and selection process at Ashoka, see http://www.ashoka.org/support/sands or Schwab Foundation for Social Entrepreneurship (e.g., http://www.schwabfound.org/sf/SocialEntrepreneurship/SearchandSelectionProcess/index.htm).

[2] See http://www.echoinggreen.org.

[3] Similar process at the Schwab Foundation for Social Entrepreneurship, see http://www.schwabfound.org/sf/SocialEntrepreneurship/SearchandSelectionProcess/index.htm.

[4] See http://www.skollfoundation.org/.   [5] See http://www.draperrichards.org/.

of geography, area of professional expertise, socioeconomic conditions, and educational background. Many of these individuals come from remote areas; some are not well educated or have no access to the Internet. These conditions make it more difficult for staff to find potential fellows and social entrepreneurs, ideally in the early stage of their professional lives when, after successful piloting, they are just starting to spread their new ideas.

Qualified candidates are everywhere, even if they come from areas so remote that they do not show up on the map. It is therefore all the more rewarding to find them – people like Dennis Ole Sonkoi, a member of the Kenyan Maasai nomadic group,[6] who is bringing development to communities based on their pastoral traditions and possibilities (introducing a special kind of sensitive tourism that does not destroy the local lifestyle)[7]; or Bir Bahadur Ghale, a Gorkha from the Himalayas of Nepal.[8] Ghale is bringing electric power to the highest mountain villages through spreading the development of micro hydropower plants, thus spurring economic development and an improvement in the local populations' living conditions and, as a secondary benefit, bucking the trend toward emigration among the youth.

To find potential candidates, Ashoka has established a network of nominators, experts in various fields, possibly covering all geographical areas. However, some early-stage candidates may not yet be known to experts, so Ashoka also resorts to other means of covering the most remote areas, such as subscribing to a news-clipping service in the hopes of identifying candidates.

The next step is to identify candidates who most likely would meet the criteria. Ashoka staff receives special training in learning to identify and distinguish social entrepreneurs from other applicants. The central and only issues considered during the selection process are the Ashoka criteria (see Chapter 1). The first stage in the process takes place on the local level in the more than seventy countries where Ashoka operates. The entire process is based on doing due diligence – researching references, holding interviews, analyzing, doubting, re-evaluating, and discussing. The interviews are in-depth, exploring the current state of the development of the candidate's ideas, future plans and strategic thinking, and, finally, how in the past the candidate's social sensitivity and passion evolved. See Appendix 3 for an illustration of some questions and candidates' responses.

---

[6] See http://www.ashoka.org/fellow/3620.
[7] Denis' organization: http://www.loita-maasai.org/site05.html.
[8] See http://www.ashoka.org/fellow/2750.

The next step takes place on the international level whereby a senior staff member from outside the region conducts second-opinion interviews, reviewing the criteria from the global perspective, thus helping to standardize the selection criteria. The third stage involves the selection panel, which comprises leading local social and business entrepreneurship and an Ashoka senior global representative. The fourth stage involves the international board of Ashoka.

SOCIAL ENTREPRENEUR OR...

Of the many challenges that searchers for candidates face is the necessity to distinguish between social entrepreneurs and social activists. Indeed, the latter do extremely important work such as helping the needy by providing food and health care, protecting children, fighting for women's rights, and saving endangered species. Nevertheless, in some cases, regretfully, these individuals are rejected by organizations that are specifically looking for social entrepreneurs.

For example, some socially engaged business leaders who participate in corporate social responsibility (CSR) programs may not meet the criteria for social entrepreneurship because their approach to solving social problems does not include the introduction of new ideas; or their attitudes do not exhibit a talent for creativity; or the impact of their projects are not far-reaching enough. Of course, other CSR business entrepreneurship *do* match those criteria and *are* elected to the Ashoka Fellowship because they have succeeded in replacing failed solutions with completely new approaches. In addition, they harness the power of their entrepreneurial skills by successfully identifying and assembling resources, motivating key players, and developing workable plans.

There are also social activists who, although they may excel at helping people, nevertheless do not meet all of the criteria. For example, they may not offer any new ideas or do not develop the project beyond local boundaries.

When brought to an organization promoting social entrepreneurship, each case must be meticulously analyzed and all pros and cons thoroughly weighed. In many cases, pinpointing the distinction is more complicated, requiring a more sophisticated assessment. In Appendix 2, we present narratives (simplified for the sake of clarity) that reflect the process of evaluating the candidates' ability to match the criteria for social entrepreneurship; in deference to the principles of confidentiality and privacy, we use pseudonyms and fictitious locations, institutions, and time frames.

It is especially challenging in the case of social entrepreneurship organizations, which invest in early-stage social entrepreneurs.[9] In that regard, one needs to analyze not only concrete achievements but also visions, plans, projections, and dreams.

CHAPTER HIGHLIGHTS

- Identifying social entrepreneurs is a huge challenge, even though they are everywhere, including remote areas; they comprise a highly diverse group in terms of geography, area of professional expertise, socioeconomic conditions, and educational background.
- Ashoka: Innovators for the Public, through the process of electing social entrepreneurs to its fellowship program, has developed a rigorous multistage process of selection.
- Although the ratio of social entrepreneurs meeting the rigorous Ashoka criteria is relatively small, in the contemporary society there is a growing prevalence of outstanding social innovators, activists, and change makers; many of them are disposed to become social entrepreneurs.

SUMMARY AND CONCLUSIONS, SECTION 1

In this section, we have presented the subject of social entrepreneurship from several angles: Two case studies were presented (Introduction), followed by a review of the literature on social entrepreneurship (Chapter 1). In Chapter 2, we presented a conceptual framework systematizing the existing definitions of five pivotal dimensions of social entrepreneurship. In Chapter 3, we presented a detailed view of the selection process and showed how its various dimensions work in practice; an analysis of two case studies (altered names and data) are annexed in Appendix 2.

Although there is a comprehensive literature on social entrepreneurship, most of the materials are far more popular in nature than academic. In any case, it is clear that there is a surge of interest in this area, a sign of the growing need for solving insurmountable and intractable social problems – precisely the kinds of problems that social entrepreneurs address with great success. However, there still exist some pending questions, for

---

[9] For example Ashoka: Innovators for the Public is an example of an organization investing in early-stage social entrepreneurs, those who, Ashoka believes, have the potential to accomplish a large-scale impact in the future. Ashoka's goal is to empower social entrepreneurs very early in their professional life cycle.

example: How do they do it? What is their unique capacity for understanding and solving social problems? What makes their impact so outstanding and remarkable?

To respond to these questions fully and knowledgably, we must first explore the processes and mechanisms of social change (Section 2), followed by the way social entrepreneurs harness those mechanisms in order to pursue their ideas. A dynamic perspective to understanding social-change processes will be introduced (Section 3). Finally, in keeping with this dynamic approach, we will introduce a new definition of social entrepreneurship and present a new kind of related leadership model (Section 4).

SECTION 2

THE DYNAMICS OF SOCIAL CHANGE

INTRODUCTION

In the previous section, we introduced the phenomenon of social entrepreneurship along with the notion that social entrepreneurs bring new solutions to pressing social needs and in so doing, they initiate a process of durable social change.

What sort of change do they generate? It is certainly not the kind of massive and rapid upheaval caused by natural disasters or political revolutions; nor is it the change created by external events, such as the opening of a new industrial plant along with the promise of economic benefits to the community; nor is it the change engendered by new inventions and technologies. In these cases, the common element of change is brought about by a force of significant breadth. For most of us, this seems to make sense: To effect major change demands the application of substantial effort.

The cases presented in this book demonstrate that social entrepreneurs use a totally different approach to the challenge of creating social change: They apply relatively small interventions that nevertheless manage to achieve disproportionately significant results. The initial stimuli are sometimes barely visible, but over time they gain in strength as their influence eventually reaches an inflection point and, in the long run, achieves an immense impact. On closer scrutiny, we understand that this result can be mainly attributed to the initiation of a bottom-up process that empowers groups and societies, turning them into key players. Presumably this was what Peter Drucker meant when he said that social entrepreneurs change the performance capacity of the society (Gendron, 1996).

Section 2 will focus on this sort of from-small-to-major-social-change dynamic. First, we will review how the existing theories relate to social entrepreneurship' ways of introducing change (Chapter 4). Next (Chapters 5 and 6), we will present a dynamical approach, looking in detail into the mechanisms of this sort of bottom-up social change.

The following narrative is illustrative of how one social entrepreneur achieved social change by starting small and, gradually gaining in significance, succeeded in creating a major impact on the entire society.

Kazimierz (Kaz) Jaworski, Poland: Empowering disadvantaged rural communities through a bottom-up process

Kazimierz (Kaz) Jaworski story[1] starts in the mid-1990s, in the most underdeveloped region of Poland, the southeast. After the overthrow of the Communist regime in 1989 and the transition to a growth economy in most regions in Poland, the district of Strug Valley, with a population of 37,000 and 4,000 homes, remained socially and economically behind the curve.

Coming from a peasant family himself, Kaz was totally committed to raising the living standards of his region. With the solid populist spirit of a veteran of the underground Solidarity movement of the 1980s, he couldn't tolerate the fact that after the 1989 turnover, when other regions were moving swiftly toward economic prosperity, this area remained stagnant. In order to succeed in changing the picture, he realized that first he would have to work to confront people's prejudices and attitudes, which comprised a deeply imbedded misanthropy and an enduring legacy of the Communist period when the government was imposing semi-cooperatives, which were exploitative and a way to nationalize family farming. Kaz reports the following revealing statements made by members of the community, which attest to the antisocial, distrustful attitudes of the people living in the region: "Smart guys want to cheat and deceive us as many others have done in the past"; "Don't cooperate with your neighbors – they will want to outsmart you"; "I want to stick to my own small farm and don't want to get involved in any community initiatives, as there is always a hidden agenda, which is to get something from me." In addition, about the education of their children: "Children should be required to help their parents perform their extremely difficult work on the farm, instead of spending too much time in school, where they teach unnecessary stuff"; "Milking and tending cows is much more important than the abstract knowledge they are teaching children in the classroom."

These attitudes brought social and economic isolation to the people of the region. The community was in a state of lethargy: No roads were being

---

[1] See http://www.ashoka.org/fellows/kazimierz_jaworski.

PICTURE 6. Education program for children initiated by Kaz Jaworski

built, the education system was fatally flawed, juvenile delinquency and the school's dropout rate was skyrocketing, and there was rampant alcohol abuse and bullying behavior in the schools.

With the failure of traditional ways of encouraging joint action to turn things around, Kaz found a way to circumvent the widespread resistance. His first step was to install a rural telephone system, the first in Poland to be independent from the state-owned telephone monopoly, which was barely operative in rural areas. His initial success was having managed to motivate people to participate in this new telephone co-op. Kaz' goal was to encourage communication, which in turn would maximize the feeling of satisfaction that comes from cooperating in a group effort. Kaz emphasizes that the independent telephone network was not a goal in itself but served as a vehicle for triggering communication and cooperation.

This telephone system connected community members to one another with free local calls, thus boosting internal communication and networking (callers had to pay for non-local calls, which generated operating revenue). People called one another often and became used to mutual communication; clearly, the telephone network initially was successful in combating apathy, resistance, and inertia. Participating in the popular telephone co-op

PICTURE 7. Kaz Jaworski

was a great source of satisfaction and opened an avenue for further cooperation.

In Chapter 2, we mentioned that according to Rogers (2003) the consequences of change are often more important than the initial change itself. The telephone network was the first impulse; the consequence was that a previously uncooperative group of people turned into an enterprising society. Currently, this community is a leader in business entrepreneurship, and the number of enterprises has significantly increased compared to other rural regions. Utilizing local spring water, the community launched a mineral water production facility and built a public sewage system. Citizens participated financially in order to make this happen, a truly revolutionary development in this area in those days (late 1990s, early 2000s). Various citizen-based educational and social initiatives were also undertaken, including efforts to close the education gap between this community and its urban counterparts. In addition, they started a health-food production and delivery business, bringing food directly from local organic farms to clients in the surrounding cities, thus eliminating the need for middlemen. The elegant win-win result of this enterprise was that on one hand, it generated significant income for the community, leaving 10 percent for extracurricular studies, such as English and computers, as well as juvenile delinquency prevention; on the other hand, the people in the cities received healthy food at a reasonable price.

The consequence of the consequence was that the success of those undertakings raised the self-confidence, the level of trust, and the prospect for further cooperation among the members of the community. Finally, the macro indicators reveal that this community boasts the highest rate of voter participation in the Polish national elections and the highest number of new enterprises compared to the neighboring counties.

4

Social-Change Theories and Dilemmas

Although the facts of this case tell a great story, our work is not yet complete, for we must move from mere fascination to a more analytical level, where we are prompted to ask several questions: How do we characterize this kind of change? Was it this passionate individual, Kaz, who brought change to the society or was it a society that desperately needed changes and was ready to take off on its own? Would the change have occurred in any case? Was it just a lucky coincidence that such a passionate individual appeared on the scene? In other words, what was the key change agent, the individual or the society?

DEFINING SOCIAL CHANGE FOSTERED BY SOCIAL ENTREPRENEURS

With the cases of Munir Hasan, Steve Bigari, and Kaz Jaworski in mind, the best departure point for reaching a suitable definition of social change would be to comb through and tease one out of the many existing designations. If we were to synthesize the characterizations of three key figures in the field – Sztompka (1993), Farley (2002), and Macionis (2010) – we would offer the following: Social change is the systemic transformation in patterns of thoughts, behavior, social relationships, institutions, and social structure over time.

Munir Hasan, Steve Bigari, and Kaz Jaworski influenced the mindsets and behavior of their target societies. They transformed the relationships into more cooperative, inclusive, and trusting ones. They modified institutions and sparked the formation of new ones. Finally, as a result, social structures were altered (Munir influenced a new, partnership-based model of relationships in education; Steve mainstreamed the previously excluded group; and Kaz brought about strong civic and economic participation).

Moreover, they used specific bottom-up methods that empowered the respective societies to take over and become the key change-making force. In that sense, they brought social development, which Sztompka (1993) describes as "the process of unfolding of some potentiality inherent in the system (p. 8)." He further maintains that one of the characteristics of social development is that change is stimulated by internal and immanent propensities of the system.

This brings us to a more comprehensive definition of social change brought by social entrepreneurs, to wit social change introduced by social entrepreneurs is the systemic transformation in the organization of society in patterns of thought, behavior, social relationships, institutions, and social structure over time, *with the use of methods that empower the society and enable the unfolding of potentialities inherent in the system.* Finally, this statement reflects the specific approach of social entrepreneurs, who not only bring about modifications but do so by empowering societies in a bottom-up process.

The last few words of the definition – "unfolding of potentialities inherent in the system" – warrant more reflection. Sztompka (1993) deems this notion to be an inherent component of the process of social development, which he sees as being stimulated by the intrinsic, internal, endogenous, or autodynamic propensities of the system.

For some sociologists, however, this intrinsic potential for change is not so obvious, provoking us to ask: Is social change endogenous or exogenous? This and other important questions will be considered after reviewing the basic theories of social change.

EXISTING THEORIES OF SOCIAL CHANGE

Ancient Greeks and the Present Time

Change has been a central issue for centuries. One school, represented by the seventh-century Greek philosopher, Tales from Millet, held that change is omnipresent and inevitable and is one of the basic features of the world. According to Heraclites, everything changes, *panta rei*: There is no permanent reality except the reality of change. Illustrating his point is his well-known saying that no man ever steps in the same river twice, for it's not the same river and he's not the same man. Social entrepreneurs often help to reinforce people's understanding that change is inevitable and that true sustainability comes with preparing and managing the change process.

In the opposite camp was the City of Elea school, which held that every-thing is eternally unchanged. Zeno of Elea went as far as to say that all motion is impossible and bolstered his argument by citing the famous Achilles-and-the-tortoise paradox, in which Achilles will never catch up to the tortoise: Whenever Achilles reaches somewhere the tortoise has been, he still has farther to go, as the tortoise during that time will, at his slow pace, move a bit farther; *da capo al fine*. Similarly, social entrepreneurs have a solid, immutable vision and operate on solid ground, taking into account border conditions and adjusting and drawing from the given geographical or historical context.

Finally, there were the Greek metaphysicists who were searching for a theory that would conflate the two basic features of the world: change and stability.[1] This is exactly what social entrepreneurs do: consolidate and harmonize the continuous process of change with solidity and stability of a far-reaching vision and from within a given context.

Sociological Change Theories

In sociology there are at least four basic categories of theories of social change (Noble, 2000; Vago, 2004): evolutionary, conflictual, structural-functional, and social-psychological. Next is a brief overview of each.

Evolutionary Theories

Evolutionary sociologists agree that there are inevitable stages of social evolution, although they differ as to the essence of particular stages:

> In the nineteenth century the works of Charles Darwin, the father of the theory of biological evolution had a huge influence on the thinking of sociologists. Previously, society had been envisioned as proceeding inevitably through fixed sets of stages; the idea of evolution was associated with the notion of progress, with each next stage on a more "advanced" level than the one before.

One of the leading nineteenth-century evolutionists, Auguste Comte (who coined the term "sociology" and is known as the "father of sociology"),

---

[1] The irony is that this ancient debate between change and immutability is currently becoming a central issue in social-change analysis. Some authors are strong advocates for the notion of change. For example, Peter Drucker (2001) states that "every organization will have to become a change leader." Others want to push back on the rapid pace of change, arguing that most efforts to impose change fail in the long run and create an enormous waste of financial investment and human energy (Kotter, 1995; Senge, 1999).

believed that there are three inevitable and irreversible stages of human development: theological (belief in the power of inanimate objects or invisible "beings"); metaphysical (belief in nature and its abstract forces); and the (most advanced) positive stage that provides explanations and ability to control events through the laws of science, a stage that we are in to this day, which Comte associated with industrial evolution. Another leading evolutionist of that time was the anthropologist Henry Morgan, who described the progress of humankind through three inevitable stages of evolution: savagery, barbarism, and civilization.

Henry Spencer, a nineteenth-century engineer (known as the "second father" of sociology, after Comte), thought that everything "in the cosmos" is gradually synthesized at ever higher levels of complexity. Similarly, he explained the development of human society as going from relatively simple patterns of organization to more complex structures. Spencer built direct analogies to the (Darwinian) concept of biological evolution, maintaining that the struggle for survival will be won only by those individuals who are best able to adapt to new conditions (change). According to Spencer, the stages of development are inescapable, even though they may occur in a nonlinear trajectory: from simple societies (based on the family unit) to compound societies (based on the clan), to doubly compound societies (based on tribes), and finally to trebly compound societies (based on the nation).

The concept of social dynamics is seen as moving gradually from lower to higher stages of development. This is similar to what social entrepreneurs do; for example, starting from a place of misanthropy, isolation, and frustration, Kaz Jaworski set off a change process that engendered trust and cooperation, eventually leading to economic and civic development. We will take a closer look at the gradual evolution of the different stages when we discuss the phases of social emergence (Chapter 6) and the buildup of social capital through social networks (Chapter 8).

Conflict Theories
Conflict theories posit that social change can be best understood in terms of tension and conflict between the group and the individual. The best-known representative of this approach is Karl Marx, who saw conflict as the vehicle for change and progress. He perceived the stages of human development through the lenses of conflicts and revolutions with regard to the issues of production. Marx suggested the stages as: tribal ownership, then ancient, communal, and state ownership accompanied first by slavery, then feudalism, capitalism, and finally – as the most progressive – communism.

The latter can be divided into two phases: the dictatorship of the proletariat and – the ideal and only stage without conflict – pure communism.

Some sociologists, like Lewis A. Coser, perceive conflict as a positive force for change. Coser says that conflict is an inherent component of the human condition and can be either destructive or constructive. When constructive, conflict opens up opportunities for resolving disagreements and, as a consequence, for building unity. Moreover, conflict frequently enhances group cohesion, as people unite around a common cause or enemy. Coser views conflict as a means of promoting social change through the distribution of social values and formation of a new social order.

Conflict is indeed an important component of the social entrepreneur's approach. However, some conflicts are destructive whereas others are constructive. The first are based on negative elements, such as hatred or prejudice, and usually tend to gain in strength retroactively. The latter are normal components of democracy, whose (1) inherent inclusiveness means creating an enabling environment for diverse groups to articulate their own objectives, some of which may be contradictory to those of other groups; (2) openness and tolerance of conflict and diversity permits negotiation and finding consensual solutions. A constructive conflict or controversy is a necessary component of an adaptive society; also readiness to confront the prevailing situation may be one of the necessary requirements for change. The example of Imam Mohammed Ashafa and Pastor James Wuye from Nigeria (see Chapter 11) shows that as long as those two were conflicted in a destructive way, their influence on the society was destructive, thereby reinforcing the tendency toward hatred and violence. However, when they began to cooperate and to bring peace into the equation, they came to a constructive place, a safe space for groups in conflict to voice their pains and frustrations and to opt for positive solutions.

Structural-Functional Theories
Social entrepreneurs focus both on functions and structures. Usually the initial phase introduces new kinds of societal relationships, which enhance trust and cooperation and, as a result, galvanize economic growth. In the next phase, social entrepreneurs usually focus on modifying structures, procedures, and law so as to enable the new idea to thrive and spread. Should one focus on modifying societal structures, such as the legal sector, or rather on societal communication, relationships, and functions? Social systems have a number of structural components, and the relationships among those components become functions.

Henry Spencer uses the metaphor of society as the body whose proper functioning depends on the "organs" working together. The best-known representatives of this approach are Talcott Parsons and William F. Ogburn, who view societies as holistic entities in which cause-and-effect relationships are multiple and reciprocal. Societies (according to Ogburn) operate as homeostatic mechanisms, and changes that upset the equilibrium produce compensating changes to restore the balance. According to Parsons, social changes, seen also as "boundary destruction" and "boundary maintenance," may have two sources: endogenous (affecting boundaries within the system) and exogenous (external). Both mutually influence one another; for instance, exogenous causes may create endogenous changes in personalities and cultural systems.

Social-Psychological Theories

Social entrepreneurs understand that societies consist of people and it is people's mindsets, beliefs, prejudices, and attitudes that contribute to the way societies are organized and vice versa. The psychological factors are essential in the process of change.

In sociology, the most prominent representative of this approach is Max Weber, whose main contribution was to articulate the major influence of Protestant ethics on the development of Western societies. This methodology (finding affinity between religions and directions of societal development) was followed by others, including Fukuyama (1996), who attributed Chinese diligence, frugality, and striving for excellence to Confucianism.

A twentieth-century sociologist, Everett E. Hagen, discovered that in modern societies there exists an "innovational personality," as opposed to old, traditional societies where the personalities were uncreative and authoritarian. The innovational personality persistently looks for new solutions and has a propensity for critically assessing the common beliefs.

Finally, the renowned contemporary psychologist David McClelland (1967) focused on economic growth and on the kind of personalities that mostly contribute to it. He identified a certain "achieving motivation," which he called the "n Achievement," a personality type that he credited with the force behind the development and perpetuation of human societies. In his best-known book, *The Achieving Society*, McClelland (1967) also analyzed the key psychological factors that contributed to economic development, exploring the characteristics of n Achieving personalities, especially entrepreneurs. Moreover, our research shows that there are common personality features of social entrepreneurs enabling us to talk of a *social-entrepreneurial personality*.

Psychological Change Theories

There are numerous psychological theories of change, although most of them relate to individual internal processes (for example, the well-known behavioral approach or Maslow's growth theory). However, germane to the understanding of the impact of social entrepreneurship is to observe how social entrepreneurs are changing societal mindsets. What is the mechanism of this sort of mindset shift?

The first indication is that social entrepreneurs by definition (Chapter 1) are creative (more on creativity in Chapter 9). Their creative motivation is intrinsic to their identities and, at the same time, tangible (Amabile, 1996). As Albert Einstein said, "Creativity is contagious. Pass it on." Indeed, when meeting and working with social entrepreneurs, one is acutely aware of their creative energy and the intensity of their motivation.[2] Sternberg and Lubart (2004) point out that "creativity may not only require motivation, but also generate it (p. 6)." We contend that social entrepreneurs, with their passion and ingenuity, are a contagious source of energy that radiates creativity and a heightened level of motivation. What is the mechanism of this influence? If Kaz Jaworski convinces the grudging community to buy into participating in the shared local telephone network, and if they like this idea, then they need to restructure their cognitive perception and modify the long-held prejudice against cooperation. The satisfaction that the new experience brings (chatting freely with neighbors as a result of local cooperation) counters the old mindset that cooperation leads to victimization of one kind or another. One has to restructure internal beliefs in order to reduce the apparent cognitive dissonance and reach a state of internal cohesiveness on this new level. This phenomenon is consistent with the accepted notion that people want to perceive themselves as cohesive and that in order to reach that goal our mind creates and maintains a perception of continuity even in the face of perpetual observed changes in our actual behavior (Mischel, 1969, 1973).

Bem (1967) holds that situational context influences cognitive structures, so that the person ends up incorporating the new behavior into a cohesive self-image. Social psychology provided several insights into the formation of attitudes; for example, people end up liking those they help and dislike those they hurt (Smith & Mackie, 1995). In other words, if a new, promising

---

[2] One of the authors, Ryszard Praszkier, as a second-opinion reviewer, has interviewed in depth more than one hundred candidates to Ashoka from nearly all continents; he has also closely collaborated with some of them.

situation is offered and accepted, even though it counters the old internal cognitive structures (e.g., cooperation with a previously antagonistic group), and if cooperation is successful (even if it relates to isolated issues), the old cognitive image is restructured in order to maintain consistency (changing the negative perception of the antagonistic group into a positive one). Consistency is one of the basic human drives, and the situational context feeds into restructuring the consistency. Research has confirmed this by, for example, observing individuals who exhibited similar levels of aggressive behavior yet differed predictably and significantly in the types of situations in which they expressed that behavior. These results lead us to conclude along with Mischel & Shoda (1995) that the situational context is much more predictive of human behavior than are personality traits.

In other words, when our actions conflict with our anterior attitudes, we often change our attitudes to be more consistent with our actions. Making a choice kindles cognitive dissonance, which is then reduced through rationalization. The phenomenon of cognitive dissonance is considered to be one of the most influential theories in psychology (Festinger, 1957; Festinger et al., 2009).

Unfortunately, this mechanism is a double-edged sword: If we are, even coincidentally, brought into a conflict situation, we will tend to restructure the previous positive image of those who were our opponents in this – even if intermediate – conflict situation and turn it into a negative so that our internal set of beliefs becomes cohesive again. This evokes more conflicts, as we begin to believe that they are really "bad guys."

This mechanism has been clearly illustrated by Morton Deutsch's *Crude Law of Social Relations* (Deutsch, 1973, Nowak et al., 2010). The characteristic processes and effects elicited by a given type of social relationship (e.g., cooperative or competitive) also tend to elicit that type of social relationship. In other words, the consequence of conflict-laden relationships is a buildup of the rationale for conflict, whereas a consequence of cooperation bolsters the rationale for cooperation. Thus, we are left with the paradox that a given type of relationship yields its own rationale.

Munir Hasan (see the introduction to Section 1) faced decades of traditions keeping Bangladesh away from the mainstream global mathematics. He achieved the major shift in societal mindsets through organizing local festivals. Those festivals brought in the key players, thanks to their vibrancy and enthusiastic public acceptance. In return, the key players restructured their cognition of the role of mathematics and accepted the math olympiads, followed by the acceptance of teaching mathematics on a higher level. The first step (festivals), which seemed innocent and neutral, produced the mindset shift through the process of striking the internal cognitive cohesiveness: High-level mathematics ought to be perceived as positive and desirable in order to harmonize the cognition of one's own enthusiastic participation in the festivals.

Social entrepreneurs probably employ this mechanism of influencing societal mindsets more than any other approach (see Chapters 10 and 12).

Historical Change: The Power of Ideas

Sztompka (1993) sees ideas as a driving force for social change. Out of the many ideas that have contributed to changing society, one of the most relevant to the subject of social entrepreneurship is the Weberian[3] concept of an innovative personality, which is defined as extremely curious and driven to explore the world, and as demonstrating a propensity for taking responsibility and searching for new solutions.

Social change in the social sector has contributed immensely to the development and empowerment of this sort of innovative and achieving personality. Drayton (2002, 2009) and Drayton & Budinich (2010) maintain that the citizen sector is in a transition from a base-building period to a very rapid and self-multiplying augmentation. It is fair to say that before the 1980s, rapid economic growth bypassed the public sector. With no competition, a huge productivity gap opened between the private and public sectors, the latter being characterized by low performance, dismal pay, and low self-esteem.

During the last two decades of the twentieth century, the citizen sector started following the business model and becoming entrepreneurial and competitive in structural terms. This created an enabling environment for "Weberian" individuals with innovative and achieving personalities to thrive and expand their impact. The avenue for social entrepreneurship became wide open.

Another illustration of the power of new ideas was Gandhi's nonviolent movement for independence and peaceful collaboration. It attracted millions and continues to influence people's mindsets. A recent example of a Gandhi-like nonviolent transformation was the Polish Solidarity movement (Kenney, 2001, 2002), which peacefully changed Poland from a totalitarian regime to a democracy merely through the power, activism, and unity of the civil society. The methods included: supporting illegal education,

---

[3] Max Weber, Germany, end of the nineteenth and beginning of the twentieth centuries; one of the pioneers of modern sociology; he coined the term "humanistic sociology."

publishing and distributing illegal books and brochures, running self-help groups, and boycotting official TV and events. Kenney (2001, 2002) cites the Orange Alternative, a loosely organized group of antigovernment individuals who participated in street theater and other activities ridiculing the regime. The Solidarity movement contributed to the transformation of Central and Eastern Europe and to the fall of the Berlin Wall. The self-esteem and self-reliance gained as a result of the movement prepared the participants to take over after the fall of communism.

CRUCIAL DILEMMAS RELATED TO SOCIAL CHANGE

The aforementioned theories imply several crucial dilemmas (Noble, 2000).

Is Social Change Endogenous or Exogenous?

Indeed, this question is often raised: Where does true change come from? Does it come from inside (endogenous) or outside of the social system (exogenous)? Do societies generate the change process or is change brought to the societies from outside? For example, at a conference when we were presenting the Kaz Jaworski case, someone suggested that the community may have been ready to take off anyway. If so, then hasn't Kaz just facilitated the process, which would have taken place sooner or later?

Sztompka (1993) indicates that the endogenous–exogenous dilemma could easily be solved by identifying the levels of analysis. For example, let's consider a hypothetical society that is becoming aware of the looming energy crisis. The members of this society start saving energy and, through several mechanisms (public events, education, word of mouth, and influence of civic organizations), saving energy gradually becomes a normal and permanent activity. This social change may be seen as exogenous because the impulse came from the global markets. However, looking from the perspective of the society as a system, the initial impulse triggered an endogenous process involving immanent autodynamics based on the mutually reinforcing elements. The result was the appearance of new societal mindsets and behaviors (engaged in saving energy), a practice that became permanent regardless of any impending market alterations.

From Kaz came the initial impulse – a specific stimulus, which he predicted would trigger an autocatalytic process.[4] His initial idea was not

---

[4] We use the term autocatalytic as the metaphor for the speeding up of a chemical reaction by a catalyst that is a product of the reaction.

merely to launch the independent local telephone network, but in so doing, he would circumvent the initial resistance and release the immanent social dynamic. From this perspective, he clearly triggered an endogenous social-change process.

Of course, various sociological schools have different ways of framing this dilemma (Noble, 2000). Conflict theories would see change as a result of wars and conflicts immanently embedded in the society, hence endogenous. Wars and conflicts create an opportunity for change, whereas periods of harmonious existence are essentially metastable as they discourage change. Jean-Jacques Rousseau would view social relationships as naturally harmonious, whereas wars and revolutions are destructive to that harmony, unnecessary, and avoidable; in these circumstances, change is imposed from the outside along with the upheavals. The evolutionists see social change as endogenous, meaning that there are several inevitable consecutive stages, and societies simply have to adjust and change along with them. Thus, change will happen regardless of what unfolds in the short term. (Structural-functional theories and social-psychological theories see social change as either exogenous, or endogenous, or both.)

Is Social Change Inevitable or Contingent?

Also posing a central issue for the study of social entrepreneurship is the question of whether change happens (or doesn't happen) occasionally. Or is change constant, ubiquitous, and inescapable? Would the growing pressure to do something about mathematics in Bangladesh sooner or later have generated some change in that field, or would the situation have remained stagnant until a young, passionate mathematician, someone like Munir Hasan, came along and seized the opportunity to modernize this aspect of Bangladeshi society?

Social entrepreneurs do not act against the societies in which they operate; instead, they find innovative ways to awaken latent tendencies, which is exactly what Munir, Steve, and Kaz were able to do. With their social empathy, passion, and creativity, they enlivened and vitalized the dormant potentials in their respective societies.

Social change seems both inevitable and contingent. On one hand, social needs create a void and a pressure to solve the pressing problems, so we may assume that sooner or later social change will happen; in that sense, it is inevitable. On the other hand, creative and entrepreneurial individuals with passion, commitment, and social empathy are a rare phenomenon, so it may be rather fortuitous to succeed in matching the need with the change maker.

Evolutionary or conflictual theories claim that social change is inevitable. However, the structural-functional theories hypothesize that the social structures occasionally exhibit a need for social change, and the social-psychological theories make the case for change as dependent on the psychological characteristics of the society.

Individuals or Societies?

There is a conviction that despite and behind all the structures, stratification, hierarchies, beliefs, and roles – all that sociologists understand as a "society" – there are simply people. This position is called "methodological idealism," a term coined by Karl Popper. It contends that only real people matter and that theoretical concepts are, by definition, abstract notions that do not exist in nature; only people and their lives can be verified, and therefore sociological analysis should focus on individual experiences.

Others hold to a belief that we are only what society has made us; we are shaped by our era, culture, rituals, gender, and location. This view is called "sociological realism." The only way to understand individual actions is by analyzing the properties of the society and its social systems and their influence on individuals (Talcott Parsons, 1972; Émile Durkheim, 1984).

This contradiction applies well to social entrepreneurship: Munir, Steve, and Kaz certainly understood and dealt with people. On the other hand, their results documented a shift in societal mindsets and in the characteristics of entire groups. Thus, by working with people they addressed and modified societal beliefs and attitudes, which, in a feedback loop, influenced the mindsets of individuals.

For evolutionary and structural-functional theorists, there is no doubt that societies are the prime vehicles of change. This is true for some conflict theories as well, although some others may see the role of special individuals as critical, for example, kings or leaders of revolutions. Social-psychological theories will focus on individuals and people as the main change makers.

Noble (2000) brings up another sociological dilemma: determining the best approach to understanding social change.

Materialism or Idealism?

Materialists hold that the research should be limited to analyzing action between and among people (procreation, fights, wars, power struggles, etc.). Other concepts, such as beliefs or relationships, are only secondary, supplemental, and decorative. This describes the Marxist way of thinking: What matters is where the real power lies.

Idealistic theoreticians hold that central to understanding social phenomena are the interactions among people. People's behavior derives from the way they understand the social situation, so it is essential to analyze beliefs and ideas. This is the general functionalists' perspective, as this approach focuses on the functions in society.

The role of symbols in the process of societal change is an important issue; Ernst Cassirer (1962), the twentieth-century idealist philosopher, says that major reformers should perceive the impossible as possible. This is the symbolic way of thinking that bolsters the effort to combat natural inertia and equips the individual with a new ability – to transform his human universe.

Again, Munir, Steve, and Kaz modified the reality as well as the ideas. Social entrepreneurs are on one hand down to earth, concrete in their planning, and on the other hand, big dreamers and visionaries. Here materialism meshes well with idealism. In the case of social entrepreneurship, these two apparent contraries mutually reinforce one another.

A NEED FOR A NEW THEORETICAL FRAMEWORK

Social entrepreneurs operate at the intersection of apparently contradictory parameters. They may bring change from the outside (exogenous), while at the same time they foster tendencies toward internal change (endogenous); their interventions seem sort of obvious and predestined (inevitability), although change may not have happened without people like them (contingency); they deal with people (methodological individualism) and at the same time they build new patterns, structures, laws, and symbols (sociological realism); finally, they are down to earth as they deal with concrete issues (realism), simultaneously influencing ideas, identification, and the level of hope (idealism); they bring direct, short-term solutions (independent telephone system) while at the same time aiming at far-reaching consequences, such as changing societal mindsets.

In the existing theories, concepts are portrayed as disjunctive: Social change is either inevitable or contingent; change is brought about by individuals or societies; and the drive for change is materialism or idealism. The social entrepreneur, however, has the capacity to blend these apparent contraries. They are able to provide a balance between extremes, creating a nonlinear process with dynamic equilibriums, feedback loops, and mutually reinforcing elements. Perhaps this can be explained by the observation that they are not *introducing change* but instead they are *acting as catalysts* for a natural change process. In the next chapter, we will present the complexity and the dynamical systems theory as a framework for capturing these sorts of dynamic processes.

CHAPTER HIGHLIGHTS

- Social change is defined as a systemic transformation over time in the organization of society in patterns of thinking, behavior, social relationships, institutions, and social structure.
- There are various theories of social change (ancient Greek concepts of change and stability; and sociological change theories, such as evolutionary, conflictual, structural-functional, and social-psychological). Another important point of view is historical, indicating that the power of new ideas has an immense influence on the course of history. In addition, the psycho-social dimension sheds some light on the mechanisms of changing societal mindsets.
- There are four crucial dilemmas related to social change: is the change process endogenous (coming from inside the groups or societies) or exogenous (coming from outside)? Is it inevitable or contingent (happens occasionally)? Are people the basic motor of change or is it that the sociological structures (roles, rules, and stratification) trigger the change process? Finally, should the research be limited to analyzing concrete action between and among people, such as procreation, fights, wars, and power struggles (materialistic approach); or should it analyze the myriad interactions, including the role of symbols or trust (idealistic approach)?

5

Equilibrium and Complexity

Social problems are characterized by extreme complexity, but it is that very same complexity that provides a way to achieve large-scale social change by exerting a disproportionately small force. Analyzing and exploring this principle will be the main focus of this chapter. We will present the theoretical framework of the complexity approach, which illustrates the complex social-system change fostered by social entrepreneurs.

It was in the early 1990s, much before the booming interest in social entrepreneurship, that Waddock & Post (1991) noted that social entrepreneurs recognize the complexity of social problems and use their understanding to become catalysts in the change process, that is to say, agents that engender significant changes with surprisingly limited resources. A deep understanding of social systems is central to the effectiveness of social entrepreneurs who are trying to effect change, and this knowledge can substitute for the lack of resources necessary for imposing change in a direct way. Pushing for change directly by applying an external force strong enough to overcome the resistance of the social system stands in sharp contrast to the entrepreneur's "catalytic" approach, which relies on facilitating a natural process. In other words, instead of acting against the forces existing in the system, social entrepreneurs, aided by their deep knowledge, use the forces within the system to achieve change by searching for the smallest and simplest possible impulses and rules.

The complexity of social processes has always been a given. However, the understanding of the *sources* of complexity has changed dramatically. In the past, the concept of complexity was directly related to the number of variables involved and to the number of factors influencing a given process. One of the most important discoveries made in the formal sciences since the 1970s has been to show that, ironically, simple rules can lead to new and highly complex properties of a system.

Complexity can be perceived as the reverse side of simplicity rather than its opposite. Many highly complex phenomena, such as self-organization and pattern formation, which are observed at the level of the system, can be explained by simple rules. Such simple rules, for example, can reproduce the patterns of pigmentation observed in living organisms or the shapes of plants and shells, which can be reproduced by the simple rules of interaction of nearby cells (Wolfram, 2002; Meinhardt, 2003). Simple rules are thus the core of complexity theory (Waldrop, 1992; Holland, 1999; Kauffman, 1995; Johnson, 2001; Wolfram, 2002).

Fisher (2009) articulates that within the well-observed world of animals collective behavior (e.g., intelligent swarms) often emerges from a set of simple rules for causing the interaction between neighbors. Understanding this process has also revealed that many of the complex patterns in human society also arise from simple rules of social interaction among individuals. Complex properties that emerge from simple rules have been observed in cognitive (Port & Van Gelder, 1995) and social psychology (Nowak & Vallacher, 1998b; Vallacher, Read, & Nowak, 2002), as well as in the field of sociology, political science (Jervis, 1998), and economics (Arthur, 1999).

This bottom-up process of simple rules leading to complex results would not occur in a linear process. Rather, for complex properties to emerge from simple rules in this bottom-up way, the relationships among elements must be nonlinear (Nowak, 2004), meaning that the reaction of some elements to others is in some way disproportional. Even systems composed of a few variables may display highly complex patterns of temporal changes, where the dynamics of such a system may be chaotic and unpredictable over longer time periods (Schuster, 1995) if the systems are nonlinear. Both order and chaos, for example, can be observed in artificial neural networks (Amit, 1989), where the basic elements are essentially binary, and in cellular automata (Wolfram, 2002), where elements can adopt one out of a few states.

Complex systems are characterized by multiple feedback loops in which there is no one easily identifiable thread of causation (A leads to B, B causes C, C influences D, and so on). On the contrary, there are multiple feedback loops, which together lead to complex results. On the highest level (culture, language, etc.) the feedback loops were beautifully captured by Hardt and Negri (2004), who say that we can truly communicate only when we use the languages, symbols, ideas, and relationships we share in common; in turn, the results of our communication are new common languages, symbols, ideas, and relationships.

Kurt Lewin's field theory, developed in the mid-1940s, provides a conceptual framework for understanding social change from the perspective of complexity theory. He was a social psychologist who laid the foundation for modern experimental social psychology.

KURT LEWIN'S FORCE-FIELD THEORY

Kurt Lewin (2004) asserted that prior to taking any action one should analyze the factors (forces) that influence a given social situation. He viewed social processes as resulting from the interplay of social forces. The configuration of the forces can be defined as a force field. Most forces have counterforces. Social systems are usually at the points of balance where the force is equal to the counterforce. This perspective provides the foundation for understanding how social change can be achieved. One must first see the situation as a whole, then analyze the mosaic of social forces that aggregate to maintain the current balance of the social field, and then finally draw out which forces are the driving movements toward desired change (Lewin called them locomotion or helping forces) and which would interfere (barriers or hindering forces). This "Lewinian" way of thinking helps social entrepreneurs find the best point of application of force, enabling the slightest impulse to release maximum energy, and leading to change.

The important property of any change process should be its permanence. Lewin pointed out that change frequently is short-lived and that the situation soon returns to the previous level. This indicates that it is critical to include permanency of change in the planned objectives, and to equate permanent change with changing the equilibrium of the system. He asked the fundamental question: "How can a situation be brought about which would permanently change the level on which the counteracting forces find their quasi-stationary equilibrium?" His response was, "To bring about any change, the balance between the forces which maintain the social self-regulation at a given level has to be upset (p. 42)" (2004). A successful change includes three aspects: unfreezing the present level, moving to the new level, and freezing the situation on the new level. Because any level is determined by a force field, permanency implies that the new force field is made relatively secure against change.[1] At that time this idea was a revolutionary discovery, to wit: It is not enough to bring change; one also needs to maintain and preserve change in the new constellation. Lewin's theory is to this day an inspiration for business and social organizations.[2]

---

[1] Lewin, 2004, p. 330.
[2] See for example http://www.accel-team.com/techniques/force_field_analysis.html, http://www.change-management-coach.com/force-field-analysis.html, and http://www.mftrou.com/support-files/lewins-force-field-analysis.pdf.

HOMEOSTASIS, EQUILIBRIUM, AND SOCIAL ENTREPRENEURSHIP

Lewin's "balance between forces," in other words, refers to a homeostatic process in which the point of balance represents the equilibrium. Thus, to achieve social change one needs to destabilize the current equilibrium, establish a new equilibrium, and then stabilize it. Changing the equilibrium requires a change in the balance of forces. Social force-field analysis is therefore critical for understanding how a permanent change can be achieved in an efficient way. Effective introduction of social change involves strengthening the forces in the system that push it in the desired direction and weaken the forces that counter the change. As a prerequisite for introducing sustainable change by affecting the balance of forces, one needs to possess a deep understanding of the forces within the system.

According to de Rosnay (1997), complex systems must be in a state of homeostasis in order to maintain stability and to survive. However, a complex system must evolve by adapting to modifications of the environment. Otherwise, outside forces will soon destabilize and destroy it. The ensuing paradoxical situation can be summed up as follows: How can a stable organization, whose goal is to maintain itself and endure, also be able to change and evolve?

Consider Martin and Osberg's (2007) answer to this probing question: "The entrepreneur is inspired to alter the unpleasant equilibrium." He or she creates a new, stable equilibrium, one that provides a meaningfully higher level of satisfaction for the participants in the system. "The new equilibrium is permanent because it first survives and then stabilizes, even though some aspects of the original equilibrium may persist (pp. 33–34)."

This approach to social entrepreneurship opens up a new avenue of inquiry, to wit: How do complex systems behave? What are the mechanisms of stabilizing new equilibria? How, actually, does social change proliferate in society?

SELF-ORGANIZATION: SIMPLE RULES LEAD TO COMPLEX RESULTS

As mentioned previously, many complex systems are based on simple rules (Nowak & Vallacher, 1998; Nowak, 2004). A set of several simple rules leads to complex, intelligent behavior, whereas a set of complex rules often leads to poor results or simply backfires. Too many traffic regulations, for example, may very well increase traffic jams. These rules are transformable into computer simulations (also called cellular automata) through assigning simple directions to each cell on the screen (see bird-flock analysis, Reynolds,

1987).[3] In each step, cells follow the programmed directions, and hundreds or thousands of such steps simulate the complex behavior of the flock.[4] For the application of the cellular automata approach to modeling social processes, we now discuss the bubbles theory.

BUBBLES THEORY

The challenge is how to model the "diffusion of innovations,"[5] especially when the flow of rapid spread of novelty is non-uniform, with "bubbles of new" appearing in the "sea of old." This process is similar to the phenomenon of phase transitions in physics (Nowak and Vallacher, 2005), as when water, at a temperature of $212°$ F, transforms into gas. In this scenario, one first observes small nucleus bubbles, which connect together, grow in size, and become large, full-blown bubbles, which eventually burst out at the surface. Using bubbles as a metaphor for dynamical change, we can say that the bubbles are the forerunners of the new state (gas), while the old state (liquid) can still be observed. Similarly, in societies undergoing rapid transition, we can find islands of the new reality intermixed with the old ones. As change progresses, the islands of "new" gradually expand at the expense of the areas of "old." In the late 1980s and early 1990s, a group of international scientists who had no knowledge of the phenomenon of social entrepreneurship took on the challenge of modeling similar social-change dynamics. Their thinking paralleled the concept of social entrepreneurship spreading their new ideas through creating clusters of "new," interconnected through a network (see Chapter 7) and spreading through clusters, or hubs, which are formed around leaders.

They began with the notion, supported by many experiments, that the magnitude of social influence depends on three critical factors: the number of sources exerting influence, the proximity of the source(s) to the target(s), and the strength of the source(s). Research in various fields has documented (Nowak et al., 1990) that influence grows approximately as the square root of the number of people involved, decreases with the square of the distance

---

[3] The ants' food search was an inspiration for computer modeling as well, see http://www
.youtube.com/watch?v=117jIuUAm8s&feature=PlayList&p=BD8B5F8BDE33EEB5&
index=5.

[4] One of the examples of simple rules that may lead to complex outcomes are some computer games; see, for example, the Game of Life at fix spacing http://www.math.com/students/ wonders/life/life.html (click Play Life in the upper right corner).

[5] The title of Everett Rogers' (2003) book is "Diffusion of Innovations."

between the source and target, and is proportional to the strength (e.g., social status and credibility) of the sources.[6]

On the basis of some research (conducted both in the United States and China), we know that the probability that two individuals will discuss matters that are important to them decreases by a square of the distance between their respective residences (Latané et al., 1995). We also know that the impact of information about the event decreases with physical distance from it (Latané, 1981): A traffic accident on one's street is likely to attract considerable attention, whereas information about a traffic accident in a distant town is likely to be ignored.

The joint influence of these two factors is multiplicative and is reflected in a clear mathematical formula.[7] Another variable, individual variation in strength and locality, and the way it dictates the dynamics of information in a social network was studied and proved to be critical (Nowak et al., 1990; Lewenstein et al., 1993).

In preparing the computer modeling, each individual was assigned a specific location in social space, represented as a two-dimensional matrix of N rows and columns. The social group, modeled in a manner resembling cellular automata, consists of n individuals located on this two-dimensional grid. Each individual has an opinion on an issue. Opinions that are in the minority form a local minority cluster.

Individuals weigh an opinion and eventually modify or maintain it according to the mathematical formula mentioned before. It is interesting to note that they weighed their opinions using in fact a very limited sample, comprising mostly people in their neighborhood.

In computer simulations, it was assumed that the opinion of the minority was more attractive than the opinion of the majority. The simulations were implemented by adding a positive constant to the total influence of the minority (as described by the aforementioned equation). A typical progression of computer simulation is portrayed in Figures 1a and 1b.

In the simulations (Vallacher & Nowak, 2007), one individual is chosen (usually at random) and influence is computed for each opinion in

---

[6] N.B.: This formula applies to various social and psychological situations, as when studying the issues of conformity, stage fright, petition signing, or interest in news events.

[7] The equation is: $I_i = \left(\sum_1^N \left(\frac{s_j}{d_{ij}^2} \right)^2 \right)^{1/2}$, where I_i denotes the total influence, s_j corresponds to the strength of each individual, and d_{ij} corresponds to the distance between individuals i and j. It follows from the formula that individuals who are strongest and nearest to the target of influence have the greatest impact.

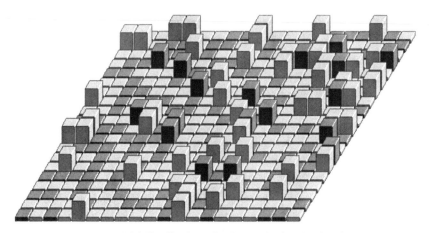

FIGURE 1A. Initial distribution of opinions in the simulated group

the group. If the resultant strength is greater than the strength of the individuals' current position, their opinion changes to match the prevailing one.

This procedure is repeated until there are no further changes, which typically requires several rounds of simulation because persons who have previously changed their position to match that of their neighbors may revert to the original one if the neighbors change their opinions. Figure 1b shows representative results of the computer simulations. In Figure 1a, there is a majority of 60 percent (light gray) and a minority of 40 percent (dark gray). The majority and minority members are randomly distributed, and

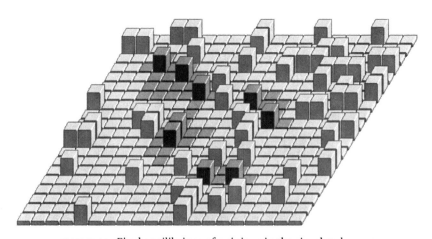

FIGURE 1B. Final equilibrium of opinions in the simulated group

each group has the same relative proportions of strong and weak members (high versus low boxes). Figure 1b shows the equilibrium reached after six rounds of simulated discussion. Now the majority is 90 percent and the minority is 10 percent. The minority opinion has survived by forming clusters of like-minded people, and these clusters are largely formed around strong individuals.

During transitions, clusters (*bubbles*) of "new" appear and grow in the sea of "old." From this perspective, interacting groups rather than isolated individuals are subject to change. Indeed, clustering of change is pervasive across a variety of social and economic phenomena (Perroux, 1950).

These cases indicate that social entrepreneurs usually do create such "bubbles of new in the sea of old"; that is, they bring into being around them areas of shared goals and ideas. The computer simulation revealed that it is enough to create such bubbles and interconnect them in order to achieve a major mindset shift, and that one doesn't need to address directly the whole society or region, which would involve huge investments; rather, bubbles will grow and the change will appear in a natural way.

Sheer analysis of this computer modeling, before even referring to social processes occurring in reality, provides some indications of how to facilitate the changes. One should establish clusters of the "new." In order to do this, one should identify social groups that are best prepared to help the transition occur. It is essential to assist those groups in creating a cluster by changing their local environment and providing some aid. This aid might be discontinued as soon as the cluster reaches a configuration in which it can survive as a minority.

Cluster leaders are of central importance in this scenario, especially at the beginning. They become the seeds of the bubbles of "new." They can help the minority to withstand the pressure of the majority when the clusters of the "new" are relatively small.

Finally, one should support the development of connections among clusters of "new." Such processes may take place on a local scale in the social space. Consider the advent of several cooperating businesses joining their efforts in order to develop a larger-scale enterprise.

It is interesting to note that comparing our practical knowledge stemming from real social processes with the results of the computer simulations lead to very similar conclusions. The simulation and its theoretical model offer some important practical suggestions for deciding how to facilitate the change process effectively, at low cost, and based on the endogenous properties and tendencies of groups and societies.

SELF-ORGANIZATION

Social entrepreneurs usually find simple solutions with simple rules that require minimum effort to adapt to and follow. In the long run, those simple rules bring about complex results.

The process by which simple rules produce complex patterns is called self-organization, mainly because there is no central director to oversee the process (Fisher, 2009). All that is needed is an appropriate set of simple (local) rules.

A good illustration of self-organization is an audience clapping in unison – a spontaneous, self-directed activity. Without direction, the applause automatically becomes synchronized into rhythmic beats created by people adjusting their clapping to that of those around them. The rules controlling this process are simple: They tell you to either speed up or slow down the frequency of your own clapping according to what you hear from your neighbors. However, there is no way to identify the linear causation. In other words, who set or increased the pace of the applause? And what was the actual mechanism, what were the dynamics of these changes?

There are many instances of complex, self-organizing systems, in which millions of interactions occur simultaneously – when everyone changes the state of everyone else (Strogatz, 2003). Consider the booms and crashes of the stock market or the emergence of consciousness from the interplay of trillions of neurons in the brain. Often, at the level of simple rules, one can see common mechanisms in phenomena that on the surface seem to be quite different from one another. Next, we will see how collective intelligence can emerge, even in systems composed of elements that are not intelligent by themselves.

In August 2000, a Japanese scientist (Nakagaki et al., 2000) demonstrated that a simple organism, *slime mold*, a fungus-like creature, can successfully navigate a maze to reach food placed at the exit. It would first align itself along the shortest route, then slowly traverse the maze and reach the food. Slime mold is composed of cells that either aggregate to form a colony or remain separate from the rest of the cells. Each cell secretes a pheromone called *acrasin*. The better-fed cells secrete a greater amount of pheromone. Each cell has a tendency to follow the scent of *acrasin*. In the beginning, a number of cells separate from the colony and wander randomly. When by chance they find some food and ingest it, following the trace of the pheromone, they find the colony. Returning cells that are satisfied leave a stronger trail of scent for other cells to follow. As more cells follow the trail, the trail becomes stronger so eventually almost all the cells come to the location of the food.

Ants in their colonies demonstrate complex, well-organized behaviors with no apparent leader orchestrating the process. The study of ant colonies has led to a new computer-modeling technique, ant colony optimization (ACO). The "wisdom" of the ant colony, especially the simple rules of interaction, has become a repository of knowledge for modeling various processes (Fisher, 2009).

Ants search for food, following a set of genetically determined behaviors (Dubakov, 2009), which are similar to the ways the cells of slime mold act:

1. Travel randomly in search for food.
2. If you find a food, take it to the nest, laying down an odor trail on the way.
3. Signal to other ants the discovery of food, which encourages them to search for it.

The newly recruited ants will follow the odor trail directly to the food source; moreover, each newly arrived ant will reinforce the odor trail for the next comers. Ants, in addition to their pheromones signaling the path to follow, also can use a "panic" pheromone to signal danger.

Similar rules also operate in human groups. Humans have a tendency to follow the behavior of others, especially in situations in which they do not know how to behave. This tendency to imitate others is called modeling (Bandura, 1976). It is especially strong when the observed behavior results in a reward.

The tendency to imitate successful behavior of others is also the key to Internet behavior. Most Internet shopping sites indicate what other visitors have bought and show the satisfaction of the customers who have bought the products.

All these examples involve enormous numbers of players linked in complex webs. In every case, astonishing patterns emerge spontaneously. The richness of the world around us is due, in large part, to the miracle of self-organization (Strogatz, 2003).

Chaos or Order?

Complex systems with their random elements (e.g., neurons, ants, stock-market traders), as well as the process of self-organization, may on the surface resemble chaos, as they are the result of many chaotic interactions (Fisher, 2009). This *randomness* of connections is one way, and the most popular, of defining chaos.

The *deterministic* approach is the other way of defining chaos, which posits that minimal changes in initial impulses produce different paths of evolvement and remarkable differences in final outcomes. The well-known narrative of the "butterfly effect" – that the flap of a butterfly's wings in one place can have a major effect on weather conditions on the opposite side of the globe – illustrates how small changes at the outset can produce astonishingly significant results (Érdi, 2008). Along the same vein, imagine a bottle drifting in the current called the North Atlantic Drift encountering its bifurcation point (Y-junction), a very slight breeze will determine whether the bottle ends up near the North American coast or close to Norway.

The chaos phenomenon is also well represented in business, in which a tiny local impulse can influence the attitudes of stock traders and aggregate into an immense global market shift. This was well conceptualized by the founder and former CEO of Visa International, Dee W. Hock (2000), who asserted that Visa owes its success and remarkable achievements to its structure, which merges chaos and order by creating a dynamic business venture that is changing, "changing change," and promoting originality and innovation. Following that train of thought, Hock coined the term "chaordic," claiming that we are currently entering a *chaordic era.* He notes that the best results are achieved when business ventures follow the chaotic principles of natural interactions (e.g., horizontal and unstructured communication), which produce, in a bottom-up process, a new order.

When he coined the term *chaordic era,* Hock was no doubt aware that complex systems are adaptive and evolve as they adapt to changing circumstances; the interactions among individuals, instead of being simply additive (e.g., more and more participants pull the rope in a tug-of-war competition) are more chaotic and hence produce a disproportional response as the process is involved in myriad feedback loops (Fisher, 2009). Later, we will return to the *chaos-to-order* concept in its many variations (vibrant networks, in Chapter 9, and building the community, in Appendix 1).

Recapping Simple vs. Complex Systems

The difference between simple and complex systems was articulated by Érdi (2008):

Simple systems:

- There is a single cause and single effect; the causation is linear: A causes B, B causes C, and so on.
- A small change in the cause implies a small change in the effect.
- The result is predictable.

Complex systems:

- The causation is circular; various feedback loops influence, or rein-force, the effect.
- Small changes in the cause may result in dramatic effects.
- The results of complex-system processes are often unpredictable; for example, new emergent phenomena may appear (for the theory of emergence, see Chapter 6).

In some cases, no matter what one does, the system reverts to its initial state. Storms may repeatedly damage the anthill, yet the ants, without any control or driving force, will rebuild it diligently and meticulously, time and time again. In some cases, however, attempts to revitalize lethargic communities fail: After presenting a spectacular event or implementing a world-class program, when the dust settles, all goes back to the initial stagnant situation. Free-floating dynamics tend to drift toward certain equilibrium.

In phase 1, natural equilibrium is controlled by a societal attractor, for instance, misanthropy and distrust. In phase 2, a force keeps the ball up – a metaphor for top-down activities. In phase 3, after the external force is gone, the system goes back to its natural equilibrium.

FIGURE 2. The system over time drifts back to the old attractor; the ball is pushed up by an external force and falls back after the force withdraws

As shown in Figure 2, one needs a constant force in order to keep the metaphorical "ball of change" up; in the absence of such a force, the environment's homeostatic mechanisms bring it back to its natural equilibrium. In modern physics, such equilibrium is called the attractor, as it "attracts" all the states of the system. An attractor refers to a subset of potential states to which a system's behavior converges over time.[8] Metaphorically, an attractor "attracts" the system's behavior, so that even very different starting states tend to evolve toward the subset of states defining the attractor (Vallacher et al., 2010). In other words, an attractor is a state or a reliable pattern of

---

[8] If there are several attractors in the system, a strong push is needed in order to move the ball to the next attractor.

changes toward which a dynamical system evolves over time, and to which the system returns after it has been perturbed. In a natural way and in an adequate period of time, independent of actions taken, the social systems will have a tendency to drift back toward the attractor (Nowak & Vallacher, 1998; Vallacher & Nowak, 2007).

In some situations, such as the aforementioned lethargic communities, there is a deeply ingrained "old" negative attractor, which could for example be based on distrust, on misanthropy, or on lack of cooperation – or all of the above – that controls the natural equilibrium. To achieve lasting, durable change requires much more than exerting force to keep the ball up. What is needed is a new attractor that would shift the natural societal balance point. It is not the external force that in the long run would alter the dynamic; it is the new societal balance point determined by new positive variables (like trust and cooperativeness) that would lead to abiding change. Figure 3 illustrates this process with the "ball of change."

FIGURE 3. Phase 1: the surface is modified (high hollow) so that the ball can fall into another balance point; a new attractor emerges with the new parameters, let's say, trust and cooperation; phase 2: the ball is pushed to high hollow; phase 3: the new attractor of trust and cooperation gains in strength, while the old one decreases in influence; the new hole over time deepens while the old attractor becomes irrelevant

Gradually, if the new attractor of trust and cooperation deepens, it becomes a permanent property of the system. Consider the case of Arif Khan from Pakistan (mentioned in Chapter 2), whose goal is to empower craftswomen and artisans, especially in remote mountainous areas of tribal Pakistan. He is leveraging their handmade products to a marketable level and is selling them under a label associated with high quality and authenticity. Together with handcrafts, Arif is bringing to the communities elementary education as well as improvements in family health and hygiene. The direct impact has been to raise the living standards of the families and communities, in addition to empowering women and enhancing the level of respect accorded them. Finally, in a kind of ripple effect, whole communities become involved in economic development.

Consider Arif Khan's approach from the dynamic perspective: Instead of pushing directly for change against the old attractor (whether it is economic or educational development, the state of hygiene, or the status of women), he is building a new attractor around an already-existing activity: crafting handmade goods. Arif Khan provides income, pushing the metaphorical ball up into a small higher hollow. This attractor is well received by the communities and, as a result, changes the deeply ingrained attitudes toward women and toward market-based activities. This enables him to introduce improved standards of hygiene (deepening the hollow and stabilizing the change), which, in turn, make the people more productive. This also enables him to introduce education for children. Trust in the new economy (and of one another) increases, further deepening the hollow. Over time, this new attractor becomes an endogenous aspect of the community and in turn spurs other activities. The new attractor deepens to the extent that if Arif Khan goes elsewhere, there are others, including women, now trusted by the community, educated enough who will ensure that the income stream and education continue.

There is one other dimension of building a new attractor in which the action also changes the regulatory mechanisms instead of grappling with the resistant dynamics. Revisiting Lewin's force field, we are reminded of the existing tendencies and potentials of groups or communities, and on the basis of those potentials, such regulatory parameters as trust, optimism, and cooperativeness must also increase. At a certain level, those parameters then create the new attractor, which, as we have seen, becomes a powerful vehicle for change. In Chapters 7 and 10, we will describe how social entrepreneurship build new attractors.

In the next chapter, using the apparatus of complexity theory, we will delve into the question: How do new social phenomena emerge and become sustainable?

CHAPTER HIGHLIGHTS

- Small initial impulses or forces can lead to huge results (whereas people usually think that big results can be achieved only through big initial investments).
- Seemingly chaotic interactions can lead to structured and complex consequences (usually people think that prestructuring and controlling interactions prevents chaos and destruction). Leaving space for unstructured interaction may lead to new, unpredicted although highly appreciated results.

- What makes the complexity nonlinear are the many free interactions and feedback loops between them and their spontaneous ideas; those feedback loops may connect lower-level structures with higher-level ones, influencing the process both ways (bottom-up and top-down).
- It is impossible to predict the results of complex interactions by analyzing single agents or through linear thinking (from A to B); often the only way to capture complex dynamics is through computer modeling.

6

Theory of Social Emergence

Social entrepreneurs are known for their intense passion and visionary aspirations to make a significant impact on society and to engender a permanent change that would mean a better world for large numbers of people. As they often say in private conversations, they want to leave behind something new, significant, and substantial. Munir Hasan, for example, can reflect on an irrevocably changed field of mathematics in Bangladesh, thanks to his efforts to transform the way the field of mathematics evolved from a neglected and undervalued aspect of public education to one in which students excelled and even competed on the world stage. Steve Bigari has created a solid approach to retaining and mainstreaming low-income workers. Similarly, Kaz Jaworski's region in the underdeveloped part of Poland is thriving, the societal mindsets changed irreversibly, prompting cooperative and enterprising behavior.[1]

It may seem at first glance that these three individuals "magically" created "something out of nothing": They addressed seemingly unsolvable problems, started with virtually no resources, and turned a totally "no-go" situation into a dynamic process, achieving significant and durable results.

However, a closer look reveals that they triggered a process of interactions on a "lower" level, fostering cooperation among individuals and increasing the number of connections, which at some point reaches a critical mass and evolves into a significant change in the society as a whole. This dynamic is what Coleman (2000) refers to when he states that there is a category of social-change processes that are characterized by an accumulation of changes on the micro level, turning at some point into changes on the macro level at which some new and significant structures emerge.

---

[1] Kaz Jaworski is currently serving as his region's Senator with the mission to spread similar bottom-up and society-empowering rural community development methods.

It is obvious that in pursuing social change, social entrepreneurs would want to leave behind a legacy of some new, lasting, and irreversible systemic structures. That is, in the language of the dynamical theory, they would want to build *emergent phenomena*. The theoretical framework for analyzing how those higher-level entities appear is called the *emergence theory*. A closer look at the new universe of emergence theory enables a deeper understanding of the process of producing new, durable, and irreversible higher-level social phenomena. It is instructive to look at general emergence theory as it applies to the fields of physics and biology as a prelude to seeing how it applies to social change.

THE THEORY OF EMERGENCE

As suggested previously, emergence may appear like something emanating out of nothing. In his widely read book, *The Tipping Point* (2002), Malcolm Gladwell described this phenomenon, whereby in some situations the process of interaction among low-level elements reaches a turning point beyond which they transform into completely new, higher-level, irreversible phenomena. The movement from low-level rules to higher-level sophistication is what we call *emergence* (Johnson, 2001). Nowak (2004) holds that "the basic idea is that the local interactions among low-level elements, where each element adjusts to other elements, without reference to a global pattern, may lead to the emergence of highly coherent structures and behaviors on the level of the whole." What probably makes emergence theory so compelling is that it relates to processes in which new entities arise without any specific body either controlling or orchestrating this occurrence, save for the interactions among elements (air particles, grains of sand, birds, ants, people, etc.) reaching a threshold (tipping point). "The emergent phenomenon typically arise in the absence of any sort of 'invisible hand' or central controller (p. 15)" (Johnson, 2009).

Emergence theory can be applied to such disciplines as philosophy, systems theory, and biology, and especially to investigating how complex systems and patterns arise out of a multiplicity of relatively simple interactions. Consider, for example, how a pile of sand takes shape: As grains of sand are spilled on top of one another, the pile "automatically" forms a conical shape. New sand spilled on the top slides down, building up the shape of a cone. The sand cone is an emergent phenomenon and it appears out of the interactions between grains of sand and gravity (Bedau & Humphreys, 2008).

According to Goldstein (1999), the following are the basic properties of emergent systems:

Radical novelty. The appearance of features that are not previously observed. For example, no matter how long and meticulously scientists (chemists and physicists) might analyze single air particles, they would never be able to predict that those particles, if brought together, would propagate sound waves! Similarly, analyzing single ants would never bring us to the conclusion that if more such ants gathered together they would cooperate in building anthills. The anthill is an emergent result of their cooperation, with no external or internal body controlling or directing them. Ants are genetically programmed to exchange information and, through that biochemical process of communication, they create complex and surprising emergent entities.[2]

Unpredictability. The creation of complex systems – in this case, anthills – can never be predicted by individually examining ants; the new property appears on a higher level as a result of the exchange of information. The features of emergents are neither predictable nor deducible from lower- or micro-level components. The v-shaped flock of birds that suddenly appears out of a randomly assembled gathering of birds on the branches of a tree could be characterized as an emergent entity. Birds are not hierarchic, and the formation of the higher-level "v" shape appears out of the unsystematic interaction of birds "on the lower level" (Reynolds, 1987). We may know from experience that at some point birds will form a v-shaped flock, but we wouldn't be able to predict the exact timing; nor would we know in advance if some groups of birds will remain separated from the main group and create their own v-shapes, or if they will first mix with birds from neighboring trees; nor would we be able to predict the order of birds in the v-shaped flock.

Coherence or correlation. Emergents appear as integrated wholes that tend to maintain some sense of identity over time. The sand pile as a whole maintains coherence (you can admire its elegance regardless of the amount of sand added on the top). The v-shaped flocks of birds, as well as the swarm of ants, are coherent; this coherence spans and correlates the separate, lower-level components into a higher-level unity.

---

[2] See, for example, BBC footage on how ants build an island out of themselves and caringly carry their queen to the other side of the river: http://www.youtube.com/watch?v= A042JoIDQK4&feature=PlayList&p=7893E947FC9954A5&playnext=1&playnext_from= PL&index=1.

Global or macro level. Because coherence represents a correlation that spans separate components, the locus of emergent phenomena occurs at a global or macro level, although components are located at the micro level. On the micro level, one can observe only single ants or single birds on a tree. The occurrence and observation of their emergent behavior is available only on the macro level.

Dynamical. Emergent phenomena arise as complex systems gradually, over time. This means that there are some processes and increasing interactions that gather momentum, as when a random group of birds on the branches of a tree spontaneously (as we interpret it) picks up and takes off and, in transit, exchanges information leading to the formation of a v-shaped flock (Reynolds, 1987). As a dynamical construct, emergence is associated with the arising of new attractors (see Chapter 5) in dynamical systems.

Clearly demonstrative. Emergents are recognized by showing themselves. One can easily spot and admire a v-shaped flock of birds; similarly, one can easily identify elegant anthills clearly visible on the forest floor.

What conditions are favorable for configuring emergent entities? According to Sawyer (2007), emergence is more likely to be found in systems in which many components interact in densely connected networks; sand grains, birds, and ants are in close contact before they transform into an emergent. However, Johnson (2001) suggests that dense connections are not enough to produce emergent phenomena; the system must also be adaptive in order to form, out of numerous interactions of elements (agents), a new pattern; this means that some random gatherings of birds may not meet the necessary conditions to take flight, such as time, space, quantity, and other features.

Global-system functions cannot be either localized or decomposed to any one subset of components, but rather are distributed throughout the entire system. The whole flock forms the v-shape and the multitude of ants creates the anthill, not individual entities. The components interact using a complex and sophisticated language: Birds exchange information regarding the exact position, orientation, and velocity of other birds (Reynolds, 1987); ants communicate via the "language" of pheromones (Vittori et al., 2006; Garnier et al., 2007).

There is also the question of autonomy: Emergence relates to phenomena that arise from and depend on, yet are simultaneously independent of, some more basic phenomena (Bedau & Humphreys, 2008). This means that the v-shaped flock of birds behaves as an autonomous, single mechanical unit, even though, as a matter of fact, it arises and depends on the coordination of individual birds.

SOCIAL EMERGENCE

Émile Durkheim[3] was no doubt one of the first sociologists to notice the importance of the appearance of new phenomena resulting from the inter-action of discrete elements. He states that the main object of sociology is to study social facts. These social facts have a meaning of their own, *sui generis*, and cannot be reduced to psychological or biological factors. Durkheim never used the term "emergence" although most of his key theo-retical concepts – such as: social facts, dynamic density, social milieu, social substratum, and *sui generis* – were actually other ways to express this idea. Both social facts and collective representations are emergent social phenom-ena and both are *sui generis* properties of a social system emerging from the association of individuals (Sawyer, 2007).

Sawyer (2007) mentions five levels of social emergence, as follows:

The first is the individual level, which consists of individual intentions, memories, personalities, and cognitive processes. We could add that at that level people represent their own personal experience, patterns of attribution, eventual prejudices, and attitudes.

The second is the interaction level, which involves patterns of discourse, symbolic interaction, collaboration, and negotiation.

The third is the ephemeral-emergent level, at which some emergent manifestations may appear, although still unstable; there may arise some common topics, frames of interactions, structures for participation, and some relative roles and statuses. However, at this point, things can be easily reversed.

The fourth is the stable-emergent level, at which we observe group structures, new language (e.g., group jargon, catchphrases), and con-versational routines. These elements are the base for final emergence.

Finally, the social-structure level, where we observe the emergence of written texts (procedures, laws, and regulations), technological or mate-rial routines, and systems of the society.

Sawyer introduces the notion of "the circle of emergence," which involves levels two, three, and four, as well as parts of levels one and five. Why only

---

[3] End of the nineteenth and beginning of the twentieth century.

parts? Because some of the elements on the individual level are not involved in the process of social emergence; for example, some societal mindsets and prejudices are related to the history of the region. Also, the fifth level includes already-existing structures, such as the political system, law, and local government.

The "circle of emergence" exemplifies the feedback loops among all those sections. For example, the shift in mindsets may influence the interactions and collaboration and, as a consequence, the ephemeral emergents; in a feedback loop, the advent of new interactional frames and participation structures may influence individual processes of attribution. Other feedback loops among those levels may occur as well, although the usual dynamic starts with the way people think, interact, and create new structures.

By definition, the notion of the "circle of emergence" implies that the process is nonlinear. Traditionally, we are used to rational, result-oriented thinking: "If we increase factor A, we will receive an increase in impact B" or "The reason for X is Y." Here we are faced with multiple reasons/results mutually influencing one another in a complex process; through myriad interactions and stages this process leads to the appearance of emergent phenomena. However, the problem is that there is no mathematical formula for emergent processes (Strogatz, 2003); the only way to explore them is through modeling computer-based simulations. For example, one can model crowd behavior and city traffic. The behavior of pedestrians or people exiting a theater, especially in an emergency, becomes an extremely complicated challenge for planners, thanks to the diversity of variables among the individuals – age, physical fitness, degree of mental focus, state of mind, to name a few – all of which add up to what we call "crowd behavior." In many cases, the result of the interaction among the many diverse individuals is an emergent order (Bonabeau, 2001, 2002).[4] In extreme cases, at some critical point, order turns into panic. It is impossible to create a formula for predicting the emergence of the panic behavior, and it is unethical to experiment in real-life situations. An experiment in which researchers stage a fire in a crowded theater in order to study the crowd's behavior could lead to physical and psychological harm. If, however, the "audience" is told beforehand that the fire is not real, the experiment is ruined. The only way to analyze panic behavior and draw conclusions for prevention (e.g., number of exits, color of signs, and tone and volume of vocal messages) is to model

---

[4] An exemplary demonstration of a computer-based simulation of high-density crowd behavior can be found at http://www.youtube.com/watch?v=KsbChtHmwfA.

such situations (Lozano et al., 2007; Smith et al., 2009). Modeling in this case would mean simulating the actions and interactions of autonomous agents with special consideration given to the effects of those interactions on the system as a whole. Emergent behavior in city traffic (unimpeded traffic flows or sudden traffic jams) is, ironically, one of the simplest examples of complex situations that do not fit into linear logic.

SOCIAL ENTREPRENEURSHIP AND THE CIRCLE OF EMERGENCE

Sawyer's circle of emergence provides a convenient framework for analyzing the change process engendered by social entrepreneurs. Let's take the example of Kaz Jaworski, which was introduced previously.

Level 1. Individual

The first step was to address people's initial negative attitudes (prejudices, lack of trust, and unwillingness to cooperate). To do so, he launched the local telephone network, the nature of which prompted the community to connect much more intensely than before and thus, to bond; furthermore, this development primed people's minds for continued cooperation.

Level 2. Interactions

The local telephone network opened an avenue for discussing how to take advantage of this success. There were deliberations over further projects: Should they invest in the sewage system? Or should it be mineral-water production? Should the community organize English and IT education? What about addressing the community-wide alcohol abuse?

As a result of the interchanges and negotiations, some new initiatives were undertaken (sewage and mineral-water production). The community was ready and set for further dialogue and negotiations for continuing development.

Level 3. Ephemeral Emergents

As a consequence, the community launched the production of organic food, with door-to-door delivery to the neighboring cities and designated 10 percent of the generated income for education and health prevention.

The success of those consecutive enterprises triggered more ideas for new undertakings. The society self-identified and self-organized around common causes, such as community development.

Level 4. Stable Emergents

Those undertakings transformed the structure of the society from a loose aggregation of isolated farms to a variety of cooperatives and venture partnerships. The distribution of 10 percent of the generated income for social investments was accomplished through a process of delegating representatives and democratic decision making.

On a macro scale, the number of new enterprises was significantly higher when compared with the average of neighboring communities, and the degree of civic participation was outstanding. The percentage of voting citizens, for example, compared favorably to nationwide and regional averages. Thus, as a result of the economic and social development, a new phenomenon emerged: civic awareness and participation.

Level 5. Structures

The collective frame of mind of the population changed from helplessness to hope, optimism, self-esteem, and identification with a successful community. Mirroring these positive developments, a new entrepreneurial language replaced the old "nothing-can-be-done" lingo. Many new enterprises based their headquarters in the area and spread their influence over the whole region. For example, the mineral-water enterprise became the main supplier for the entire area.

However, a bare description of the levels of emergence per se falls flat without an understanding of the dynamical process of the various systemic feedback loops among all the levels. The second level (interactions) influenced the individual way of thinking: People started perceiving themselves as ready for success and cooperation, which influenced changes on the individual level. The third and fourth levels (ephemeral and stable emergents) and the success of the first few enterprises built trust and the propensity for collaboration, which influenced the second level (interactions) and the first level (attitudes of individuals). The new thinking and achievements accelerated the drive for new successes, which in turn influenced the self-image of the group and increased sociability. The fifth level (structures) built, in a feedback loop, a new cognition and new self-identification (first level), and accelerated the spirit of cooperation (second level).

The new community, now structured around achievement instead of self-defense, is full of hope and optimism, feeling empowered and future-oriented. We can consider this new state as emergent, because it is stable, irreversible, and not reducible to the simple sum of its elements. The overall potential of the society has significantly increased as a result of its multifaceted development.

From the perspective of the dynamical systems theory, the whole process started with introducing a new positive attractor, which became the nucleus for further development.

CHAPTER HIGHLIGHTS

- The accumulation of changes on the micro level may turn at some point into changes on the macro level, at which some new and significant structures emerge; these newly appearing structures are called "emergent phenomena."
- What probably makes emergence theory so compelling is that it relates to processes in which new entities arise without any specific body either controlling or orchestrating this occurrence; the emergent phenomenon typically arises in the absence of any sort of "invisible hand" or central controlling agent. As stated in Chapter 4, social entrepreneurs often enable the endogenous change process instead of controlling it. Through a deep understanding of the Lewinian forcefield (Chapter 5), they often operate as if "from the inside."
- Emergent phenomena are clearly observed in physics, biology, and sociology. Similarly, social entrepreneurs foster a process leading to the emergence of new, irreversible social structures, mindsets, and symbols.

SUMMARY AND CONCLUSIONS, SECTION 2

In this section, we introduced a dynamical approach to social entrepreneurship through the portrayal of a new case. Chapter 4 outlined several essential sociological theories and dilemmas related to social change, as well as the basic social-change theories. Chapter 5 presented the dynamical systems theory and the complexity theory; an example of modeling the extent of change was provided (bubbles theory). The theory of emergence and its application to social entrepreneurship was introduced in Chapter 6, including the concept of the circle of social emergence, which was introduced in the case at the beginning of this section. We reached the conclusion that the process initiated by social entrepreneurs is nonlinear and consists of several feedback loops modifying the "performance capacity of the society."[5]

Instead of directly addressing and pushing for solving problems, social entrepreneurs trigger a durable process. The process is usually nonlinear, with various feedback loops and mutual reinforcements. One of the differences between simple and complex systems is that in the first there is a single cause and single effect, whereas in the latter there is circular causality and feedback loops (Érdi, 2008).

The process initiated by social entrepreneurs leads, through various feedback loops, to a creation of emergent entities, such as an enterprising community, and is usually actuated with small and simple initiatives that behave as a trigger. (This relates to another difference between simple and complex systems: In the first, a small change in the cause implies a small change in the effects; in the latter, a small change unleashes vast consequences; Érdi, 2008). Those initiatives, which forge the next change process, are essential when working with people, groups and societies, as they allow the creation of new, positive attractors regardless of the intractability of the problem being addressed.

In the next section, we will present how this sort of social-entrepreneurial approach empowers and strengthens the performance capacity and self-reliance of societies. We will delve into many related questions, such as: What sort of personality traits fosters this sort of change dynamics? What kind of leadership ensures its cultivation and generation? We will also redefine social entrepreneurship in light of the dynamical systems theory.

[5] After Peter Drucker; see Gendron, 1996.

SECTION 3

SOCIAL CAPITAL BUILT BY SOCIAL
ENTREPRENEURS

INTRODUCTION

The previous section illustrated the complex properties of the change process spawned by social entrepreneurs. We observed how the new attractors become a gateway for pursuing social entrepreneurs' goals (covering education gaps, protecting endangered species, and developing disenfranchised communities) and, moreover, how they empower societies in a generalized way, whether it be economically or in the area of civic participation.

In this section, we will illustrate how this process builds and strengthens social capital and how social capital, in a feedback loop, empowers societies (Chapter 7). The subject of social networks, which are the foundation of social capital, will be presented in Chapter 8. We will next analyze what kind of personality traits facilitate the process of building social capital, with a closer look at the differences between social entrepreneurs and other leaders (Chapter 9). The departure point, again, will be through an illustrative account of social entrepreneurs in action.

Reza Deghati, Afghanistan: Advancing the status of women and youth through journalism

Reza Deghati,[1] born in Iran, now a citizen of France, is a world-renowned photojournalist whose photos have been published by some of the most prestigious magazines, such as *Time, National Geographic,* and *Life.* Prompted by the profound belief that through his images he could foster social change, Reza Deghati crossed the globe for decades, focusing on areas devastated by war and conflict.

[1] See http://www.ashoka.org/rdeghati.

75

He was especially concerned with the situation in Afghanistan, and he traveled through the country, using his camera to document what he saw. He understood that true change could only be achieved as a bottom-up process through the power of communication and education. In 2001 he founded AINA,[2] whose mission is to contribute to the emergence of civil society through actions in the areas of education (particularly focusing on women and children), information, and communication; AINA promotes the development of independent media and cultural expression as a foundation of democracy.

The question was how to pursue this critically important mission. Reza's strategy was two-fold: on one hand to train Afghan women in media, culture, and communication, so they could develop long-term autonomous and sustainable business entities; on the other, to educate children for long-term peace and progress in their home country.

Women were encouraged to become local journalists, receiving training in photojournalism and video production, as well as in radio and broadcast management. AINA also used print media and innovative film shown to millions across the country at multiple venues, presenting topics as varied as disease prevention, tolerance, cultural history, and democracy. Through AINA, female citizens receive the necessary education and skills to create media, reinforce democratic values, resist oppression, and speak out in a country where they have been voiceless for generations.

The beginning was not easy, as initially there was a total communication void; therefore, Reza Deghati's first step was to organize a pool of "master trainers" in media and communication. These filmmakers, photographers, radio journalists, and writers, mostly women, comprised the core training team. More importantly, Reza Deghati began to identify potential managers and administrators, recognizing that such individuals would be key to the long-term success and growth of any independent media enterprise. This led to building a self-multiplying community of media professionals, which transformed the media landscape in Afghanistan, particularly with respect to women's voices.

In the end, AINA trained hundreds of Afghans and as a result dozens of sustainable media businesses flourished, including female-led radio stations that disseminated information on health, nutrition, domestic violence, education, and more. One of the most notable radio stations, Afghan Women's Voices, airs nine hours daily and is completely autonomous and sustainable. It reaches more than five million listeners. One of the most successful

[2] See http://www.ainaworld.org.

PICTURE 8. Reza Deghati

PICTURE 9. AINA women's radio

PICTURE 10. Afghan girls reading *Parvaz* in Pashto

PICTURE 11. AINA Media Center in Afghanistan

publications, *Kabul Weekly*, with a circulation of close to three million, is designed to accurately reflect the concerns and desires of Afghan citizens.

AINA also created the first Afghan television serial titled *Palwasha* (rays of the sun). The serial follows a female judge (the heroine) who within each episode deliberates and rules on issues such as domestic violence, gender equality, drug addition, child abuse, and others. In 2005, the first documentary produced by an all-female Afghan team, *Afghanistan Unveiled*, was nominated for an Emmy Award given by the Academy of Television Arts and Sciences.

Reza Deghati also initiated *Parvaz*, a bimonthly magazine for Dari- and Pashto-speaking girls and boys ages seven through fourteen, and Afghanistan's first (and only) children's magazine. It is a colorful, visually rich educational tool whose stories and illustrations teach children (and their families, as it is read by many family and community members) about health issues, brotherhood and tolerance, sharing, and the history of Afghanistan, among many other topics. *Parvaz* was launched, not only as a means of educating and entertaining children, but also as a way of bridging gaps between parents and children. To date, fourteen editions have been produced, the press run averaging 40,000 copies per edition, with a readership of several million children and adults. *National Geographic* reports that one of the young *Parvaz* contributors, Masoud, was delighted when a boy stopped him in the street yelling, "You are Masoud! I have seen you in *Parvaz!*"[3]

Reza Deghati and AINA have championed a spirit of volunteerism among Afghanistan's people and have given women the freedom to express themselves – a privilege most Afghan women never dreamed of. This process restored self-esteem and encouraged them to participate in the development of Afghan civil society. Reza Deghati is planning to spread his idea to other countries heavily affected by wars, such as Sudan, Kurdistan, Burma, and Burkina-Faso.

[3] http://ngm.nationalgeographic.com/ngm/0311/online_extra/index.html.

7

Social Capital

Reza Deghati uses a bottom-up process, empowering the target groups (women and youth) and, by extension, the whole society. The capacity of bottom-up change mechanisms is generally seen as pivotal in introducing social change (Piven, 2008), in eradicating poverty in rural areas (Blair, 2005), or in promoting health care (Carey, 2000; Edwards et al., 2003).

Another illustrative example of the bottom-up process of change is the case of a social entrepreneur who was working with post-Soviet communities[1] whose social fiber was totally shattered by the regime that lasted more than seventy years. He started by organizing teachers' discussion groups, starting with simple issues. Gradually the groups self-organized and became action- and solution-oriented, leading to the next step – becoming role models and seedbeds of social change in the field of education and, finally, vehicles for the buildup of civic awareness and engagement.

Restoring trust and the propensity for cooperation was pivotal to igniting self-reliance and hope for change. These factors are the key parameters that typify social capital, which is deemed to be critical for sustaining bottom-up mechanisms (Woolcock, 1998). As such, social capital is increasingly becoming one of the central concepts for analyzing related social processes.[2]

In this chapter, we will present the various definitions and characteristics of social capital, followed by a review of the hypothesis that social entrepreneurs pursue their mission by building social capital.

---

[1] Krzysztof Stanowski from Poland. See http://www.ashoka.org/fellow/2920.

[2] Putnam and Gross (2002) mention that prior to 1981 there appeared 20 articles on social capital, 109 between 1991 and 1995, and 1,003 between 1996 and 1999. This increase is also reflected by the citation index (see Field, 2008).

DEFINING SOCIAL CAPITAL

Social capital is seen as a form of capital, although unlike other forms of capital, it is integral to the structure of relations between and among actors (Coleman, 2003). In simpler terms, social capital means features of social life – networks, norms, and trust – that enable participants to act together more effectively (Putnam, 1996). To simplify even further, some say that the idea at the core of the theory of social capital is that social relationships and networks matter and have value (Putnam & Gross, 2002; Field, 2008). In other words, a person's family, friends, and associates constitute an important asset, one that can be called on in a crisis or enjoyed for its own sake (Woolcock & Narayan, 2000).

The notions of financial and social capital are comparable in the sense that social networks also create tangible value, both individual and collective, and that we can "invest" in networking. Social capital is productive, making possible the achievements of certain ends that are impossible to accomplish without it (Putnam & Gross, 2002; Coleman, 2003).[3]

Borgatti et al. (1998) and Grootaert et al. (2004) illustrate two different, yet related, ways of discussing social capital. Borgatti contends that individual social capital refers to the resources, such as information, ideas, and support, that individuals are able to acquire thanks to their relationships with other people. These resources can be seen as *capital* (as they refer to tangible assets) and as *social* (as they are only accessible in and through relationships) (Burt, 2001; Lin, 2001). This approach is reflected in Bourdieu's definition (2003): Social capital is the aggregation of actual or potential resources that are linked to possession of a durable network of more or less institutionalized relationships.

We will refer to Putnam's, Fukuyama's and Grootaert's interpretations of group social capital, which refers to the nature and extent of one's involvement in various informal networks and civic organizations. "From chatting with neighbors or engaging in recreational activities to joining environmental organizations and political parties, social capital in this sense is used as a conceptual term to characterize the many and varied ways in which a given community's members interact. So understood, it is possible to construct a map of a community's associational life, and thus with it a sense of the state of its civic health" (Grootaert et al., 2004, p. 3). Social capital in this view

---

[3] The difference is that financial capital is homogeneous – one bit looks much like another; ownership of financial capital can be transferred and put to another use.

is seen as a quality of groups or, often, whole societies (Putnam, 2000). It is thus partly cultural, partly socio-structural, and includes such things as rule of law, social integration, and trust (Fukuyama, 1996).

It is also important to distinguish between two types of social networks, which correspond to Putnam's (2000) concepts – *bridging social capital* and *bonding social capital*. He defines the former as creating connections across diverse social groups, and the latter as doing so only among homogenous groups. Each mode serves an important purpose: The "bridging" form links groups and communities with the outer world, whereas the "bonding" type builds internal connectivity.

THE SEVERAL DIMENSIONS OF SOCIAL CAPITAL

The essence of social capital is related to the variety of groups and networks people belong to and participate in. Hence, *groups and networks* are then the central dimension of social capital (Grootaert et al., 2004).[4]

In the case study presented at the beginning of this section, Reza Deghati was building from scratch groups and networks of journalists comprising women and young people – groups that had had no voice in the society. They were linked to various groups and networks, both related directly to journalism as well as beyond.

Trust and solidarity are also essential dimensions. Trust, as it exists among neighbors, peers, and group members, leads to a high level of solidarity. It is the key driver for undertaking cooperative actions (Coleman, 1990; Putnam, 1993; Fukuyama, 1996; Bourdieu, 2003).

Reza Deghati aimed directly at setting the standard of trust and solidarity, seeing both as pivotal for building a civil society. The networks are vibrant because participating women and youth are encouraged by mutual trust, which reinforces their motivation to take bold actions.

Based on trust, the next dimension, *collective action and cooperation*, reflects the way people are willing to cooperate. Again, in Afghanistan, the mushrooming journalism and photojournalism initiatives (radio, TV, newspapers, and magazines) are the direct result of networks built on trust.

The way people communicate and access information brings about the dimension of *information and communication*. It is obvious that the circulation of information is at the core of Reza Deghati's strategy: He saw communication as a gateway to the buildup of the social fiber; this approach works, especially in isolated areas.

---

[4] Authors through several studies conceptualized the six pivotal dimensions of social capital.

The question arises as to how cohesive and inclusive the social networks are. The related dimension is *social cohesion and inclusion*. This dimension reflects the distinction between social capital's *bonding* and *bridging* functions (Putnam, 2000). Bonding, which represents the factors that enhance reciprocity and solidarity among group members, is exclusive and limited to inside the group. Bridging is inclusive and represents linkages to external assets and enables the diffusion of information among networks. Bonding provides internal group identities and generates the inner strength of the group, whereas bridging social capital can generate broader identities and reciprocity. A balance between those two dimensions provides both assets: access to internal as well as external assets. Moreover, Putnam (2000) argues that those two kinds of social capital, bonding and bridging, do strengthen one another, and research proves that the highest group performance appears with unlimited relationships both within the group as well outside the group (Burt, 2001). Reza's and AINA's networks are both bonding and bridging. They provide some identity for participants and are also open to other community members, especially men.

Finally, it is critical to observe how much the society is empowered and ready to undertake common actions, which is reflected by the dimension of *empowerment and political action*. The mission of Reza's AINA is to contribute to the emergence of civil society through actions in the area of education (particularly focusing on women and children), information, and communication. The idea is to empower civic participation through integrating the many dimensions of social capital.

IMPACT OF SOCIAL CAPITAL

Impact on Individuals

Individual social capital, through the diversity of connections, opens up avenues to various, previously inaccessible resources; it also empowers the individual to take some risk and explore new opportunities (Coleman, 1988; Brehm & Rahn, 1997). For example, college graduates often retain their student e-mail addresses and use Facebook™ to stay in touch with the college community. Such connections often have strong payoffs in terms of jobs, internships, and other opportunities (Ellison et al., 2007). Adler and Kwon (2002) point out that individual social capital generates concrete gains, such as career success (Burt, 2001) and helps job seekers find employment (Granovetter 1983, 1995). An important advantage of possessing individual social capital is the access to updated, comprehensive information. In addition, social capital may provide strong solidarity, which can be especially important in critical situations (Burt, 1997).

Impact on Groups and Societies

Social capital is seen as a driving force for the development of societies. Communities with strong social capital are more successful in combating poverty, resolving conflicting issues, and taking advantage of new opportunities (Woolcock & Narayan, 2000; Praszkier et al., 2009).

In economic terms, social capital and trust among entrepreneurs, employees, suppliers, and customers are the vital underpinning for creating business networks that lead to sustainable economic growth (Neace, 1999). Social capital might seriously influence a community's long-term economic performance through a chain of circular causation with trust as its pivotal element (Maskell, 2000). As for emerging economies, the indirect role of entrepreneurs (business or social) is to act as agents for creating social capital, thereby creating a seedbed of civil society, a crucial element in sustainable economic development (Neace, 1999). Putnam (1993) offers an even larger view, stating that social capital is starting to be seen as a vital ingredient in economic development around the world.

WHAT MAKES SOCIAL CAPITAL SO PROMISING?

The roots may be traced to as early as the first half of the nineteenth century, when the French writer Alexis de Tocqueville in his book *Democracy in America* (2003) expressed his fascination with the vibrant associational life that bolstered American democracy and economic strength. For de Tocqueville, personal interaction in voluntary associations provided the social glue that helped to bond individual Americans together (Field, 2008). This "social glue" was probably on Emile Durkheim's mind when he coined the idea of *organic solidarity* (1984) and also may be related to Francis Fukuyama's concept of *spontaneous sociability*[5] (1996). This social glue, seen as a blend of networks, trust, and cooperation (Putnam, 1996; Putnam, 2000), is the essence of social life, which perpetuates development, empowers people, raises their self-esteem, and makes people happier and more optimistic.

---

[5] Fukuyama (1996) articulates that organizations are constantly created, destroyed, and modified; hence, the most useful kind of social capital is the capacity to form new associations and to cooperate within the terms of reference they establish (p. 27).

SOCIAL ENTREPRENEURS BUILD SOCIAL CAPITAL

Given enough time, and regardless of the actions taken, many social systems have a natural tendency to drift back toward the previous state, known as the attractor (Chapter 5). According to the tenets of dynamical social psychology, true change is achieved, not by just temporarily disrupting the equilibrium, but rather by building a totally new attractor to which the system will then naturally tend to drift (Nowak & Lewenstein, 1994; Vallacher & Nowak, 2007).

In some situations, there is a deeply ingrained "old" negative attractor comprising distrust, misanthropy, or lack of cooperation – or all of the above – that controls the natural equilibrium. As shown in Figure 2 (Chapter 5), one needs a constant force in order to keep the metaphorical "ball of change" up; in the absence of such a force, the attractor pulls it back to its natural state. The traditional approach is to confront the problem directly, disrupting the status quo; this has been the modus operandi of many social leaders, especially if, according to the aforementioned bubbles theory (Chapter 5), leaders create "bubbles of new in the sea of old" and enhance connections among one another. The result is often either neutral (over time, the system drifts back to the old attractor) or negative (the dynamics of the system backfire, e.g., when communities, instead of taking responsibility, expect more actions from outside – and sometimes become frustrated when the external program expires). Figure 2 (Chapter 5) illustrates this process using the graphic symbol of a ball.

Achieving lasting change, however, demands much more than exerting a force to keep the ball up. What is needed is to build and deepen a new attractor, as seen in Figure 3 (Chapter 5), which would shift the natural societal balance point. Gradually, if the new attractor of, let's say, trust and cooperation is strengthened, the community will know instinctively how to keep it up the next time it faces a new challenge.

The new attractor can emerge through simple interactions on the micro level leading to a significant change on the macro level (according to the emergence theory, Chapter 6). It is therefore possible that even seemingly minor situations can lead to the emergence of a new attractor (Vallacher & Nowak, 2007).

Our conjecture is that social entrepreneurs, to pursue their goals, build networks that are the backbone for creating and augmenting social capital. Specifically, they modify certain characteristics of the social networks, such as trust and the propensity for cooperation – essential ingredients in the building and reinforcement of social capital. It is this creation of social capital that makes it possible to achieve, with exceptional efficacy, core goals such as helping children with disabilities, empowering women to succeed in the job market, developing economically disenfranchised areas, and addressing health issues, poverty, and education. Moreover, in a kind of chain reaction, success with one set of challenges (the social entrepreneur's goals) also becomes an additional value in the newly empowered society and helps to cope with other challenges.[6]

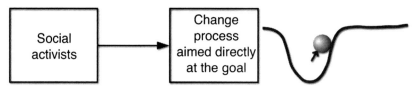

FIGURE 4. Social activists addressing the problem directly; the ball is pushed up by external force within the same old attractor

We submit that social activists – as opposed to social entrepreneurs – take a different tack: They address the issue directly (see Figure 4).[7] Operating within the old attractor, they are able to bring change through an external "force." This change is reversible, however, and can only be sustained as long as this force is operating. On the other hand, social entrepreneurs, rather than attacking the problem head-on, circumvent it and instead begin by building social capital (see Figure 5).

In the next step, the social entrepreneur creates a feedback loop between the first successes (see Kaz Jaworski's telephone network or Reza Deghati's women journalists) and social capital. Success gives hope and opens new perspectives, thus reinforcing trust and the willingness to cooperate, which deepen the new attractor (see Figure 6).

Finally, the social entrepreneur addresses goals directly, with efforts mutually reinforced by the emerging social capital (see Figure 7)

The hypothesis that social entrepreneurs pursue their goals through building social capital was verified and confirmed in qualitative studies in Poland, where the research target cohort were all Polish Ashoka Fellows.[8] First, surveys and questionnaires were prepared to interview the experts

---

[6] Field analysis reveals that in areas where social entrepreneurs operate, the society copes better with natural disasters such as floods; this hypothesis has to be confirmed through further research.

[7] It is important to emphasize once again that the work of social entrepreneurs does not in any way devalue the extraordinary contributions of social activists.

[8] This was the dependent variable; the independent variables were the Ashoka criteria for selecting social entrepreneurs (http://www.ashoka.org/support/criteria). In other words, the hypothesis held that the Ashoka definition of social entrepreneurship implies building social capital. (Praszkier, R., 2007. Methods used by social entrepreneurs for introducing

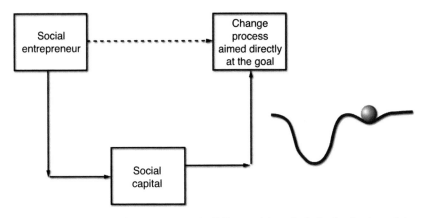

FIGURE 5. Step 1: social entrepreneur building social capital; the beginning of the new attractor

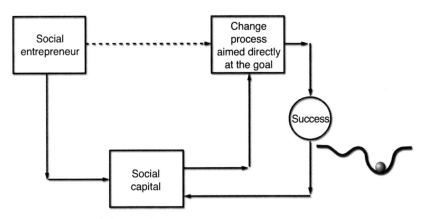

FIGURE 6. Step 2: feedback loop between success and social capital; the positive attractor intensifies, and the negative one decreases in power

participating in the Ashoka selection process;[9] other questionnaires were generated in order to analyze the case studies; and to evaluate the results, the methods of qualified judges were used.[10] The results of all the research confirmed significantly that social entrepreneurship do build social capital.[11]

social change. Unpublished doctoral dissertation, Psychology Department, University of Warsaw.)

[9] Selecting social entrepreneurship for Ashoka fellowship (see http://www.ashoka.org/support/sands).

[10] Raters were appointed; they individually assessed the materials.

[11] The bonding type of social capital; it would be compelling to verify the conjecture that they build the bridging type of social capital as well.

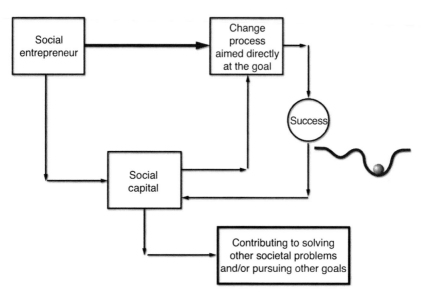

FIGURE 7. Step 3: pursuing the social goal; social capital is the transforming parameter; the new attractor becomes well established.

An additional qualitative survey proved that for working with hypothetical groups, social entrepreneurship chose (from a list provided to them)
methods that build social capital. They aim their techniques at increasing
the unexploited (sometimes latent) potential of the communities, and they
tend to convey the value of drawing from and building on the communities' own resources. Moreover, they avoid top-down methods and those
based on external resources; for example, they tend to minimize reliance on
external experts to "come and preach," thus avoiding top-down aid; they
instinctively understand that the latter approach threatens to maintain the
society's dependence on external forces. As contrasted with the comparison
group (leading social activists, not selected as social entrepreneurs),[12] social
activists also chose social-capital-building methods, although they equally
preferred methods based on external resources (non-social-capital-building
methods).

This research provides another helpful path leading to the understanding of the differences between social entrepreneurs and social activists (as

[12] Both groups were equal, N = 52; social activists were randomly selected from the database
out of a shortlisted group of those meeting rigorous criteria (in order to compare authentic
high-quality leaders representing both groups).

continued in the analysis in the last segment of Chapter 2): social entrepreneurs use bottom-up methods, which build social capital, and avoid top-down methods, which may disempower the society, whereas social activists use both methods equally and eagerly.

CHAPTER HIGHLIGHTS

- Trust and the propensity for cooperation are pivotal to ignite self-reliance and hope for change. These factors are key parameters characterizing social capital, which is seen as critical for sustaining bottom-up mechanisms.
- Social capital is seen as a form of capital, although unlike other forms of capital, it is integral to the structure of relations between and among actors. Social capital's similarity to economic capital is that social networks also create tangible value, both individual and collective, and that we can "invest" in networking. Social capital can be defined as an aggregation of actual or potential resources, which are linked to the possession of a durable network.
- Social capital is seen as a driving force for the development of societies. Communities with a strong social capital are more successful in combating poverty, resolving conflicts, and taking advantage of new opportunities. Social capital is deemed to be a vital ingredient in economic development around the world. In many cases, social capital produces economic capital.
- Social entrepreneurs pursue their mission by building social capital, which helps to build sustainability of their projects and also becomes a societal asset far beyond their stated goal.

8

Social Networks: Bedrock of Social Capital

As we said in the previous chapter, social networks can become the bedrock of social capital; in other words, in order to connect, communicate, cooperate, and build trust, one has to be involved in multiple relationships. This grid, commonly known as a network, is also sometimes referred to as "a web without a spider" (Barabási, 2003). Because social networks play a crucial role in the buildup of social capital (Putnam, 1996; Lin, 2001; Putnam & Gross, 2002; Coleman, 2003; Field, 2008; Praszkier et al., 2009), it is important to explore this subject further.

SOCIAL NETWORKS: WHAT ARE THEY?

Social networks are social structures made of individuals or organizations (called nodes) that are connected by way of specific interrelations (Wasserman & Faust, 1994; Degenne & Forsé, 1999). Those nodes exchange information, either via personal interaction or through communication technologies.

The structure of a given network – who interacts with whom, how frequently, and on what terms – has a major bearing on the flow of resources through it. Those who accumulate the most connections in the network (Gladwell [2002] calls them "connectors") are deemed to possess more social capital than their peers, precisely because their position in the network accords them greater access to more and better resources (Burt, 2001; Grootaert et al., 2004). In its simplest form, a social network is a map of all of the relevant ties among all the nodes under observation.

SMALL NETWORKS

Let's simulate a hypothetical startup of small, informal groups. The diagrams in Figure 8 represent the dynamics of initial informal relationships between the participants of two groups – A and B (based on Degenne & Forsé, 1999).

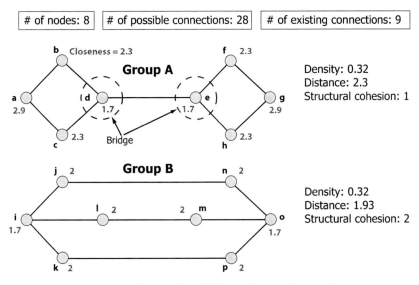

| # of nodes: 8 | # of possible connections: 28 | # of existing connections: 9 |

FIGURE 8. Groups A and B (8 nodes in each group)

The diagrams show structures of two different types of informal relationships: In group A, there are two subgroups linked through nodes d and e (which *bridge* the network)[1]; if either of the two nodes is absent, the subgroups break apart. In group B, there is the same number of informal relations, but the integrity of the group holds whether or not any of the participants is absent; moreover, two nodes, i and o, play a special role because they hold three connections, whereas others are connected by two nodes.

Social network analysis (SNE) can be done through a visual examination of the graphs, which is often sufficient. For instance, we may predict that network B is more immune to breakdowns (it survives the absence of any one participant), whereas network A is less exposed to the spread of epidemics, as removing only one participant (d or e) detaches the rest from the "disease."

SNE can also be done in a quantifiable way. For instance, one of the network's properties is *density*, which is defined as the number of existing connections divided by the number of potential connections. The potential connections between 2 nodes (participants) are calculated from a factorial formula $\frac{n!}{[(n-2!)*2!]}$. In the case of networks A and B, n = 8, so the number of

---

[1] A node is said to be a bridge if deleting it would cause its endpoints to lie in different components of a graph.

potential connections works out to a total of 28. In both cases, the number of existing connections is 9, so the density is the same, and equals 0.32.

The other property is the *closeness* of the nodes, which adduces the average distance from all the other nodes. Let's take student a from class A, who has one step to reach two students (b and c), two steps to reach one student d, three steps to reach another student e, four steps to reach two students (f and h), and five steps to reach the last student (g). This means that if student a needs to send a different message to each of the other students, the total number of links that need to be traversed by the messages is 20.[2] Because there are 7 other students, the average number of nodes that a message needs to transverse is $20/7 = 2.9$. This is called the *closeness* of student a. Similarly, the closeness of student d is 1.7: 1 step to 3 students (b, c, and e), 2 steps to 3 students (a, f, and h), 3 steps to 1 student (g).[3] The greater the closeness the longer the distance to others; this would imply that the more promising position as to the potential for cooperation within the entire network is the one with the lowest closeness factor.[4]

Whereas closeness is the property of a single node (participant), it would also be interesting to identify the aggregated closeness of the entire network. This network's property is called *distance* and calculates as a sum of the closeness of all the nodes divided by the number of nodes. In the case of class A, the distance is 2.3; and in the case of class B, it is 1.93. This means that in network B, the average distance between participants is smaller than in network A, which makes it shorter on average to send messages between nodes.

The *distance* of our personal network is quite a peculiar parameter, as we are all increasingly interconnected globally and locally. Participating in various networks (family tree, Facebook, school alumni discussion group, collectors of car models, sponsors of art museums, local community membership, etc.) we finally form a so-called small-world (Milgram, 1967; Duncan, 1999), where almost anyone in the global network can be reached with no more than six links. This means that any one of billions of individuals is no more than six degrees away from anyone else (Watts, 2003). It is a highly rewarding exercise to draw the graphs of our various networks, identifying our position and interconnectivity. In some cases, it can also be a bonding

---

[2] $1 \times 2 + 2 \times 1 + 3 \times 1 + 4 \times 2 + 5 \times 1 = 20$.

[3] $1s \times 3 + 2s \times 3 + 3s \times 1 = 12; 12/7 = 1.7$

[4] For example, the person in the center of the eight-person star-like network would have only one step to every other of the seven members, so the closeness factor would be 1 (7:7); all the other members' closeness would then be 2 (14:7) in this case.

activity, for example, drawing a multigenerational family tree, as it reveals our roots and cross-generational patterns (McGoldrick & Gerson, 1985).

Another important feature is *betweenness*, which reflects the number of people with whom a person is connecting indirectly through their direct links. This measure takes into account the connectivity of the node's neighbors, giving a higher value for nodes that bridge highly connected hubs.

Perhaps the most important property of a network is its *structural cohesion*, meaning exposing the network's vulnerability to fragmentation into disconnected parts. In network A, the structural cohesion is as low as 1, as you need remove only one person (d or e) to fracture the entire network. Network B is more immune to disruption, as it requires the removal of two persons to destroy the network (e.g., j and o, or i and p). The higher the level of the network's structural cohesion, the more alternative paths it provides to counteract the impact of the absence of some nodes, thereby ensuring that the communication remains intact.

Let's further posit that the groups evolve over time and more informal relationships are established. A new structure appears (group C), see Figure 9.

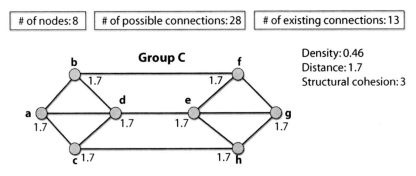

FIGURE 9. Structure of relationships after adding more connections

To achieve this point from group A, four new relations were established (between b and f, c and h, a and d, and e and g). In group B, the same network could be reached by additional relations between b and d, c and d, e and f, and e and h. The total number of existing connections increases to 13, so the density grows to 0.46.

The closeness of all nodes, as well as the entire network's distance, is 1.7. The structural cohesion is 3, because in order to destroy the network, at least 3 persons have to leave. It may be observed that the growing number of relations decreases the entire network's distance and may increase its structural cohesion.

Considering small networks, such as our sample of groups A, B, and C, we can conclude that C is potentially the best configuration to produce a vibrant network that could eventually give rise to new initiatives, as participants are connected in multiple ways with little distance between them, making communication easy and the entire network relatively immune to potential upheavals. (We will see, however, that this may be true for small networks and not larger ones.)

Obviously, the networks are dynamic entities. Over time the amount of information exchanged or the density of connections between nodes may grow or decrease. Also new members may join, or others may drop out. Networks may become dormant or, on the contrary, vibrant, yielding what many social leaders call "the network effect."[5]

LARGE NETWORKS

Networks A, B, and C are small, so all members can get to know and establish relationships with one another. But what happens when networks bloom and the number of nodes grows to hundreds, thousands, and even millions? First, the network analysis obviously becomes much more complicated and requires special software. Second, at some point it becomes impossible for individuals to establish relationships with everybody; in fact, in large networks, if each person was somehow able to communicate with every other person, ironically, chaos rather than order would certainly ensue.

Social entrepreneurs tend to expand their networks. Reza Deghati started with women from a few villages and gradually expanded the network to more than one thousand persons trained in media and communication skills, more than 90 percent of whom are currently employed using their acquired skills. Currently thirty educational films have been viewed by more than one million Afghanis, and female-led radio programs have been broadcast across the country. All these women-led teams are linked, providing mutual support and peer-to-peer consultancies; the network is expanding and breeding new offshoots.

Another example of large networks is provided by Daniel Ben Horin, a social entrepreneur through and through. Daniel launched TechSoup, a global network for know-how exchange between technically oriented

---

[5] Originally understood as the phenomenon whereby the connections become more valuable as more people use them, thereby encouraging ever-increasing numbers of adopters (Metcalf's law); currently also understood as the value added, generated by the sole existence of a vibrant network.

specialists and the social sector.[6] Technology products, services, and information are transferred to the civil society,[7] and social values are being passed on to the technical communities.[8] More than 45,000 international organizations received technical support, and the scale of the network may be best illustrated by the fact that there are monthly online forums that draw more than 115,000 participants.

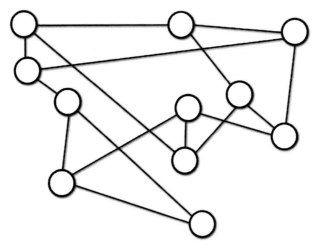

FIGURE 10. Random paradigm: nodes have more or less the same degree

What happens to large networks? How do they self-organize? Initially (from the late 1950s to the mid-1970s), there was a belief that large networks are random (Figure 10) and that the majority of nodes have the same degree (number of links) as the typical (average) node does, following the bell curve (Barabási, 2003).

Following this philosophy of randomness, in the mid-1960s noted psychologist Stanley Milgram discovered the phenomenon of the "six degrees of separation," which is that the distance between one individual and any other person in the world is always reducible to six steps, meaning that the path to finding any person on any continent would require passing through no more than five other persons; for example, one friend knowing another friend on another continent, who knows someone in the related field, who will know the boss of the wife of our target person (Duncan, 2003). Milgram,

---

[6] See http://www.ashoka.org/fellow/5891 and http://www.techsoupglobal.org/.

[7] More than $312 million worth of technology products were donated and distributed.

[8] More than 400,000 visitors from 190 countries access the TechSoup Web site monthly.

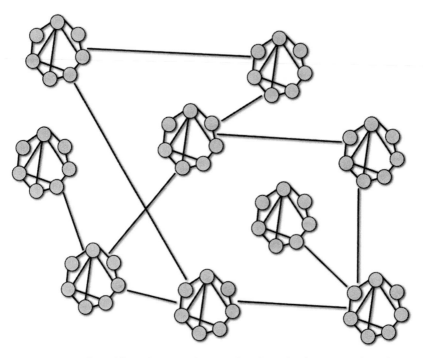

FIGURE 11. Small worlds with internal strong bonds and a few external weak ties that connect all clusters and nodes to the entire network (i.e., to any other node)

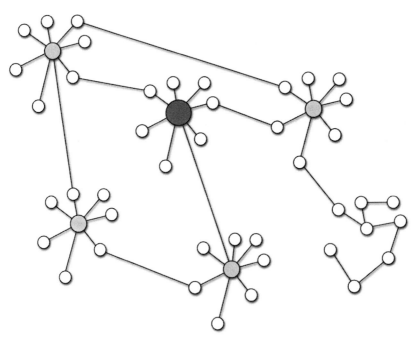

FIGURE 12. Scale-free network: all nodes are connected through the high-connectivity hubs; the central is a super-hub, characterized by high "betweenness"

however, overestimated the distance, as one may not be aware of unexpected shortcuts; for example, if you are looking for the path to the president, you may not know that the neighbor at the dinner table went to school with the First Lady, which shortens the path to two steps. Not knowing the map of social connections, we may not be aware of the shortest paths; this means that in reality, with good network mapping, the distance can be less than six (Barabási, 2003). The idea of the small-world social network was born: Most nodes are *not* neighbors of one another, but most nodes *can* be reached from every other by a small number of steps; the networks contain small groups (meaning subnetworks) that have connections between almost any other groups in the network.

However, we are all surrounded by close friends. Society is structured into highly connected clusters in which everybody knows everybody else. No matter where your old school buddies move or whatever job they take, you may keep track of their e-mail addresses. Your friends are always one click away, which creates your own circle. There is, however, a flaw in the concept of small circles scattered through the entire network, as this would mean that those small worlds form isolated islands. The solution emerged along with discovering in the late 1970s the *power of weak ties*: Granovetter (1983, 1985) proved that the truly helpful connections are not the closest ones but rather ones that are loosely knit. Asking people who helped them get their jobs, he found out that significantly more respondents benefited more from acquaintances than from close friends (Figure 11).

Even a few extra links (weak ties) among clusters are sufficient to drastically decrease the separation of nodes. The network was then envisioned as a universe full of small worlds that are interconnected through a relatively small number of weak ties (Barabási, 2003).

This vision was based on conjecture that the nodes are randomly distributed on the score of their *degrees* (i.e., numbers of connections per node). However, nodes of very high connectivity[9] were seen, as well as nodes with exceptionally low numbers of ties (Figure 12). The distribution is far from random, where extremely high-degree nodes as well as low-degree ones are equally possible (the formula following the power law).[10] This sort of grid is called a scale-free network, the name indicating that there is no one representative (typical) node (it was the previous random distribution with its bell curve that easily pointed to the most "average" node).

---

[9] Called "connectors" in Malcolm Gladwell's (2002) book *Tipping Point*.

[10] Power law means that the number of nodes with exactly k incoming links, that is, $N(k) \sim k^{-\gamma}$; γ was found to be between 2 and 3.

Power law (observed in so-called scale-free networks, it means that there are many individuals with a small number of connections and a decreasingly small number of highly connected individuals) emerges where systems move from chaos (random distribution) to order (Barabási, 2003). The mechanism is simple: There is a combination of two laws – growth (one node added at a time) and preferential attachment (probability of attaching to a particular node is proportional to the number of connections of that node).

At first glance, it would seem that newcomers would prefer to connect to the highest-degree hubs, and that as a result winners take all (the best-connected attract more connections). However, the reality is not so simple, and many new participants have a chance not only to create hubs but also to surpass the older and most-connected ones (Barabási, 2003). One of the reasons is that in the competitive environment each node has a certain *fitness*, which is an ability to link others in; some participants may be especially gifted with this knack and thus create new growing hubs.

Scale-free networks usually provide better coordination and flow of information and are resilient and impervious to failure, a property called *robustness* (Barabási, 2003). Consider the World Wide Web, the iconic twenty-first-century communication network: Various experiments have demonstrated that one can remove as many as 80 percent of all nodes, and the remaining 20 percent will still ensure the network's overall connectivity. A study found that at any moment hundreds of Internet routers malfunction with no negative consequences; it means that the Internet displays a high degree of *robustness* against router failure. It is worth mentioning that the robustness of random networks is much lower, as it is much easier to remove a few nodes to tear the network apart.

The supposed downside of scale-free networks is that they are susceptible to viruses: If a virus hits the hub, it spreads instantly to all nodes connected to this hub and to other nodes as well. On the other hand, this may be an advantage, as scale-free networks could spread innovations with the same agility as they spread disease.

We will discuss further the hypothesis that the networks woven by social entrepreneurs are scale-free and thus ensure an easy communication flow, high interconnectivity, and robustness.

VIBRANT NETWORKS

While observing the way social entrepreneurs weave their social networks together, the term *vibrant networks* kept coming to our minds. It seems that social entrepreneurs are asking the question: What makes their network vital and productive? (This was, for example, a passionate issue discussed with Daniel Ben Horin, the founder of TechSoup, mentioned earlier in this chapter).

The following question arises: How do we transform a potential structure of relations into a network that is lively and bubbling with initiatives? Perhaps this is the central issue essential for future development in business (growing through networking); civic engagement (discussing, watching, and electing representatives); education (peer-to-peer learning models); and, finally, social change and social entrepreneurship.

Answering this question has become one of the challenges of the first decade of the twenty-first century.[11] One of the examples of analysis in this direction is the appealing idea of *augmented social networks* (understood as enhancing person-to-person interaction and group formation), especially at the point where authors aim at building identity and trust into future networks (Jordan et al., 2003).

It seems that we are on the verge of understanding how networks transform into producers of emergent phenomena. Here we can share some conclusions drawn from the field experience with social entrepreneurs' networks.

Social entrepreneurs usually start with a small social network based on their friends, where everybody knows everybody. In the process of growing and expanding the project, they involve more active supporters so that the network grows to a critical point, where close friends are now the minority. Next, the program spreads to other locations, some of them quite distant. At this point, the challenge becomes how to organize the connection and information flow among all those associates: Should it be top-down, random and horizontal, or all of the above? If the idea keeps spreading, then the social network becomes large (hardly anybody knows other participants personally) and the communication flow becomes quite complicated: Imagine a few hundred associates communicating with one another scattered across United States. And what if the program grows globally?

Our conjecture is that there are four subsequent stages of vibrant network development:

- First stage: Enabling Structure
  - This is the physical basis, the bedrock for further filling in with the substance of human relationships. The properties of this structure create numerous possibilities: For instance, when starting with a small network, *high density* provides opportunities for multiple

---

[11] One receives more than one million responses to a Google "weaving networks" query.

relationships; the shorter the small network's *distance*, the easier
it is to reach other participants; and the higher level of *structural
cohesion*, the more dropout-proof the network is. The appropriate
adjustment of those properties may provide a foundation for launching a vibrant social network (see Chapter 5 with regard to regulating
parameters of change instead of pursuing change directly).

- When the network surpasses the threshold where everybody can
  know everybody in person, then it seems most important to foster
  the most enabling structure – the *scale-free* network: Several hubs
  provide high connectivity for all nodes and ensure a high level of
  structural cohesion. This would mean in practice delegating several
  regional or programmatic leaders to provide a communication hub;
  those leaders should be interconnected, and there should also be
  several connections among nodes from various hubs (following the
  rule of *the power of weak ties*). The latter could be provided either
  through occasional conferences assembling participants from various hubs or through encouraging online connections with people
  from other hubs.

- Second stage: Rewarding Content
  - The network's structure may be ready, although participants may
    not yet see a real motivation to be active, especially because of the
    time investment it may involve. Some initial incentives are needed to
    captivate people's attention and attract them so that they would be
    willing to invest their time in network activities. The network may for
    instance deliver something new; in the case of social entrepreneurs, it
    may be a new and realistic opportunity to solve some pressing social
    problems that had been considered intractable and insurmountable.
    For young people, it can be the message that they can make a real
    difference in the world. Some other sort of incentives may also be
    considered: access to a resource center (database), media coverage,
    and so forth. Participating in this sort of network should be seen as
    beneficial and advantageous. Moreover, some authors indicate that
    benevolence should be a strong reinforcing and attracting compo-
    nent in "net-weaving."[12]

- Third stage: Network Identity
  - In the previous stage, the network was perceived as a source of
    some gains. At some point, the situation may reverse so that the

---

[12] For example, http://www.weavingnetworks.com/2009/05/almost-book-review-on-net
works.html.

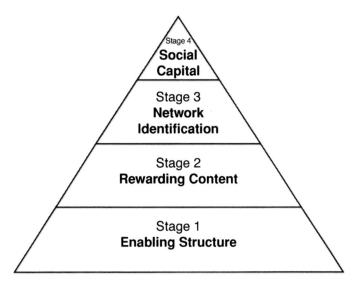

FIGURE 13. The stages of a vibrant network's development

motivation for actively participating in the network supersedes the initial benefit; this happens when the feeling of belonging becomes the overriding magnet. The new network identity (Watts et al., 2002; Jordan et al., 2003; Castells, 2009) and the desire to be linked in and brought up to speed becomes the central drive. The network possesses some properties that enhance the feeling of belonging, for example, the logo, feeling of belonging to an exclusive club (in the case of social entrepreneurs, it could be spearheading a changemaker's club).

- Fourth stage: Social Capital
  - In some cases, the network's relationships may generate a high level of trust and propensity for cooperation, which would enable the rise of social capital. Trust is pivotal for the development of communities (Putnam, 1993; Fukuyama, 1996) and for the growth of solidarity-based relationships (Parsons, 1972). Social capital may lead to some common undertakings, and in the feedback loop success may enhance social capital that, in turn, may augment success. The network at this point becomes truly vibrant, bubbling with various initiatives and with new emergent phenomena appearing and providing a feeling of participation in a vital and successful community.

This sort of four-step process (see Figure 13) happens only with some networks, probably only with a very small percentage of them. Many remain a potentiality (*enabling structure*) or become temporarily vibrant when related to some concrete issue or products (reaching only the *rewarding content* phase). Some become a source of identification and do not move forward (*network identity*). A few become resonant and self-perpetuating, generating emergent phenomena and social capital.

NETWORKS CREATED BY SOCIAL ENTREPRENEURS

Our conjecture is that social entrepreneurs use networks for building social capital and, in a feedback loop, social capital then enhances the network effect. This was verified in a field survey in communities where social entrepreneurs operate (Zablocka-Bursa, 2010).[13]

Strong networks were identified around social entrepreneurs. Participants cooperated on a voluntary basis and carried out a variety of social projects. They also provided mutual exchange of information and support.

One of the regions surveyed was an underdeveloped, mountainous community (Bystrzyca Klodzka), which was developing dynamically due to the involvement of the social entrepreneur Dorota Komornicka.[14] Her idea was to launch a community endowment and use its accrued interest for covering the rural-urban gaps in education. However, the community was poor, which made the contributions coming from local resources rather limited. Dorota's innovation was to use the endowment's modest interest income in a way that would yield a high impact. She triggered the process by launching competitions for social projects in schools. The projects were small, for example, to clean the river bank, and so was the requested donation: a shovel and a bucket for garbage. Many children's initiatives were documented and displayed in annual photo exhibitions, which became a great treat for the whole community, making families proud to see their children's achievements. In return, more contributions flowed into the community fund, especially from the businesspersons who saw the results and their significance. The growing endowment yielded higher income, which in turn supported more educational investments, such as stipends. Children

---

[13] Research conducted in Poland by the Center for Complex Systems Research, University of Warsaw, in 2009; targeted at local communities in which social entrepreneurs operate. (Zablocka-Bursa, A. [2010]. Social change developed by social entrepreneurs. Unpublished doctoral dissertation, Institute for Social Studies, University of Warsaw.)

[14] See http://www.ashoka.org/fellow/2874.

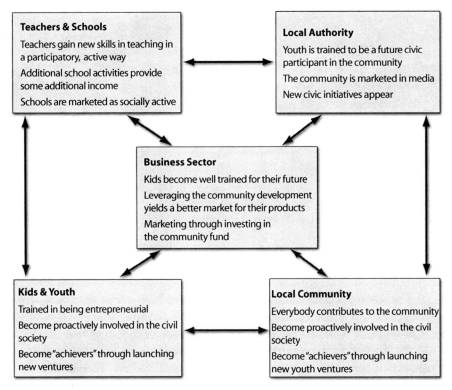

FIGURE 14. The feedback loops involved in the social-capital creation and community development (Bystrzyca Klodzka)

became more socially involved and educated, the society became socially aware and active, the business sector was involved in the community, and the teachers were more open to linking education with the social environment. This, in turn, triggered more donations to the community endowment. Figure 14 captures the multiple feedback loops involved in the community development.

This complex undertaking involved multiple relationships and networking, which was studied in the aforementioned research. Other informational diagrams from this project (Bystrzyca Klodzka community) are presented in Figures 15 and 16.

One can see the social entrepreneur's super-hub (BK29), as well as several other hubs (BK8, BK5, BK9, BK16) that denote a scale-free structure, which is, as indicated earlier, the most resilient, robust, and best configuration for facilitating the smooth flow of communication.

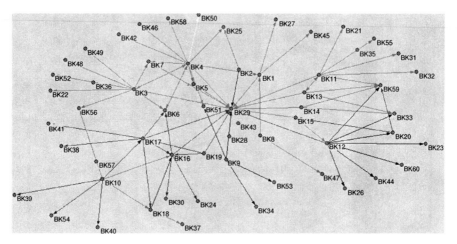

FIGURE 15. The network of the flow of information related to social projects in Bystrzyca Klodzka

The research revealed that in all five communities, one of the results of social entrepreneurs' activities was established networks characterized by high levels of trust and cooperation. It is worth highlighting that nearly all the original volunteer participants were subsequently engaged in their own businesses, although they continued to remain active. The assembled data analysis showed that in areas where social entrepreneurs operate, a significantly stronger and more durable social capital had been developed. Moreover, the profound change accomplished by social entrepreneurs in

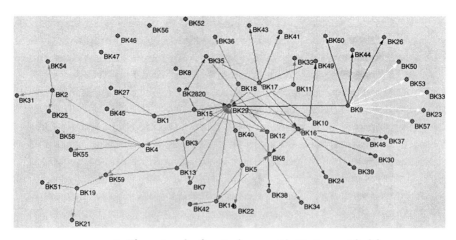

FIGURE 16. The network of mutual support in Bystrzyca Klodzka

the societies was relatively cost-effective, mostly thanks to weaving the networks.[15]

The same field survey confirmed that communities where social entrepreneurs operated achieved a significantly higher level of social capital as compared to the average in Polish society: There were more diverse relationships and more cooperation with regard to social activity as well as to mutual support.

In this chapter, we focused on the ways social networks play a crucial role in the buildup of social capital. The research indicates the significant role of social entrepreneurs in weaving vibrant, productive networks; researching this phenomenon, especially on an international level (e.g., how the local and global networks are interconnected, structured, and productive) is definitely called for.

CHAPTER HIGHLIGHTS

- Social networks are social structures made of individuals or organizations (called nodes) that are connected by specific interrelations. Those nodes exchange information, either by personal interaction or through communication technologies.
- *Social network analysis* can be done through a visual examination of the diagrams and through identifying and comparing a network's properties, such as density, closeness, distance, "betweenness," or structural cohesion.
- Large and vibrant networks self-organize in a scale-free way: The number of connections per node is distributed according to the power law; no one node is "typical" as opposed to random networks, where there is a typical network identifiable in the center of the bell curve. Scale-free networks usually provide better coordination and flow of information and are resilient and impervious to local failure.
- Creating vibrant, productive networks has four subsequent stages: establishing *enabling structure* (physical basis for further filling in with the substance of human relationships); *rewarding content* (some initial incentives are needed to captivate people's attention and attract them to participate in the network's exchange); *network identity* (the desire to participate and identify with this concrete network becomes the central drive; the network possesses some properties that enhance the feeling of belonging); and *social capital* (the network's relationships

---

[15] With a few start-up community events involved.

generate a high level of trust and propensity for cooperation, which enable the rise of social capital; the network at this point becomes vibrant, bubbling with various initiatives; new emergent phenomena appear and provide a feeling of participation in a vital and successful community).

9

Personality Traits That Facilitate the Building
of Social Capital

In the previous chapters, we put forward the view that social entrepreneurs build social capital. We now assume this view to be correct, which prompts us to ask the following questions: (1) What makes social entrepreneurs capable of dealing with groups and societies in a way that empowers others? (2) What personality characteristics are essential for growing and fostering social capital? (3) In short, how do we best describe the people we define as social entrepreneurs?

Elkington and Hartigan (2008) refer to social entrepreneurs as "unreasonable people," paraphrasing the playwright George Bernard Shaw's quip that reasonable people adapt themselves to the world whereas the unreasonable ones adapt the world to themselves, implying that for progress, we do well to depend on the latter. It has been suggested that many social entrepreneurs were characterized as "crazy" by family and friends because of their propensity for going after intractable problems, taking huge risks, and forcing people to stretch the limits of the possible.[1] According to Sternin (2002), social entrepreneurs may be thought of as "positive deviants," because, when it comes to finding the best solutions, their uncommon behaviors or practices enable them to surpass others who share the same resource base. Sternin asserts that identifying and studying these positive deviants can reveal hidden resources, already present in the environment, from which they devise solutions that are cost-effective, sustainable, and internally owned and managed.

---

[1] This also was confirmed in a pilot survey targeted at social entrepreneurs; responding to the question asking them what happened to them after they got involved in pursuing their idea, some said: "All of my friends abandoned me as they thought that I am nutty." "I divorced." "I became totally lonely as nobody understood why I am working with street children instead of taking some decent job."

This observation raises further questions: What are the specific personality traits that come together to create a social entrepreneur? How can we go about empowering future social entrepreneurs? What capacities and areas of potential should be seeded and cultivated?

We know from the definition of social entrepreneurship adopted throughout this book (see specifically Chapters 1 and 2) and from the criteria for selection that social entrepreneurs are creative and entrepreneurial.[2] This raises the question: What forms do creativity and entrepreneurial qualities take? This is the topic of the following section.

Some other properties (mentioned later in this chapter) may appear to be an indirect consequence of this definition.[3] The question is: If we identify individuals who practice social entrepreneurship according to the definition provided in Chapter 1, does this commonality of features give rise to another level of shared characteristics? If yes, do those characteristics also differentiate social entrepreneurs from other leaders?

CREATIVITY

The definition of social entrepreneurship adopted throughout this book (Chapters 1 and 2) implies that creativity is one of the pivotal personality traits of social entrepreneurs. Indeed, during the selection procedures (see Chapter 3), creativity is thoroughly examined, especially during the interviews. In the case of Munir Hasan (see the introduction of Section 1), for example, the idea of mathematics festivals indicated a creative approach; those festivals were appealing, and key players were buying into the idea; in the long run, a change-producing social process was triggered. There were also other, small indications that Munir was creative: He tried (and succeeded) to influence the school authorities to incorporate the festivals into the curriculum and to organize them on weekdays – which was a treat for teachers and students. Steve Bigari (see Section 1) was also labeled as a creative person, because he caused the entrenched practice of firing low-income workers after they failed to show up at work to make a complete U-turn. He accomplished this by treating the employees with dignity and used the situation as an opportunity to conduct training in preventive coping skills. Kaz Jaworski (see Section 2) invented a method of convincing the previously resistant-to-change society to buy into the idea of establishing

---

[2] These factors serve as independent variables; it wouldn't make sense to verify independent variables, as it would only help to confirm if the criteria are well "translated" into operational guidelines and selection practices.

[3] These traits would be dependent variables and as such can be verified in research.

the telephone system, which offered free local calls; this triggered cooperativeness followed by a plethora of new ventures. Reza Deghati (see Section 3) discovered that journalism can be a powerful tool for empowering women and youth in Afghanistan and other conflict areas.

What is creativity and what does it mean to be creative? In short, creativity is the ability to produce work that is both novel and appropriate (Sternberg & Lubart, 2004). More broadly, it can be seen as a confluence of intrinsic motivation, domain-relevant knowledge and abilities, and creativity-relevant skills. The latter include (a) a cognitive style that involves coping with complexities and making one's mental set more plastic during problem solving; (b) knowledge of heuristics for generating novel ideas, such as trying a counterintuitive approach; and (c) a work style charged by concentrated effort, an ability to set aside problems, and high energy (Amabile, 1996).

Creative persons demonstrate a specific way of thinking called *lateral* (De Bono, 1990), *divergent* (Runco, 2007), or *quantum leap* (Mapes, 2003), all of which generally mean:

- A new look at the situation, possibly from outside the box and from different angles perceiving and accepting new options and possibilities
- Reframing the problem in a way that provides a chance for new problem solving
- Readiness to relinquish rigidity in perceiving and understanding the world

A good example is the way Steve Bigari reframed the problem of the high rate of turnover among low-income staff, so that instead of a negative action (firing those who have had coping problems), it became perceived as a positive opportunity for educating and raising the level of staff loyalty.

The ability to think and communicate in effective, appropriate, and imaginative metaphors is also a clear marker of a creative mind (Runco, 2007). Such an ability permits one to address a problem in a more contextual, multidimensional way, rather than approaching it in an "in-your-face," aggressive way.

Csikszentmihalyi (1997) interviewed more than ninety world-renowned creative individuals whose stories were of great help in understanding the nature of creativity. Most of the interviewees recalled an *aha!* experience, when some major solution to a problem crystallized in their minds. Mapes (2003) and others label this kind of experience as *quantum leap* thinking, using the analogy of the electron rapidly changing its orbit and yielding a portion of its energy; others see it as *lateral thinking*, characterized by using an indirect approach to solving problems, being receptive to ideas that may not be accessible through traditional, step-by-step logic (De Bono, 1990).[4]

Creativity, according to Davis (1993), implies being confident, independent, risk taking, intuitive, flexible, as well as demonstrating the courage to dare to differ, to make waves, to challenge traditions, and to "bend a few rules."

Davis (1993) looks at the traits of creative individuals from still another angle: He asserts that creative individuals possess an abundance of enthusiasm, curiosity, and wide interests, whereas others have a tolerance for complexity and ambiguity and an attraction to the mysterious. Davis holds that to be considered a creative thinker, one must be able to work with incomplete ideas, where relevant facts are missing, rules are cloudy, and "correct" procedures are nonexistent (the latter trait is especially essential for dealing with complex systems; see Chapters 5 and 6).

Creativity is sometimes seen as the fundamental source of social and economic growth. The creative individuals are the ones who become the leaders in contemporary society and as such are creating a new social class – the creative class (Florida, 2002).

THE ENTREPRENEURIAL PERSONALITY

The entrepreneurial personality is thoroughly examined by Ashoka, which is constantly testing its assumption that there is strong evidence of specific entrepreneurial qualities.

Munir Hasan motivated all the key players, spurring them on to take the lead in carrying out his idea: The schools volunteered to organize mathematics festivals; the teachers established their own association, elevating the level of teaching mathematics; the students had their own volunteer organization; and the publishers became strongly motivated to produce materials on mathematics. Munir Hasan's entrepreneurial qualities led to the creation of a well-oiled, self-perpetuating, win-win machine, while he himself remained in the position of an inspirational creator.

Reza Deghati would not have been so successful without deploying his business acumen: He understood that there was no point in training women and youth to become journalists if they weren't going to be able to generate

---

[4] Psychologists also use the term *divergent thinking* for a process or method used to generate creative ideas by exploring many possible solutions, for example, brainstorming.

revenue from their new profession. So, intrinsic to his plan was the goal of helping them establish ventures, thus enabling them not only to support their families but also to enhance their position in society. This makes the AINA project not just "social" in nature but also a self-supporting business enterprise.

What then does it mean to be entrepreneurial? What are the unique qualities of an entrepreneur (if any)? We will address these questions with the understanding that we will establish a divide between business entrepreneurs (which most of the literature deals with) and social entrepreneurs. (It is instructive to note that in researching the subject on the Internet, the descriptive phrases attached to the concept of "entrepreneur" include such attributes as "street smart,"[5] "superstar," "artist," "fireball,"[6] "Jack of all trades, master of none,"[7] "good health," and "a need to control and direct"[8] to "paranoiacs" and "insomniacs."[9])

On the other hand, some scholars express a degree of skepticism with regard to establishing a rock-solid aggregate of traits. For instance, Aldrich and Zimmer (1986) indicate that the proposed list of entrepreneur-specific personality traits is nearly endless, although rigorous empirical research has had trouble identifying any traits whatsoever associated with entrepreneurship. Chell (1985) goes even further, asserting that it is impossible to identify reliably a trait that characterizes entrepreneurs and distinguishes them from other business persons. Rauch and Frese (2007) pointed out that a number of reviews reported inconsistent and conflicting empirical evidence for the relationship between personality traits and entrepreneurship.

In the literature of the 1960s and 1970s, there was agreement about some of the characteristics, to wit: Entrepreneurs are highly achievement-oriented (called nAch, n-achievement); they are moderate risk takers; and they prefer to take personal responsibility for their decisions and seek concrete knowledge of the results of those decisions (McClelland, 1967; Brockhaus & Horwitz, 1986). There was also speculation as to the internal locus of control (i.e., to what extent people believe they can control and influence events that affect them). Rotter (1996) believed that the need for achievement correlates with internal locus of control, although Brockhaus & Horwitz

[5] http://www.morebusiness.com/getting_started/primer/d943458887.brc.

[6] http://sbinformation.about.com/cs/development/a/personality.htm.

[7] http://www.atalasoft.com/cs/blogs/billbither/archive/2006/01/03/inception-of-a.aspx.

[8] http://www.aw-wrdsmth.com/FAQ/characteristics_successful_entre.html.

[9] http://www.16thletter.com/2008/02/25/10-less-than-great-personality-traits-of-entrepreneurs/.

(1986) report no difference in the locus of control between entrepreneurs and non-entrepreneurs.

Two additional important insights merit our consideration:

> Locke and Baum (2007), in reviewing various motivations of entrepreneurs, mention *vision*, saying that the entrepreneur's vision exists in full detail inside his or her head. "The entrepreneur defines the nature of the business, sees parts, sees the whole, and sees how each part relates to the whole (p. 96)."

Many authors highlight the capacity to *see and seize opportunities* as special skills of an entrepreneur (e.g., Drucker, 1985; Dees, 1998; Krueger, 2005; Martin & Osberg, 2007). It is our belief that entrepreneurs do indeed look at the environment as a source of potential opportunities and are able to recognize those opportunities where others do not.

MORE PERSONALITY TRAITS: WHAT ENSUES FROM THE DEFINITION?

The qualities of creativity and entrepreneurs in general are embedded in the definition of social entrepreneurship in particular. Our conjecture is that the selection criteria for identifying social entrepreneurs (Chapter 1) indirectly imply other personality traits. For instance, a high level of *optimism* and belief that things that initially look unchangeable can be changed enable the entrepreneur to focus on seemingly insurmountable, hopeless social issues. In addition, a certain degree of *social empathy* is necessary for weaving social networks and motivating people to actively participate.

However, pinning down personality traits in a way that would be operational and verifiable is a tall order. Expressions such as "making waves" may be excellent for communicating in a dramatic way how an author envisions those unique individuals, but how do we introduce such language into a serious study? A closer look at the way social entrepreneurs pursue their mission, whether it be through interviews, field studies, analysis of resources, or interviewing those who benefit from a given project (see Chapter 3), offers some hints as to the specific personality qualities that enable the process of change.

Our hypotheses (verified in research discussed later in this chapter), initially based on practice and analysis of the literature, are that the social entrepreneurs mentioned so far in our case histories all demonstrated a high level of the following traits and psycho-social attributes.

Trust and Optimism

We not only intuited these traits when talking to them, but they were the reasons behind their success. Munir Hasan, as a child, was convinced that he could change the country's attitude toward mathematics. He also had prodigious capacity for trust in the people he involved in the program, and so he did not hesitate to offer them responsible missions. Steve Bigari, acting against the routine and discouraging attitudes of his colleagues, was optimistic that the lives of low-income employees could be radically improved. Kaz Jaworski rose above the overall resistance of the rural community in Poland and optimistically dreamed of a rural society overtaking urban ones. He demonstrated enormous trust in people, even when they remained skeptical. Reza Deghati believed that women can spearhead societal change, even in a highly structured society.

The passionate way social entrepreneurs bring new hope and new possibilities to society can only be effective if accompanied by their own optimism (Casson, 2005; Gifford, 2005) and a high level of trust in people and societies (Coleman, 1990; Putnam, 1993; Fukuyama, 1996). Uslaner (1998) indicates that optimism and trust are the foundation for introducing change to the society and that these two attributes are closely related: Optimism shapes trust, which in turn plays a powerful role in effecting civic activism.

Cooperation

Cooperation is undeniably the keystone of bottom-up societal transformation. Munir Hasan wouldn't have been able to transform Bangladesh into a country saturated with the pursuit of mathematical knowledge without the many teams he sparked and collaborated with (student volunteers, the teachers' self-education association, and local governments, to name a few). Reza Deghati worked in teams, fostering the growth of master trainers and cooperated with many editorial offices, in each case delegating responsibilities.

Individual (non-entrepreneurial) leaders, even if charismatic, usually bring only short-term change, which is mostly based on personal energy and commitment. According to Elkington and Hartigan (2008), social entrepreneurs are willing to share their innovations and insights for others to replicate. Building social capital empowers others and is achieved through cooperation (Woolcock, 2004).

Individual Social Networks

The "Lone Ranger" approach, however, disregards the need for support from others and is therefore doomed to fail in the long run. As observed, social entrepreneurs usually have their own strong individual social networks, which help them attain their complex mission. This kind of personal social capital is also perceived as a source of support, which in many cases is critical to a successful outcome, considering that social entrepreneurs usually act against all odds, struggle with many obstacles, and pursue a seemingly impossible mission.

Mechanisms for Coping with Adversity

Introducing new solutions involves moving against the mainstream, which is usually a continuous, overwhelming struggle. In the cases of Munir, Steve, Kaz, and Reza, all faced multiple barriers and drawbacks. Social entrepreneurs have the knack of turning those obstacles into opportunities and finding innovative solutions in the most difficult circumstances (Bornstein, 2004; Krueger, 2005; Elkington & Hartigan 2008). Their success, however, depends on their own mechanisms for coping with adversity.

Risk Taking

Elkington and Hartigan (2008) say that social entrepreneurs are risk takers who "jump in before ensuring they are fully resourced." Although McClelland (1967) indicated that an entrepreneur has only an average tendency to engage in risk-taking behavior, this assessment was made long before the dramatic worldwide escalation of the phenomenon of social entrepreneurship and long before Drucker's (1985) observation that "entrepreneurship is risky (p. 29)." Rauch and Frese (2007), focusing strictly on business entrepreneurship, hold that the propensity for risk taking has a significant impact on business performance. As was clearly visible in the interviews, social entrepreneurs are often so passionate about their vision that as a result they often risk their professional careers, their family life (many reported that when they got involved in pursuing their social mission, they faced severe marital problems), and financial resources (they often leave well-paid jobs) in order to pursue their passion. Some of them go even further and during the early launch period sell their properties to invest in their budding projects. Risk taking is highly embedded in the act of exploiting new opportunities and making decisions in the face of uncertainty (Lumpkin, 2007), which often goes along with social entrepreneurs' struggle to maintain sustainability.

Belief in the Malleability of People and the World

What motivates social entrepreneurs? They are mission-driven individuals who believe in the capacity for change among people and, by extension, in the world. This belief accounts for their persistence, tenacity, and commitment in pursuit of their mission (Dweck 2000, 2006). Entrepreneurs are convinced that with their ideas they can bring change by influencing the key players, potential beneficiaries, and sometimes an entire field or market. Munir Hasan believed that he could change the negative attitudes of Bangladeshis into respect and love for mathematics; he also strongly believed that math teachers, although initially resistant, could eventually become enthusiastic about the mathematics olympiads. Similarly, he believed the parents and students would eventually buy into the new "regime," as would the initially dismissive educational publishers, who in the end became allies, publishing math books as well as puzzles in the media. Social entrepreneurs also believe strongly that it is possible to effect change, not only in structures or procedures, but most of all in people's mindsets so that they become carriers of the new concept. According to Dweck's (2000, 2006) theory, they believe in the malleability of people and the world.

VERIFYING THE HYPOTHESES

In preparation for conducting our research, we quickly understood that it is quite a tall order to verify a hypothesis that embodies all seven traits. First, one needs to turn each of those seven hypotheses into one, preferably short, questionnaire in deference to time constraints (in pilot interviews, interviewees mentioned that they can't afford to spend more than one hour on the study). This precludes using already existing questionnaires, each related to one of the seven suggested traits, because the respondents would simply refuse. This leads to the challenge of constructing one new, possibly shortened, questionnaire encompassing all seven traits; this would require verification of the reliability of the new questionnaire in a series of pilot tests.

Second, one needs to identify a target group of social entrepreneurs. The parameters of who is and who is not a social entrepreneur could follow the Ashoka selection process, which would ease the burden of identifying the target group.

Third, there is a need to establish a comparison group in order to ascertain not only whether the social entrepreneurs have the proposed seven traits, but also to determine if in fact they differ from other groups, such as social activists. It would also be beneficial to compare the results with the societal average, which would require checking out a representative sample.

In the first decade of the twenty-first century, the team of the University of Warsaw's Complex Systems Research Center[10] took on the task of verifying the aforementioned hypotheses. The target group was identified as fifty-two Polish Ashoka Fellows.[11] The comparison group, N = 52, was randomly selected from the national database of nonprofit organizations, after customizing the list to include only those who met high-bar criteria; this was done with the aim of creating a methodologically comparable group.[12] An initial assessment revealed that this comparison group (social leaders) did not differ from the research group (social entrepreneurs) in terms of gender and educational level. A second comparison group, a representative sample of the society, N = 1002, was randomly selected by a company specializing in conducting national surveys. The seventy-two-question survey, titled Social Entrepreneurs' Personality Characteristics, was constructed by associating several categories with each of the seven personality traits; it was then piloted and standardized.[13]

The results were interesting (Praszkier et al., 2009): Both groups – social entrepreneurs *and* the leading social activists together (N = 104) – were shown to differ significantly from the rest of society in each of all seven specific personality traits; this means that they all are well equipped to pursue their social missions. They have a higher level of optimism, which allows them to believe in the success of their mission. They trust others more

---

[10] See http://www.complexsystems.edu.pl.

[11] All were elected Poland Ashoka Fellows from November 1994 (when the program was launched) to the end of 2005.

[12] (1) The founder of the organization is its current leader (similar to social entrepreneurs); (2) the organization has a high status (in Poland, one has to meet several criteria and undergo a screening process to achieve this status); (3) it is operating nationwide; (4) it has relevant (updated) information in the database; and finally, (5) the selected leaders were not Ashoka Fellows.

[13] The questionnaire was piloted with a group of university graduate students, N = 50 (39 female, 11 male; ages 22–24) in order to verify its discriminating power and reliability. It was standardized on a 1,002-person probe, randomly selected sample of Polish society (482 male, 520 female), between the ages of 16 and 90 years old (M = 48,35; SD = 18). The result was that all seven scales did not diverge from normal distribution. (Zabłocka-Bursa, A., Praszkier, R., & Nowak, A. [2006]. Questionnaire: Social entrepreneurs' personality characteristics. Unpublished research materials, Institute for Social Studies, University of Warsaw.)

than the average person does, which enables them to delegate and share responsibility. They are more willing to take risks, which enables survival on the shaky social market. They all have wide individual support networks. And they truly believe that change is possible, which bolsters their change-making mission. Their tendencies and abilities to be cooperative are above average, which opens the door to teamwork, cooperation, and dialogue. Finally, they are equipped with a higher ability to cope with adversity, which allows them to overcome the many natural obstacles usually associated with a social mission.

However, the results also showed that the social entrepreneurs differed from social activists in two dimensions:

- They have a higher readiness for risk taking. This seems logical considering the definition of social entrepreneurship, which includes passion and total commitment to disseminate innovative ideas nationwide and regionwide (in many cases worldwide). Social entrepreneurs often put their own quality of life and private wealth at risk; they also often risk their professional development as they abandon their professional identity (e.g., doctor or teacher) and take on a new role in the society – the role of a social entrepreneur.
- They have a much deeper belief that people, societies, and the world can be changed, so that the effectiveness of their mission is backed by their profound convictions.[14]

SPECIAL INDIVIDUALS BEHIND CHANGE: IS THE PROCESS ENDOGENOUS OR EXOGENOUS?

We might conclude at the end of the chapter that behind the change process there stand special individuals with several exceptional personality characteristics. This would indicate that the change they bring is exogenous, brought by those individuals, and contingent (see Chapter 4) – occurring only as a result of their special passion, talents, and personalities.

However, there is more to the story than meets the eye. Social entrepreneurs most likely possess other abilities that make them uniquely sensitive to social processes, most notably the gift of being able to use minimal interventions in order to empower the society while pursuing change. Finally, although sparked from outside, change is in the long run pursued

---

[14] It may be interesting, however, to compare the seven personality traits with a less rigorous sample of selected social activists; the "leading social activists" selected in this research as a comparison group are positioned relatively close to the group of social entrepreneurs.

by society. From this point of view, then, the change could be perceived as endogenous.

This ability to be empathetic with social processes, that is, to understand what is possible – what the dormant potentials and latent attractors are – seems to be another essential distinguishing feature of social entrepreneurs, much in the way Michelangelo Buonarroti was said to cut the stones for his sculptures: He had a strong instinct to follow the natural tendency of the material and would diligently search for the line along which the stone would naturally break – instead of imposing his vision of how the stone should be cut.

However, this personality characteristic is yet to be verified and still needs further research. We piloted a qualitative survey,[15] posing such questions as:

- Do you think she/he has an ability to look at the society as a whole, seeing it as a complex dynamic system?
- Does the subject have skills that allow him/her to mentally envision the models of the society in which she/he operates, and through that imagery understand its structure and dynamics?
- Does the person have a feeling for the often-latent needs, potentials, and the latent motivations of the society with which she/he is involved?
- Does the person operate in a delicate, sensitive way?

In this pilot, we received statistically significant "yes" responses to all these questions (and more), although it was administered on too-small a sample to definitively infer that this is true for all social entrepreneurs; however, this opens a gateway for further research.

CHAPTER HIGHLIGHTS

- Social entrepreneurs have by definition a creative and entrepreneurial personality (independent variable). Creative people are imbued with enthusiasm, curiosity, and wide interests; they are also tolerant of complexity and ambiguity and are attracted to the mysterious (problem solving). It is one of the core motivations of social entrepreneurs to create (and leave behind) something new and sustainable for society.

---

[15] This was piggybacked to the aforementioned research (Praszkier et al., 2009) through (a) interviewing Ashoka experts who were involved in the selection process and (b) evaluating interviews with Ashoka Fellows.

- The entrepreneurial personality sees the environment as a source of potential opportunities to pursue their mission; entrepreneurs have a gift to recognize those opportunities where others do not.
- The definition of social entrepreneurship implies some more personality traits, for example, trust, optimism, propensity for cooperation, individual social networks, adversity-coping mechanisms, risk taking, and belief in the changeability of people and the world (dependent variables).
- Research has revealed that social entrepreneurs and leading social activists significantly differ from the society's average in all aforementioned seven personality traits. However, social entrepreneurs differ from the leading social activists in having a much higher belief in the malleability of the world and people; they are also likely to take a higher risk in order to pursue their mission.

SUMMARY AND CONCLUSIONS, SECTION 3

In this section, we asserted that social entrepreneurs build social capital. In Chapter 7, the concept of social capital was presented, followed by the theory and practice of social networks, which are the bedrock for building social capital (Chapter 8). Chapter 9 provided an overview of social entrepreneurs' personality characteristics, especially highlighting those traits that allow the building of social capital.

Sections 2 and 3 led to posing a fundamental question: Shouldn't we reframe and broaden the existing definitions of social entrepreneurship so that they encompass the social entrepreneur's understanding of the processes of social change (Chapter 4), complexity (Chapter 5), creating emergent phenomena (Chapter 6), building social capital and social networks (Chapters 7 and 8), and possessing specific personality characteristics that enable this process?

In the next chapter, we will address this question, positing a new, dynamic definition of social entrepreneurship.

SECTION 4

A NEW KIND OF LEADERSHIP

INTRODUCTION

In the previous sections, we introduced the definition of social entrepreneurship, the social-change process that social entrepreneurs trigger, the dynamical theories of social change, as well as the social capital social entrepreneurs are capable of building and the specific personality traits that enable them to do so.

In this section, drawing from those theories, we will provide an overview of the phenomenon of social entrepreneurship from the dynamic point of view (Chapter 10) and the new kind of leadership manifested by social entrepreneurs (Chapter 11). Next, we will show how this approach works in practice, especially in seemingly insurmountable social challenges (Chapter 12).

10

Social Entrepreneurship: A Dynamical Account

The consensus among those who have had the opportunity to talk to social entrepreneurs is that it is usually a unique and powerful experience in which these individuals exude passion, commitment, and energy. Most likely these special attributes are responsible for helping to rouse people initially from a state of lethargy, passivity, or protracted dejection. Having accomplished that first step, what happens next? How do social entrepreneurs trigger the long-lasting, irreversible process of social change?

In this chapter, we want to delineate our understanding of the phenomenon of social entrepreneurship from the point of view of change theories (Chapter 4), dynamical systems theories (Chapters 5–6), and social capital and social network building (Chapters 7–8).

Additionally, we will follow the process of thinking, learning, and strategizing from the point of view of a social entrepreneur. The narrative we present is based on the case and archives analysis, as well as on the interview with a Nepali environmentalist and Ashoka Fellowship[1] candidate, Megh Ale,[2] whose mission is to "restore, conserve and protect the rivers of Nepal through affirmative action and education, while maintaining the cultural integrity of local riverside communities."[3]

The intention is to reveal the cognitive process, whereby small things can lead to big solutions, and the process of thinking alternates, like a spiral, with exploring, learning, and acting. This process is often far from the linear business planning model, instead resembling an instinctual method of getting from point A to point B, with various insights and *aha!* reactions along the way. Following social entrepreneurs' passionate and nonlinear way of thinking is like tracking an unfolding trajectory of turning points, each

---

[1] Second-opinion review of candidates, see Chapter 3; Katmandu, June 03, 2007.
[2] See http://www.ashoka.org/fellow/4364.   [3] See http://www.nepalrivers.org.np.

opening new avenues leading to more critical points, which in retrospect reveal how each element forms a coherent whole.

Megh Ale's comments will be followed by our own reflections on the approach of social entrepreneurs.

CATALYSTS FOR CHANGE

It is worth mentioning that the uniqueness of social entrepreneurship was well noted a decade *after* Bill Drayton coined the term "social entrepreneurship." Waddock and Post (1991) wrote that the successes of social entrepreneurs are not intended as ends in and of themselves, but as catalysts for increasing public awareness of an issue and fostering eventual societal and organizational change.

Acting as a catalyst is different from directly pushing for change; rather, it implies searching for the smallest and simplest possible impulses to trigger a natural process. This insight is at the core of what makes social entrepreneurs so distinctive: They act not as *activists*, focused on a direct goal, but instead as *catalysts* for a durable, irreversible social change process. As seen in this chapter, Megh Ale's passion is complemented by self-constraints with regard to his role in the change process.[4]

Megh Ale, Nepal: Turning environmental protection, including the natural river-flow, into a vehicle for economic development of rural communities

Q: *So then what actually is your goal?*

A: *The Nepali rivers are a world heritage, and almost all are beautiful and clean. For example, the origin of the holy Bagmati River is Bagdwar, the Shivpuri National Park – and it is one of the best examples of the harmony of nature, though very much threatened by civilization and by the construction-industry lobbies; for example, it enters the capital city and becomes the most polluted river in our country. I feel strongly that I have to help conserve the natural habitat and the purity cleanliness of the river, as well as to help the villages located along the riverbank to thrive and benefit from keeping the river unpolluted and unindustrialized.*

Q: *How are you going to make this happen?*

A: *I know that I can't do it for them; I can't come and teach; I can't be preachy or pushy: Those villagers have been there for generations and have their own traditions and shared wisdom. So then who am I and what is my role? I need to find a way for those people to feel happy and in harmony with*

---

[4] The interview was conducted in June 2007, so Megh Ale uses the future tense; by 2010, many of those plans had already been realized.

their lives; my role here should be to help them to find their way, not to push or be in the lead, but rather to be the catalyst for unleashing their own wisdom. . . . Sounds like a mission impossible, doesn't it?

THE MAGIC OF CREATIVITY

This "mission impossible" means that there is a need for new solutions and for atypical, nonlinear thinking and acting (*for lateral, divergent,* or *quantum-leap thinking,* see Chapter 9), which is possible with a creative approach. Creativity is considered one of the core attributes of the definition of social entrepreneurship (see Chapters 1 and 2).

Creativity is contagious (see Chapter 4) and can be seen as one of the ways of influencing the societal-change process: The creativity of social entrepreneurs enables one to see things from outside the box and thereby find new paths; it prompts one to embark on new behaviors and actions. It is especially important where there are reasons for the old attractor (for the attractor theory, see Chapter 5) to be deeply entrenched: "Contagious" creativity leads to finding new solutions and attractors. However, in order for this phenomenon to "have legs," social entrepreneurs must first understand and feel the context; otherwise, they may find themselves feeling their way in the dark rather than clearly seeing their approach toward initiating a durable, well-thought-through change process.

The following interchange illustrates how Megh Ale realized that the Nepali tea-drinking ritual could lead to a key solution:

Q: *What would be the best way to win over those dwellers, have them buy in to your vision?*

A: *We need to be cautious: The community may not take well to new solutions. We have to introduce something old and something new at the same time. . . . Let's think. . . . The river-rafting tourists, what would they like to have at stopovers? Tea, of course, a delicious Nepali tea, with milk. . . . Yes! What about teahouse rafting – encourage villagers to host rafters by serving them tea? They will earn some money, and the rafters will stay connected with the local culture. . . . This is the idea: Teahouse Rafting; I will definitely spread this across the country.*

UNDERSTANDING THE FIELD OF FORCES: SOCIAL EMPATHY

Small changes and small impulses can yield big results. Simple rules produce a complex process. In order to find the best way to launch the process of change, one needs to deeply understand Kurt Lewin's *force-field theory* (see Chapter 5); this requires some hands-on experience with target groups and communities, that is, participating in their lives, talking to people, and learning about their troubles, dreams, and constraints. Some social entrepreneurs are involved personally, for example, many of those who deal with disability issues are disabled themselves or have a disabled family member. In some cases, analyzing and understanding the force-field theory involves a hands-on learning phase before the takeoff.

Social entrepreneurs seem to have a knack for visualizing the force field; educated or not, they seem to have an instinct for developing in their minds cognitive models of societal structures and mechanisms. Moreover, they have the ability to construct models of the society in their minds so that they can simulate various options and proceedings.

They usually are either "insiders," one of the members of the group or society (for example, Kaz Jaworski), or they take the time to perform a hands-on exploration of the societal context, spending time and becoming a temporary member of the community (for example, Reza Deghati). The change process they foster is hence endogenous (see the discussion of change dilemmas, Chapter 4), with an exogenous stimulation (from outside the box) reviving existing (though sometimes dormant) capabilities.

> Q: *What next?*
>
> A: *Teahouse Rafting is a great idea, though by itself, it is not enough by far. I needed to learn more, live more with the river and its people, and feel their lives and their vibrations. . . . I wanted to see who is actually involved and who the key players are.*
>
> *The river communities are most important; given the right incentives, they have the capacity to help save the river; however, they may be just as likely to be lured by the construction-industry lobbyists, who may entice them with promises of jobs associated with building dams. At the end of the day, these jobs never materialize as they are offered to low-paid immigrants who are by definition not part of the established communities. The challenge, then, is to come up with some incentives beyond teahouses that would keep these people aware and involved . . .*
>
> Q: *Will serving tea change their attitudes?*
>
> A: *Teahouse Rafting is only the trigger; we must also explore the educational systems in the river communities; could schools play a role?*
>
> *There are also the rafting guides, most of whom hail from the river communities. As the decision makers as to where to stop, what stories to tell, and so on, they are absolutely essential! As are the tourists. The challenge is how to shift their focus from picture taking and gain their support and involve them in the clean-river idea.*
>
> *Finally, it must be said that the mission has a subtext, and that is the understanding that it involves more than just one river, but that it rests upon*

the culture of respect for the natural world and the indigenous peoples who inhabit it.

ALTERING THE EQUILIBRIUM, BUILDING NEW ATTRACTORS

Martin and Osberg (2007, p. 35) call building the new attractor (for the theory of attractors, see Chapter 5) "altering the equilibrium" – saying that social entrepreneurs are:

- identifying a stable but inherently unjust equilibrium
- identifying an opportunity in this unjust equilibrium and developing a social-value proposition that would challenge the status quo
- forging – finally – a new, stable equilibrium that releases trapped potential or alleviates the suffering of the targeted group, and through imitation and the creation of a stable ecosystem around the new equilibrium, ensuring a better future for the targeted group and even society at large

This is exactly what we meant (Chapters 5 and 7) by stating that instead of pushing directly for change and, as a result, confronting the old equilibrium head-on, social entrepreneurs build a new attractor, usually around some new sort of project. The new attractor generates trust and cooperation; the new attractor, over time, renders the old one irrelevant, while the new attractor grows and fosters durable change.

Megh Ale looks for an alternative way of engendering the whole process:

Q: *Will this require your personal involvement?*
A: *At the beginning, yes. But that should change.*

> *Okay, there is the river, villages alongside it, rafting guides, and the tourists. Obviously, we can't just simply talk them all into becoming environmentalists; it doesn't work like that. At the beginning there must be something easy and compelling, something motivating all the key players. This "something" should then be self-sustaining, so that there would be no further need for continuous prodding and monitoring. I need to set this into motion, make sure it works with one river, then leave and go to other rivers, such as Kali and Sunkoshi, to launch the same process all over again. Moreover, I want to create a huge national movement, so the sooner it becomes self-perpetuating the better.*

DEPARTURE POINT: BETWEEN INNOVATION AND TRADITION

To do so, however, one needs to find something that could trigger the entire process. On one hand, it should be innovative (all the other traditional approaches have failed); on the other, it should call for an approach that is deeply embedded in the groups or societies – in their trends, capabilities, or hidden capacities. The challenge is to take the first step to garner social interest and participation in a situation that members of the society generally receive with skepticism and resistance, keeping in mind that the existing attractor maintains the status quo. The launch should definitely provide some obvious benefits as a result of a participatory process, which engenders a sense of identification and coauthorship.

This is the most subtle and sophisticated of processes – striking a balance between the old and the new in a creative way, drawing from the natural potentials and traditions, while at the same time offering a new opportunity. Social entrepreneurs sometimes find something light, acceptable, easy to employ, and often elegant in its solution, which generates the appearance of an alternative attractor (see Chapters 5 and 9).

> Q: *What would motivate the guides?*
> A: *Seems that I am close to finding the solution. The notion of Teahouse Rafting is central to the process, as it involves all the players: the river communities, the tourists, and the guides. Okay, but how do we motivate the guides to bring the tourists into the river teahouses? Guides . . . They are key to making things happen, not only because they decide where to stop over, but mainly because they are in a position to influence the tourists: They engage them in conversation, they tell stories. . . . What if they were to become the clean-river ambassadors? Make the rafting tour also an educational adventure, so that they become aware and even become active in spreading environmental sensitivity? Wow!*
> Q: *How would that influence other key players?*
> A: *Okay, now back to the dwellers: It starts with serving tea, but actually should lead to their deeper involvement and understanding. . . . Well, it feels quite challenging as it seems that I am entering the field of changing mindsets. . . . So then the vision is that rafting guides would inform and at the same time entertain the tourists through simple and appealing stories that address the subject of nature and the balance between the river and the land, the water, and the various species of animal life, and the plants and the people. Moreover, the Teahouses will provide the opportunities for the tourists to meet with the river communities and learn more about their lives. Yes, but that would also mean having to prepare dwellers to talk to tourists. . . . Quite a challenge. . . . How to do that?*

LAUNCHING AUTOCATALYTIC PROCESSES

Based on the target groups' own energy (sometimes latent), social entrepreneurs launch a process that doesn't actually rely on their hands-on involvement. Rather, it depends on the combined potential of the people, the groups, and the communities, plus the creative launch idea and the smart way of linking several key players and incorporating levers into a self-perpetuating autocatalytic process (for autocatalytic process, see Chapter 5).

Megh analyzes what could possibly motivate the parties involved:

Q: *So then, how would you build in the motivations so that the key players remain continuously interested?*

A: *Well, the dwellers will initially gain financially through the Rafting Tea-houses. How will we motivate the guides? More clients would be the best motivation, but let us not discount the value of the guides' own competencies, credentials, and prestige. The tourists would no doubt be attracted by the unique beauty of the rivers and surrounding habitat; what about turning some rivers into well-marketed "Himalayan River Heritage" sites? That should be a real hit!*

Q: *And the guides?*

A: *Okay, back to river guides: Let's start with a training program from which they will graduate as licensed "ambassadors of river conservation." Elegant diplomas to be awarded at a media event will make it compelling and visible. Another idea: Let's design a "code of conduct," which would establish the ground rules for interactions of the guides and tourists with river communities, as well as the behavior of the guides among the tourists. This code of conduct would be a first in the field of river conservation, definitely a first in Nepal, and perhaps even in Southeast Asia. Alumni of the training program will be able to proudly announce that they are licensed river-conservation ambassadors and, as such, that they follow the code of conduct – which would be a true novelty and a magnet for tourists. Obviously, this program will contribute to preserving the natural habitat (which is, after all, the ultimate goal).*

CHANGING SOCIETAL MINDSETS

As said in Chapter 4 (psychological change theories), psychological change is based on the power of the situational context, which influences the individual's cognitive structures and, in that way, influences societal mindsets. Consistency in cognition is one of the basic human drives acted out when people incorporate a new behavior into a self-image that was modified to be cohesive. The new situational context prompts for restructuring and striking consistency on a new level. If people start some action, they build up their cognition in a way that renders this action intellectually justified, and the new cognitive structures promote new attitudes and behaviors.

PICTURE 12. Megh Ale organizing the River Festival

Finally, the new cognition, reinforced by the propensity for growth, creates new symbolic representations. Symbols are powerful, as is demonstrated by their ability to bolster societal mindsets in the feedback loop (more on symbolic change in the Epilogue).

Megh is thinking about education as the key vehicle for sustaining the change process:

Q: *What do you want to change: the way things are being done or the way people think?*

A: *Both. Initially communities will buy into the new idea through the Teahouse Rafting concept. They will host tourists, enjoy the profit, and participate in communication; at the same time, the guides will translate and explain their culture. The communities will also participate in discussing environmental issues and the importance of preserving the river and its natural habitat. At*

PICTURE 13. River Festival, water- pouring ritual: a Buddhist monk pouring holy water

PICTURE 14. River Festival, water- pouring ritual: a Hindu priest pouring holy water

PICTURE 15. River Festival guests "Sadhus"

PICTURE 16. River Festival guests (b)

PICTURE 17. Interfaith water ritual at the River Festival; Christian, Hindu, Buddhist, Jewish, and Muslim religious leaders together

some point, they will identify themselves with the clean-river paradigm and become true believers and supporters of the idea.

The next step would be cultivating new generations of supporters for the project.

Q: *How will you do that?*

A: *Schools should be established along the river banks and in river valleys, teaching community forest development, sanitation, and hygiene (or this should be included into the curriculum of the existing schools) – as to prevent further pollution and to sustain the natural balance. Moreover, let's provide scholarships for passionate students and community members to participate in more in-depth river conservation, cleanliness, and tree-planting initiatives. This way, the next generation will be prepared to combat global warming and climate change.*

Children and community environmental leaders will then affect a strong influence on their families to the point that they would know how to resist the deceptive incentives of the construction-industry lobbyists when they come to call.

IMMENSE IMPACT WITH SMALL INVESTMENTS

As mentioned in the Preface and Chapter 1, social entrepreneurs achieve an immense impact, transforming whole fields in their countries or regions. They do so through minimal investments. They usually don't have governmental or financial resources; on the contrary, they often start out by pawning their own property. Steve Bigari (Section 1) needed to change the way the calls to the workplace from low-income employees were being handled by adding some local social ventures ready to participate in a network of "social emergency." The costs of Munir Hasan's (Section 1) festivals were all covered by small local funds, which grew into a powerful process of improving the country's teaching of mathematics and its position in the International Mathematics Olympiads movement. Kaz Jaworski (Section 2) changed the overall economic performance of his region starting with a small initial investment in the local telephone system.

Megh Ale's grand vision reaches far beyond one river and one community.

Q: *What next, after the first pilot river?*

A: *The big dream is to transform the way people understand the value and economic potential of Nepal's and Southeast Asia's rivers. The first step is to evaluate the economic impact of tourism: It appears that just one tourist on Nepal's rivers can lead to the engagement of eleven local people! This means that tourism by itself is an effective lever. Including the fee, the entire plan translates into higher incomes for rural people and a greater local and national respect for ecotourism activities as alternatives to dams.*

Q: *Will rafting be enough?*

A: *The impact could be strengthened through creating other ecotourism activities, such as hiking and kayaking.*

Q: *Will you need a legal entity to support your ideas?*

A: *I definitely need a structure, a social organization that will provide smooth management. Let's call it the Nepal River Conservation Trust (NRCT), which will provide a multipronged approach to educating and empowering river communities and the rest of society.*

Also, I see the need for a highly visible kind of promotion using something that is already rooted in the Nepali culture – colorful festivals . . . yes! River Festivals! Let's start with the Bagmati River Festival and replicate it at other river sites. The festivals could easily attract people and create some water rituals that would embrace all religions, given that water is a factor in most religious practices. Such activities would certainly attract the media, which is the most effective way to get the message across to the entire population, including local governments and lobbyists. Perhaps out of this will also sprout a movement to include some of the rivers on the list of World Heritage sites.

SOCIAL CAPITAL AND SOCIAL NETWORKS

In Chapters 7 and 8, we noted that social entrepreneurs build social capital around their projects; they launch vibrant and trusting social networks, linking people and prompting mutual cooperation. This has been verified both by research as well as by observing cases of social entrepreneurship operating in various fields and cultures. Indeed, studies of regions other than those mentioned so far have validated this notion. In Japan, for example, Sakurai (2008) found that when building projects for the Japanese elderly,[5] social networks increase the likelihood of mobilizing resources and social capital, which plays an important role in social entrepreneurship (often even better than in commercial entrepreneurship). Another example involves the Novgorod region of Russia, where nobody could explain the exceptionally high level of economic performance. Petro (2001) traced the causes of this outstanding performance and attributed it to the elevated degree of social capital and the symbolic belief in the historical image of Novgorod as a vibrant mercantile democracy. His study shows that local governments can do much to establish social capital, which in turn becomes a carrier for economic growth.

Megh Ale is thinking about exchange and cooperation platforms.

Q: *The idea of the River Festivals is exciting and definitely worth pursuing, even though the festivals are only once a year.... Will that be enough?*

A: *There is a high potential much beyond the once-a-year event: People may get connected, exchange cards, and continue discussing the festival and its impact on their the community's lives through e-mail or in person. After all, it could conceivably bring together many partner organizations and thousands of volunteers! Also, corporations may participate – building their image as good corporate citizens. I am totally determined to change this into a vehicle that will successfully transform the way Nepalese society thinks about and cares for its rivers and waterways; and that impact should be ongoing, based on the newly established relations.*

Q: *And the communities alongside the rivers?*

A: *The dream goes beyond influencing their mindsets: I want to help them to become trustful, cooperative, and thriving communities. They should feel their own power and possibilities. The exercise in self-reliance, power, and spirit – presumably a new experience for all – should help them grow and cover the civilization gap.*

---

[5] "Takurojo" – innovative and alternative care facilities for the elderly.

And beyond that: In the next step shouldn't I create a platform for all those river communities to remain connected, exchange experiences, and build common projects? Wouldn't that be even more of an influence on the national and regional policies?

To lobby on behalf of Nepal's river environment, I should do some more networking with national and international groups and, finally, become a member of the pan-Nepali Sustainable Tourism Network.

COMPLEXITY AND EMERGENT PHENOMENA

Waddock and Post (1991) assert that social entrepreneurs in some cases provide the necessary vision, drive, and resources to galvanize the efforts within a complex network of individual and organizational actors toward resolution of a complex problem. They do so when multiple efforts by organizations or public agencies have failed, and the multifaceted dimensions of the problem and their reach into society have become obvious to the social entrepreneur.

In other words, according to Waddock and Post (1991), social entrepreneurs start where other efforts (especially top-down attempts) have failed. Furthermore, they realize that the social problem they are dealing with is multifaceted and complex, which indicates that linear methods do not apply. Instead, they trigger a bottom-up process of interactions that leads to the appearance of a new order on a higher level. This *chaos-to-order* process is typical for complex systems (see Chapter 5). The result is often an emergent phenomenon – a new structure and culture of communication and problem solving, often followed by procedures and rules (Chapter 6). In a way, social entrepreneurs create and manage the process of emergence – leading to the appearance of new, irreversible structures and order.

Megh Ale's dream is to create an emergent new quality in the national approach to the rivers' natural flow and habitat preservation:

Q: *So then what would you want to leave behind?*
A: *I want to leave behind something important and solid; I want to be sure that the rivers are clean and safe in perpetuity, that the harmony between nature and people is maintained, and that the entire nation of Nepal is aware and involved in conservation. More than that: that this enterprise will mushroom and spread to Southeast Asia and beyond!*
Q: *That is quite a dream, isn't it?*
A: *Yes, and a bit scary, especially that I have no initial resources, and my organization has no endowment. The big money is on the other side, with the construction industry and all those who think they will benefit from building dams.*

The only way to realize this impossible dream is through educating the village communities about the causes and effects of water pollution and degradation. And of course through providing some concrete profits so that they will become the key champions and protectors.

The triangle comprising guides – tourists – villagers is one of the core solutions; the idea is to set in motion a process where those groups mutually reinforce the good deed.

In order to sustain that effort, I also need to raise the awareness for conservation on a national scale, involving the existing organizations to lobby for new laws.

A DAUNTING YET COMPELLING CHALLENGE

According to Villani (2010), "The truth of the matter is that entrepreneurship is hard. It's really hard. Venturing out on your own. No steady stream of income. No way to know that your idea will be the one that works, not the one that fails. No stability. No demarcation between life and work. People constantly questioning your progress. You get the picture. It's hard."

This statement probably would be seconded by all social entrepreneurs. They all articulate both the highlights as well as the difficulties. They suffer bouts of insomnia while wrestling with finding a solution; they become so possessed by their ideas that often their social and family relationships are shattered in the process. Yes, they experience failures, which often provide opportunities for finding new solutions; on the other hand, they became so intensely involved that they sometimes take failures personally.

This makes social entrepreneurship a compelling challenge, both professionally as well as personally. In this book, we have highlighted the positive sides: high impact, various success stories, supportive social networks, and satisfaction from building social capital and facilitating the process of emergence. However, it would be a mistake to come away with the notion that the life of a social entrepreneur is inherently and exclusively accompanied by a high degree of satisfaction without making note of the likelihood that there will be periods of dejection and disappointment.

PRÉCIS: HOW DO THEY DO IT?

Let us revisit the ways social entrepreneurs facilitate the change process. Social entrepreneurs initiate and manage the process of emergence (for emergence, see Chapter 6). To trigger this sort of process, one has to overcome and surpass the schematic and linear A-to-B, B-to-C way of thinking;

it requires setting a foot in the world of nonlinear flows (which include feedback loops) and complexity and uncoordinated interactions on the lower level. It also requires having a conviction that this process will yield, on a higher level, irreversible, emergent social phenomena (for complexity, see Chapter 5).

Social entrepreneurs achieve this result by creating an enabling environment for initiating one's own bottom-up social networks (for social networks, see Chapter 8), as well as by providing the opportunity for social coordination, so that the networks operate in a cohesive way, leading to emergent occurrence. They change the properties of the social system by modifying such parameters as trust and the propensity for cooperation, which builds social capital. This becomes the bedrock for the new social context, which influences people's mindsets and attitudes: Individuals are more prone to communicating, sharing, and cooperating. They also become receptive to creative solutions; this is especially important because the social problems they face require innovation. This also changes the structure of the networks: The previously isolated groups become open to establishing *weak ties*, which connect those groups with the (much bigger and most vibrant and resilient) *scale-free* network. Such a network creates a propitious environment for the appearance of emergent social phenomena, which become a solid part of the society. As an additional effect, it prompts a problem-solving culture, essential for addressing possible future problems.

CHAPTER HIGHLIGHTS

- Social entrepreneurs are catalysts of the social-change process; instead of pursuing change directly, their objective is to make sure that in the long run, the change dynamics will lead to durable, irreversible social change.
- To catalyze the change process, they need to possess a deep understanding of the context (Kurt Lewin's *force-field theory*) and be able to walk in the shoes of others, leading to a greater understanding of existing or latent tendencies, capabilities, and strengths. On the basis of this recognition, they find creative ways of triggering a bottom-up change process, often achieving an immense impact with minimal investments.
- In the first round, social entrepreneurs creatively craft and employ positive attractors, which build social capital and increasingly work as seeds, spores, and launchers of the autocatalytic change process;

in this process, elements mutually reinforce one another and thereby augment the impact.

- This process may involve changing societal mindsets as well as structures, policies, and laws; using the power of the *chaos-to-order* paradigm, they reach a level of emergent phenomena, which become durable and irreversible assets of the society.

11

A New Kind of Leadership

Clearly, in keeping with our definition, social entrepreneurs can without a doubt be considered as leaders, although leaders of a new sort. Moreover, as Dees (1998) articulated, there is also no doubt that society has a pressing need for different leadership types and styles. We will try to identify the kind of leadership represented by most social entrepreneurs and see how it relates to other kinds of leadership.

DEFINING LEADERSHIP

There has been an explosion of literature about leadership (McNamara, 2010). Indeed, a search for the word "leadership" on Google[1] results in 116 million entries.

An article by Chemers (2000) takes a historical perspective, dividing the analysis into four periods: (a) the period prior to the presentation of Fiedler's (1964) contingency model; (b) the period from 1965 to 1975, focusing on the development and elaboration of contingency theories; (c) the period from 1975 to 1985, when cognitive theories and concerns about gender differences arose; and (d) the period since 1985, which has focused extensively on transformational theories and cultural influences. Our analysis of the literature is followed by a presentation of an integrative framework and a suggested direction for future research regarding leadership styles of social entrepreneurs.

The traditional way of seeing leadership is as a process of social influence in which one person can enlist the aid and support of others in the accomplishment of a common task. Chemers (2000) and Northouse (2010) define leadership as a process whereby an individual influences a group of

---

[1] September 2010.

individuals to achieve a common goal; Hersey et al. (2001) see it as a process of influencing the activities of individuals and groups in efforts toward goal achievement in a given situation. Yet another way of defining leadership: It is about creating a way for people to contribute to making something extraordinary happen (Kouzes & Posner, 2008).

The ethical component of leadership is worth consideration, especially given that the attribute of ethical fiber is one of Ashoka's criteria for judging the quality of social entrepreneurship. Northouse (2010) names five characteristics of ethical leaders:

- respecting others
- serving others
- showing justice (demonstrating a sense of justice and fairness)
- manifesting honesty
- building communities

The ability to build a climate of trust is another important component of ethical leadership (Kuper, 2006; Kouzes & Posner, 2008). The more trusted people feel, the more innovative they become. Trust helps develop collaborative goals and roles (see social capital, Chapter 7).

KINDS OF LEADERSHIP

Kurt Lewin et al. (1939) identified various styles of leadership: *autocratic* (the leader takes decisions without consulting with others); *participative* (the leader involves the people in the decision making, although the process for making the final decision may vary from the *autocratic* approach to deciding by *consensus*); and *laissez-faire* (minimal involvement of leader). Macionis (2010) characterizes three leadership styles: *authoritarian* (similar to Lewin's *autocratic*), *democratic*, and *laissez-faire*. The democratic style is defined as including everyone in the decision-making process, drawing on the ideas of all members to develop creative solutions to problems.

Recently, the most prevalent approach to identifying ways leaders perform their roles is through distilling three kinds of leadership: transactional, transformational, and laissez-faire, as described next.

Transactional Leadership

Transactional leaders elicit cooperation by establishing exchanges with followers and then monitoring the relationship (Bono & Judge, 2003; Burns, 2003; Judge & Piccolo, 2004; Bass & Riggio, 2006). They do not take into account the needs of subordinates, and they are influential because the subordinates are convinced that it is in their best interest to do what they are told to do (Northouse, 2010).

Judge and Piccolo (2004) have identified two components of transactional leadership:

- Contingent reward, which is understood as the degree to which the leader sets up constructive transactions or exchanges; the leader clarifies expectations and establishes the rewards for meeting them.
- Management by exception is defined as the degree to which the leader takes corrective action on the basis of the results of leader-follower transactions. More active leaders monitor follower behavior, anticipate problems, and take corrective actions before the behavior creates serious difficulties. Passive leaders wait until the behavior has created problems before taking action.

Transformational Leadership

Transformational leaders (Bono & Judge, 2003; Judge & Piccolo, 2004; Bass & Riggio, 2006) or transforming leaders (e.g., Burns, 2003) garner support by inspiring followers to identify with a vision that reaches beyond their own immediate self-interest. They stimulate and inspire followers to achieve extraordinary outcomes and, in the process, develop their own leadership capacities (Bass & Riggio, 2006).

Four components of transformational leadership have been identified by Bass (1985), Burns (2003), Judge and Piccolo (2004), Bass and Riggio (2006), and Northouse (2010):

- The first component of transformational leadership is called *idealized influence,* which basically refers to charisma; charismatic leaders display conviction and appeal to followers on an emotional level. Because their style tends to be so spirited and energetic, they generate admiration, respect, and trust. Followers see them as having extraordinary capabilities, persistence, and determination, and they can therefore serve as role models.
- The second factor is called *inspirational motivation,* which is understood as the articulation of a clear, appealing, and inspiring vision. Leaders who use inspirational motivation challenge followers to meet high standards, communicate optimism about future goal attainment, and provide meaning for the task at hand (Bass, 1985; Judge & Piccolo, 2004; Bass & Riggio, 2006; Northouse, 2010).

- The third component is called *intellectual stimulation* – sparking followers' creativity by questioning assumptions and challenging the status quo. The transformational leader challenges assumptions, takes risks, and solicits followers' ideas.
- The fourth dimension of transformational leadership is *individual consideration*, which is attending to and supporting the individual needs of followers.

Laissez-Faire

Laissez-faire is the avoidance or absence of leadership and is, by definition, most passive. According to nearly all researchers, it usually is the most ineffective style (Bass & Riggio, 2006).

SOCIAL ENTREPRENEURS AND A NEW KIND OF EMPOWERING LEADERSHIP

Our conjecture is that social entrepreneurs represent a specific kind of leadership that differs from those just mentioned. We have observed that the leadership styles of social entrepreneurs seem to epitomize what Lewin and Macionis have characterized as *participative* and *democratic*, respectively: They involve people in the decision making and draw on the ideas of all members to develop creative solutions.

Also, following Kouzes and Posner (2008), social entrepreneurs obviously is about paving the way for something extraordinary to happen, although (1) it is aiming at durable processes, not only at one single extraordinary "thing" or event and (2) it is more than "a way for people to contribute" – it is enabling them to identify with the idea and take ownership of it.

The leadership of social entrepreneurs (as depicted in Chapter 10) could therefore be defined as a process of affranchising the capabilities of groups, communities, or societies and enabling them to identify and take ownership of the idea and pursue it through making something extraordinary happen; "something" in this case means triggering a durable change process aimed at meeting social needs. We call this sort of leadership *empowering leadership (EL)*.

The main focus of this kind of leader is in setting up the process of change, launching the self-perpetuating and autocatalytic process. In this case, the leader does not have to be in place indefinitely but for just enough time to usher in the phase of building initial social capital (trust, cooperation, and self-reliance), as social entrepreneurs are usually not driven by the prospect of maintaining the position of leadership. This sort of approach differs significantly from transactional leadership, which is focused on maintaining the status quo of relationships between the boss and the subordinates; the latter are better off if they obey the leader and the leader controls the relationship through agreements and *transactions*.

The style of leadership that comes closest to embodying the qualities of empowering leadership is transformational leadership, which is similarly based on a far-reaching vision, but which depends neither on the presence of charisma in the leader nor on submission of the followers. Often, it is simply setting a path for the autocatalytic change process to occur (with the group's, the community's. or society's leaders celebrating the success as their own).

It is true that social entrepreneurs in the role of empowering leaders often need to articulate a clear, appealing, and inspiring vision – although, again, not to "followers" or "subordinates" but to the group, community, or society members. However, the new vision may appear insufficient to alter the existing societal attractor (equilibrium), so empowering leaders often build a new attractor, which becomes the departure point for social capital and for the subsequent change process.

The traditional way of seeing the role of a leader is as someone who continuously maintains their dominant position. Although Bass and Riggio (2006) say that "it is important for leaders to develop leadership in those below them (P. 2)," this statement indicates that there are those above and below and that presumably the newly developed leaders will maintain the "below-above" structure as well. However, the concept of empowering leadership places the individual only temporarily in a "higher" position, just for as long as such a posture remains indispensable for catalyzing the process of change – to the point when it becomes self-catalytic. This would imply that neither charisma nor being visible is necessarily involved – the empowering kind of leader may operate from behind the scenes, unrecognized by the media. In this leader's vision, it is the society and its representatives who, by identifying themselves with the process of change, should become visible spokespersons and the future celebrities of their success.

Lucky Chhetri, Nepal: Bringing education and a better way of life to girls from Himalaya Mountain communities through training to become local guides

High in the Himalayan Mountains there are nearly completely inaccessible, isolated villages where life is harsh for the inhabitants – it is a three-day trek to the nearest bakery, shop, school, or neighboring community.

Men work mostly in the Katmandu Valley or serve in the military (for example, the Ghurkas who serve as UN peacekeeping troops), gradually leaving the Himalayan communities to be populated more by women and girls than men and boys.

However, the girls in those villages have no access to education. There have been several top-down attempts to solve this problem, none of which survived, owing to the virtual impossibility of transporting teachers to those high-mountain communities, a journey of several days.

Lucky Chhetri, a Himalayan trekking guide, dreamed of helping those girls by finding a way to educate them in harmony with their cultural background and their natural environment rather than having them follow a standardized curriculum. The solution came to her in a kind of *aha!* moment: Why not create an agency that hires female trekkers? Lucky felt that rural women would be ideal candidates for female trekking guides. To become a guide, one needs to speak English; to know the local geography and be able to provide directions; to understand the biology of the natural habitat; and last, but most important, to know about personal hygiene and grooming, given that most of the girls did not even know what a comb was.

Lucky opened a new pathway to success. Her program, Empowering Women in Nepal, trains women as guides for Nepal's booming adventure tourism industry. A normal school curriculum is more or less being taught, although embedded in a natural way into the guide training. The girls are highly motivated to learn to become guides, and their families are supportive of their daughters' guide training, as they understand the prospects for new economic opportunities. Trainees learn English, history, geography, and environmental preservation, along with skills for mountaineering and business management. Lucky's additional goal for her students is to convey the newly acquired knowledge to other girls when they go back home during the off-season periods.

The success of this venture inspired Lucky Chhetri to broaden her training program and to reach many more women. With already more than one hundred alumni, her program is gaining recognition and proving that Nepali women can successfully compete on the job market.

As guides, these women found economic independence, countering the discrimination that has hindered Nepalese women for hundreds of years and building a new image of women's potential. The Empowering Women in Nepal school for guides became well known and gradually outperformed the traditional male-driven schools; one reason given for this was that women demonstrated a high degree of empathy, being most caring and delicate in their roles as guides.

PICTURE 18. Lucky Chhetri

Lucky Chhetri also built economic sustainability into the program, not only through tour fees, but also through an array of handmade add-ons, such as knitted water-bottle holders to carry mineral water on the trekking tours and to collect garbage from the mountains; thus, at the same time as they are raising additional money for the project, they are also encouraging their clients to protect the environment. Moreover, Lucky has established a mutual loan program that supports them in funding local development projects. In addition, she has opened a culinary school, leveraging the ethnic culinary skills of her women to add a delicious element to the travels of adventure tourists. She connects trainees in an alumni network where members can share ideas and plan collaborative projects, thereby building values through mutual inspiration and cooperation.

Empowering Women of Nepal has attracted significant media attention: It has been featured on CNN, NPR, Japanese television, and other national and international media outlets. The media outreach leads to new

PICTURE 19. Lucky Chhetri and guide trainees

PICTURE 20. Climbing sojourn

business for her trainees and elicits a surge of applications from disadvantaged women in remote districts.

Lucky Chhetri's strategy for expansion relies also on *traveling* training programs. She launched a suite of such programs in western Nepal in 2004 and is replicating them throughout ten other districts. She has also partnered with the Nepal Tourism Board and Trekking Agents Association of Nepal, who have given high priority to her program. With their help, she has reached deep into the Indian Himalayas, and she intends to export her project to Tibet. The vibrant alumni network that she has created (as mentioned previously) is one of the most important vehicles for the program's continued success, and it has been instrumental in transforming the image of women in Nepali society. Lucky is proud to say that this change comes all the way from the Himalayan Mountains.

In 2003, Lucky started a global program, "Women's Initiative in Eco-Tourism." The idea is to train women how to generate revenue using local resources, for example, producing and selling tourism products and preparing local cuisine hygienically. These efforts dovetail with raising awareness about health, hygiene, and sanitation for their daily living as well as for tourism. Lucky Chhetri also created "Women Trek for Peace and Development," another organization with similar goals, which provides an exchange among women from different parts of the world with the focus on community development.

COMPONENTS OF EMPOWERING LEADERSHIP

The idea of defining a new kind of leadership appeared in the early 2000s when the authors of this book were researching the phenomenon of social entrepreneurship. In Chapter 7, this research was mentioned in relation to the building of social capital by social entrepreneurs; in Chapter 9, it was mentioned with regard to their specific personality traits. During the research, the question arose as to the specific methods used by social entrepreneurs to build social capital and to achieve durable and irreversible results. Initially, the conjecture was that they trigger a bottom-up social process followed by more concrete and detailed questions of methodology. Finally, we came up with several hypotheses, which we verified in qualitative pilot studies, drawing from the knowledge of the Ashoka experts participating in the selection process of Ashoka fellows and from the case studies analyzed by qualified judges.[2] This pilot

---

[2] Investigators were appointed and individually assessed the materials.

confirmed[3] the following approaches used by social entrepreneurship (Praszkier, 2007):

- Social empathy:
  - Understanding (in many cases instinctively) the various types of potential, sometimes latent, embedded in groups and/or societies.
  - Understanding the pains, needs, and frustrations of groups and/or society, as well as their hidden dreams and desires.
  - Being aware of the latent tendencies, that is, in which direction groups or societies could potentially go.
  - Identifying areas in which groups/societies would eagerly cooperate and where the likelihood of success is relatively high (the first success is critical for triggering the process of change); and identifying areas of motivation through responding to some important needs (may seem invisible).
- Empowering groups, avoiding disempowering methods:
  - Facilitating the change process in a way that empowers people and groups.
  - Ensuring that others fully experience the reality of their success.
  - Avoiding a patronizing, top-down teaching style; this means, for example, avoiding bringing experts from the outside as opposed to launching an internal educational mechanism that would trigger a process of mutual learning within the groups or communities.
  - Minimizing and gradually diminishing one's own role so that the community could generate its own leaders.
- Modifying parameters:
  - Instead of confronting problems head-on, modifying parameters such as trust, optimism, hope, propensity for cooperation, and bringing groups/societies to the point where it becomes natural to come together over a given idea.
- Identifying the best starting point:
  - The starting point is usually innovative, being the seed for the new attractor; it is constructed in a way that leads to the first success; the groups/societies experience and enjoy this first success and, as a result, are motivated to demonstrate further cooperation.

---

[3] This pilot, however, requires more confirmation focusing on larger and more diverse groups than the fifty-two Polish social entrepreneurs we studied; some quantitative methods could also be incorporated.

- The starting point could be something other than the real goal, as the latter is often the area of a core conflict or a long-term struggle and resistance.

At this point, we realized that this list of approaches/methods may also serve as a basis for formulating the components of empowering leadership:

- The first component is about social empathy: the basic foundation for empowering leaders is the social empathy for the capabilities, sometimes dormant, embedded in groups and/or societies. Prior to acting, they understand what are the latent tendencies and strengths of the groups and societies they work with and tend to harness those potentials and tendencies into the dynamical change process.
- The second component is about empowering groups and avoiding disempowering methods. Empowering leaders tend neither to patronize nor to rely on external resources; instead, they prefer to rely on existing capabilities, launching, for example, a peer-to-peer learning system or platforms for exchanging ideas and methods that have worked elsewhere. The empowering leader is focused on creating an enabling environment for a durable process that stimulates and draws from the capabilities of individuals, groups, and societies.
- The third component relates to approaching problems and obstacles: Instead of addressing them directly, they modify the parameters; for example, they create a trustful and cooperative environment, facilitating creative brainstorming and finding innovative solutions. Doing so, they identify the best starting points, enabling the buildup of new positive attractors; these attractors become the nucleus for the ensuing change process and may not necessarily be directly associated with the goals.

An important caveat is that in some situations social entrepreneurs may need to combine different kinds of leadership; even in such situations, though, the final outcome is the empowerment of others. The following account illustrates the important point that there are situations in which personal charisma becomes a necessary component of change.

Imam Mohammed Ashafa and Pastor James Wuye, Nigeria: Bringing peace to highly conflicted areas through interfaith dialogue

Pastor James Wuye, a Christian priest, and Imam Mohammed Ashafa, a Muslim cleric,[4] founders of Interfaith Mediation Center of the Muslim-Christian Dialogue Forum, are bringing peace and peace-building education to Nigeria, especially in areas where Christian-Muslim violent conflicts erupt frequently. They believe that the only way violence can be eradicated is by having leaders of each faith promote religious teachings of peace and nonviolence. Their organization is run by Muslims and Christians in equal proportions, and is influencing schools, houses of worship, and community centers to prevent violence and intervene when conflicts erupt.

They organize Christian-Muslim youth camps, creating new mindsets among youth and influencing the schools' curricula. The camps encourage a spirit of cooperation for handling many practical issues in a natural way. They have influenced the educational system through introducing the Ethical Code for Religious Instruction in Schools. They are now using the power of their faith and the example of interfaith cooperation to prevent and intervene in religious and politically motivated conflicts in Nigeria, and especially to educate youth in building avenues to peaceful cooperation. Through TV programs and a portfolio of educational projects, they are changing the model of reacting to any stimulus with violence into a model of dialogue and understanding. They also have published a book comparing how such issues as forgiveness, love, and expiation are understood in Islam, Christianity, and Judaism.

Pastor James Wuye and Imam Mohammed Ashafa also help communities identify and use traditionally accepted peace-building methods that may have been forgotten or abandoned. In addition, they have set up peace clubs in preschools and primary, secondary, and tertiary institutions; each child who goes through the training is encouraged to plant a tree to symbolize commitment to building, and not destroying, their communities. They have also developed a peace-education curriculum, which is used in schools and by other organizations interested in peace building, as well as the Ethical Code for Religious Instruction in Schools. As for prevention, they have developed an early-warning mechanism, which alerts the communities to signs of trouble and to ways to immediately defuse whatever is provoking the tension.

However, the most compelling and influential message derives from the personal story of these two individuals: In the past, they were both

---

[4] http://www.ashoka.org/fellow/3875, http://www.ashoka.org/fellow/3874; see also http://imcnigeria.org/index.html.

PICTURE 21. Imam Mohammed Ashafa and Pastor James Wuye

members of mutually hostile militant youth groups, chasing, hating, and harming one another (James Wuye lost his arm in a clash with Mohammed Ashafa's group). At some point, in a moment of mutual enlightenment, they understood that instead of fighting one another, by operating together they could bring peace and understanding between their respective religions.

Indeed, together the imam and the pastor are becoming role models for cooperation and interfaith dialogue. Their story of mutual hate and willingness to kill one another reverting to understanding and cooperation changed attitudes of many Nigerians and prevented acts of violence: For example, they traveled together to violence-ridden areas and talked together to both conflicted communities, conveying the peace message.

The imam and the pastor would not have been able to pursue their mission without the power of their charisma and their compelling personal story. This would indicate that in some cases, the nature of the mission and the nature of the idea can determine the kind of role played by the leaders. In this case, James Wuye and Mohammed Ashafa would rather be considered transformational leaders, as they – according to the definition – obtain support by inspiring followers to identify with a vision that reaches beyond their own immediate self-interest; they stimulate and inspire followers to achieve extraordinary outcomes. They use all three components of transformational leadership – idealized influence, transformational leadership, and intellectual stimulation (for example, both highly educated, they organize and stimulate public debates and interfaith dialogue). Their story implies that some social entrepreneurs manifest a mixture of styles; in that case, we can probably say that they use both styles of leadership: empowering and transformational.

EMPOWERING LEADERS IN BUSINESS

Whereas the business sector obviously includes several styles of leadership in its "tent," we see that there is also a place for empowering leadership, which is more traditionally associated with the nonprofit community. For example, Peter Senge, director of the Center for Organizational Learning at the MIT Sloan School of Management, says that the way to success is to activate the self-energizing commitment and energy of people around changes that they deeply care about (Senge, 1999). He also says, "The biological world teaches that sustaining change requires understanding the reinforcing growth processes and what is needed to catalyze them (p. 8)."

At Unilever, one of the world's largest consumer goods companies, management instituted a program aimed at strategic change called Catalyst, which – through art – enhanced innovation and strengthened the corporate culture. The results exceeded expectations, giving rise to a new corporate willingness to take risks in developing an *enterprise culture*, together with an increase in savvy leadership. New product development increased, and the company was able to attract and retain creative people and boost the company's marketing efforts, all of which resulted in a concrete improvement in financial performance and shareholder returns (Boyle & Ottensmeyer, 2005). This narrative shows that instead of pushing for change directly (i.e., toward increasing managerial skills), sometimes it may pay off to modify control parameters, in this case, through art, increasing managers' creativity. The new creative approach increased the ability to perceive the challenges from outside the box and, hence, the ability to identify new solutions; moreover, there was an increased ability to stimulate new-product development, attract and retain creative people, and boost the company's marketing efforts. This approach (through increasing creativity) is similar to the empowering leadership style, substituting "social needs" with "institutional needs." Hence, the modified definition would be: Empowering leadership is a process of affranchising the potential of groups, communities, or societies and enabling them to identify and take ownership of making something extraordinary happen; "something" in this case means triggering a durable change process aimed at solving some pressing social or institutional problem.

It is our firm conclusion that most (though not all) social entrepreneurs are empowering leaders and that this style of leadership can also be found in the business sector, where a durable change process is fostered through empowering people to take joint ownership of a shared vision.

CHAPTER HIGHLIGHTS

- The leadership style of social entrepreneurs can be defined as a process of affranchising the vast potential of groups, communities, or societies and enabling them to identify and take ownership of making something extraordinary happen; "something" in this case means a durable change process aimed at meeting social needs. We call this kind of leadership *empowering leadership.*
- Empowering leaders possess an outstanding degree of *social empathy* (understanding the potential, sometimes latent, embedded in groups and/or societies; understanding their needs and pains); they set in motion the process of change in a way that builds social capital and empowers groups; in so doing, they minimize their own role – a pivotal difference when compared with traditional kinds of leadership.
- Empowering leaders often do not directly confront problems head-on; instead, they modify the system's control parameters, such as creativity and ability to think outside the box. Empowering leadership is the prevailing style of social entrepreneurs, although some of them, because of their specific mission, may use the methods embedded in the transformational kind of leadership.

12

Addressing Insurmountable Problems and Conflicts

As said before, effecting change means attempting to alter the status quo and as such is not always easily accepted – especially if the status quo is well grounded because of some historical, cultural, or other important reasons. In other words, those who are addressing seemingly unsolvable problems usually find themselves in conflict with the existing attractor. The bigger and more pressing the addressed problems, the more attempts have probably already been undertaken and the more failures have aggregated the magnitude of the existing attractor.

As mentioned in Chapter 7, some activists address problems or conflicts directly, which means that they are engaged in a process of disrupting the status quo. In situations of protracted social problems or conflicts, the result is often neutral (the system over time drifts back to the old attractor; see Figure 1, Chapter 7) or negative (the dynamics of the system may also backfire, leaving damage in its wake).

This might prompt the search for a smart way to circumvent the conflict situation. For example, in the lethargic and underdeveloped community in which Kaz Jaworski operated (see the Introduction to Section 2), there was a growing epidemic of juvenile delinquency, including the prevalence of bullying as a lifestyle. A traditional approach, that is, addressing the problem directly, failed. Instead, Kaz Jaworski addressed and resolved the problem through an indirect approach: He introduced dance lessons for the boys. The idea was based on his observation that during community parties the boys who did not dance were usually the ones who drank and instigated fights leading to a cascade of revenges, whereas the boys who took part in the dancing behaved appropriately. As a result of the boys' participation in the dance lessons – as far-fetched as it may have seemed at first glance – dancing became trendy and, indirectly, alleviated the conflicts. Dancing became a way to circumvent the old "bullying" attractor. Instead of penalizing the perpetrators or patronizing them, the empowering leader offered appealing dance lessons, which built a new positive attractor, making the previous one automatically irrelevant (see Figure 2, Chapter 7).

Actually, all social entrepreneurs presented so far have addressed daunting social problems and conflicts, and, as was described, all were in search of ways to avoid grappling directly with the old attractor by circumventing it and building a new one. Next are three more examples of this strategy. In the first round, we will portray the intractable situations; later in this chapter, the solutions.

David Kuria, Kenya, part 1: Addressing a sanitary disaster through a bottom-up process empowering slum dwellers

This narrative is about the Kibera slums, the biggest slum in Nairobi and the second largest in Africa, after Soweto. It is home to 800,000 people, about one-third of the entire population of Nairobi, squeezed into a territory occupying one square mile. The critical issue is sanitation; the top-down solutions (e.g., the efforts of the UN, WHO, and the Kenyan government) summarily failed, as in the process, they also violated the taboos and prejudices of the local people. Those solutions brought from outside were seen as arrogant and resulted in growing resistance, eliciting a "they-want-to-impose-things-on-us-against-our-will" response. The community objected to solutions brought from outside, vandalized the facilities, and continued to maintain an unsanitary disaster area. This greatly increased the potential for fostering epidemics.

Sanitation issues by themselves created a conflict situation with the governmental health authorities. Other conflicts were lurking around the high juvenile crime rate and cross-tribal violence.

For David Kuria,[1] a young university alumnus, this situation became a life challenge. To learn more, he became part of the community and in doing so developed a deeper understanding of local beliefs and habits (from the point of view of and in the language of our theory, we would say he developed his cognition of the field of forces). An architect by profession and a social entrepreneur by spirit, he quickly understood that crucial to the change process is helping the community members identify with the changes. He was looking for something that could become the first and culturally acceptable step that would, in the longer term, trigger further changes. The initiative that would be most likely to activate the community,

[1] See http://www.ashoka.org/fellow/4356.

he thought, should be to familiarize clean toilets so that the people would want to identify with them.

Manon Barbeau, Canada, part 1: Restoring cross-generational bonds in First Nation communities with a shattered social fabric

Residential Schools in Canada was an organization whose goal was to force the assimilation of the Aboriginal peoples into European-Canadian society. A book on the subject, written by a historian Milloy (2006) and titled *A National Crime*, reveals that between 1879 and 1986 around 150,000 Aboriginal children were forcibly taken from their families to distant residential schools where they were compelled to abandon their native language. Soon, the already high rates of tuberculosis and death skyrocketed to 69 percent. Those who survived returned home unable to speak their original language (which was brutally rooted out while in the residential school) and thus couldn't communicate with their families.

Clearly, the intention of assimilation backfired, causing suffering, high mortality, and a total shattering of the community's social fiber, as cross-generational communication was devastated. The long-term results were the disempowerment of communities and high rates of alcohol abuse. The many current government programs[2] have minimal positive results against the negative attractors, which have developed over decades.

Manon Barbeau,[3] a filmmaker by profession, was always deeply engaged in the situation of marginalized individuals and communities. She has chosen to be a documentary filmmaker in order to capture the injustices and to contribute to ameliorating the plight of the individuals within those societies. Traveling to distant First Nation communities and documenting their lives, she became deeply involved in finding a way to redress the shattered social fiber. She thought that the answer lay in the involvement of youth and rebuilding the younger generation's bonds with the elder community members, an approach that did not impose top-down efforts, which, for the most part, had failed. Her challenge was how to overcome

---

[2] In 2008, the Canadian prime minister publicly apologized to native Canadians who were taken from their families and forced to attend state-funded schools aimed at assimilating them. Before then, the Australian prime minister made a similar gesture to the so-called Stolen Generations – the continent's Aboriginals, who were forcibly taken from their families as children under assimilation policies that lasted from 1910 to 1970.

[3] See http://www.ashoka.org/fellow/5696.

the community's resistance to and prejudice against new initiatives coming from the outside.

Dr. Ebrahim (Eboo) Patel, part 1: Removing interfaith barriers among youth

America is a religious country, says Dr. Eboo Patel,[4] and this makes the nature of interactions so critical. According to Eck (2001), America is the most religious country in the world: More than 85 percent of the United States population identifies itself as Christian, Jewish, Muslim, Buddhist, Hindu, Wiccan, Sikh, or some other religious persuasion. Many institutions turn that diversity into an opportunity to foster bias, distrust, and hate. Young people (12–25 years old) are especially vulnerable to being drawn by adults into antagonisms, hostility, fighting, and even killing. Hate crimes motivated by religious bias are second only to crimes motivated by racial bias, accounting for 19 percent of reported hate crimes.

Dr. Patel started as a teacher and understood how easy it is to mold young people toward destructive or constructive directions and to kindle conflicts among youth that were nearly impossible to eradicate. Since he began observing these phenomena, he has been thinking about how to replace religious conflicts by building interfaith bridges for understanding and tolerance.

INSURMOUNTABLE SOCIAL PROBLEMS AND CONFLICTS

As said before, there were numerous efforts (for example, on the part of the UN and the Kenyan government) to solve the drastic situation in Kibera, and all failed because the inhabitants simply opposed top-down attempts at change. Those failures added to the gravity of the perceived situation, making the inhabitants even more resistant (deepening the negative attractor). The Kibera story (attempts to improve the sanitary situation on one side versus resistance on the other) indicates that some social problems can easily be perceived as conflict situations. According to Praszkier et al. (2010), a conflict per se may not necessarily be well structured or clearly delineated (hard to capture and specify, despite the existence of interpersonal and intergroup tension) and may not be well manifested (instead, latent and lurking below the surface). However, detecting and addressing the early indicators of those potential conflicts may help to defuse them.

Next, we will delve into the nature of intractable conflicts, keeping in mind the analogue to intractable social problems.

---

[4] See http://www.ashoka.org/fellow/3151.

Intractability

Some conflicts (social problems) are protracted and intractable. Coleman (2003) defines them as recalcitrant, intense, deadlocked, and extremely difficult to resolve, with the emphasis on the enduring nature and intransigence of both the structure and experience of such conflict. Social entrepreneurs are the ones who attack intractable problems (Elkington & Hartigan, 2008).

Bar-Tal (2007) holds that intractable conflict situations are experienced by the participating parties as total and existential, often having a multifaceted nature and involving various spheres of life. Moreover, intractable conflicts are perceived as zero-sum games (gains of one side are seen as losses of the other). Kriesberg (1998) additionally posits that intractable conflicts have a violence component (although in the social arena, intractable problem situations do not necessarily involve violence).

Socio-Psychological Aspects of Intractable Conflicts

The social implications of a conflict extend beyond the particular site of conflict per se (Miall, 2004). Intractable conflicts in societies lead to developing an appropriate socio-psychological infrastructure, which includes collective memory, an ethos of conflict, and collective emotional orientations (Bar-Tal, 2007). Societal beliefs (providing a collective "narrative" and a sense of what is unique to the society) are the basic components of collective memories and an ethos of conflict. Societies in intractable conflicts usually develop characteristic emotional orientations, such as collective fear or hatred.

The socio-psychological infrastructure has several adaptive functions, that is, it fulfills the epistemic function of illuminating the conflict situation and is functional for coping with stress created by the conditions of the intractable conflict. It also creates a sense of differentiation and superiority and prepares the society's members to be ready for the threatening and violent acts of its enemies. Moreover, it provides motivation for solidarity, mobilization, and action and strengthens the social identity (Bar-Tal, 2007).

Morton Deutsch's Crude Law

Morton Deutsch, the founder of modern conflict resolution theory and practice, and the founder of the International Center for Cooperation and Conflict Resolution (ICCCR) at Columbia University, goes even further, asserting, paradoxically, that the consequences of the intractable conflict influence its roots. Deutsch's Crude Law of Social Relations says that "the characteristic processes and effects elicited by a given type of social relationship (e.g., cooperative or competitive) tend also to elicit that type of social relationship; and a typical effect of any type of relationship tends to induce the other typical effects of the relationship" (Deutsch, 1973, p. 365). In other words, the effects of a relationship affect its roots in a feedback loop.

This paradoxical thinking leads to recommendations that are quite solid. When a conflict is viewed by the parties involved as a mutual problem to be resolved cooperatively, it mainly leads to a constructive process of conflict resolution with mutually satisfactory outcomes. On the other hand, a competitive, win-lose orientation to a conflict mainly leads to a destructive course of conflict resolution, with both sides losing or with the stronger party defeating the less powerful one. From the "crude law," one would expect that when the typical effects of a cooperative process are introduced into a conflict situation, the conflict is likely to be characterized by a constructive process, whereas the typical effects of a competitive process are apt to produce a destructive process of conflict resolution (Deutsch, 1973; Nowak et al., 2010).

One of the leading mechanisms of this phenomenon is that the evolved socio-psychological infrastructure becomes a prism through which society members construe their reality, collect new information, interpret their experiences, and make decisions about their course of action. This infrastructure becomes hegemonic, rigid, and resistant to change as long as the intractable conflict continues. It ends up serving as a major factor fueling the continuation of the conflict, thus becoming part of a vicious cycle of intractable conflict (Bar-Tal, 2007).

Morton Deutsch's Crude Law served as a theoretical framework for computer modeling of conflict situations (Nowak et al., 2010). The conclusions drawn from the various simulations confirmed Lederach's and Bar-Tal's concept of the significance of the socio-psychological context: Local mechanisms were found to be crucial for determining the global dynamics of conflict. Moreover, conflicts grow exponentially in places with the highest incompatibility of interests. Disruption of local constraints (e.g., enabling movement through free travel) can paradoxically reduce the conflict. Simulations also suggested that seemingly intractable conflicts can be transformed by creating a fast-growing, positive process in the vicinity of their center.

CONFLICT TRANSFORMATION AND CIRCUMVENTING THROUGH NEW ATTRACTORS

Such adaptive structures generated by intractable conflicts in a feedback loop become self-perpetuating and counteract change efforts; they serve as attractors, preserving the equilibrium around the status quo. Addressing such situations head-on, with direct conflict-resolution or peace-building approaches, usually fails, as the dynamics of the attractor, in the longer run, makes the situation revert to the initial state. Hence, the essential challenge is to *transform* the socio-psychological context (Lederach, 2003; Miall, 2004; Lederach, 1996 so that it becomes a peace-enforcing environment or to *circumvent* the conflict situation by building alternative attractors (Praszkier et al., 2010).

Lederach (2003) indicates that the term "conflict transformation" is more appropriate than "conflict resolution" or "conflict management." Conflict transformation must envision and include the entire social and cultural context (Lederach, 1996) and could be defined as perceiving and approaching the conflict dynamics as an opportunity for creating constructive change, in other words, envisioning conflict positively – as a natural phenomenon that creates potential for constructive growth (Lederach, 2003). As such, indicates Miall (2004), conflict transformation becomes a process of engaging with and transforming relationships and interests; in that way, a constructive conflict is seen as a vital agent or catalyst for change. Hence, conflicts should be transformed gradually through a series of smaller or larger changes involving a variety of actors who may play important roles. Similarly, from the dynamical point of view, real change could be created by building new attractors toward which the system will naturally tend to drift; this could be achieved by initiating small changes in the basic rules of interactions between people and groups, which can result in significant changes on the macro level over time (Praszkier et al., 2010).

ETHNOEMPATHY

Conflict transformation or circumvention requires an ability to identify latent societal tendencies and capabilities, which, in turn, requires the capacity for deep intuition or a kind of psychological "radar" for detecting social dynamics. Such insight, called "ethnoempathy" by Bar-Tal and Rosen (2009), is impossible without immersion in the everyday life of the society and developing a feel or instinct for what is possible. On the other hand, ethnoempathy is essential, as the new structures must meld with the society's indigenous cultures, beliefs, and rituals. Therefore, in searching for a new attractor, it is of utmost importance to identify an undertaking embedded in the society's culture so that it will be naturally sustained.

CIRCUMVENTING A PROTRACTED SOCIAL PROBLEM – THREE EXAMPLES

David Kuria, part 2: Solution

As a result, the search for something that could become the first and culturally acceptable step, David Kuria from Kenya initiated many small-group discussions, accompanied by actual illustrations drawn by members of the group, over the way they would envision "a dream public toilet of their own." This process engaged the community and led to associating the idea with the people. From all the drawings, David put together realistic architectural schemes, and he showed those plans at the assembly of community members and asked if they really want such toilets of their dreams. Hearing an enthusiastic *yes* response, he said: "Then go ahead and build it."

With some seed money, along with the volunteer work of the community members, they built the toilet. The human waste was transformed into biogas, making it easier for women to cook. Clean and shining, the toilet became a focal point of interest. The community imposed some fees on the use of the toilets and showers, with a family monthly discount. It was such a positive development, and it was really "their own," so they started thinking in an entrepreneurial way of how to generate revenue for maintenance and for building the next group of toilets. For instance, they reserved one wall for advertising at the facility, on which Kenya's largest telecommunications company and a local real estate firm purchased space. In addition, Kenya's leading manufacturer of shoe polish has also bought into the idea and is providing shoeshine services.

As the toilet became the only sparkling clean place in the community, inhabitants brought add-on services, such as the aforementioned shoe/boot polishing services, soda machines, and a cafeteria. Using those facilities became trendy, made people proud of the place, and triggered many other business initiatives, highlighting the positive impact of this success by strengthening and empowering the social capacity of the community. David's role was to provide technical support and, decreasingly, management advice to the committee.

This soon became a draw for the media, which, for example, covered the VIPs of Kenya visiting and getting their shoes polished. Through his organization, Ecotact,[5] David Kuria is spreading the clean-toilets initiative in Nairobi and throughout the entire country.

David Kuria decided to circumvent the conflict around sanitation instead of addressing it directly: He started playfully, drawing "dream toilets" and building identification with the designs made by the community members themselves. The protracted and insurmountable conflict around sanitary issues was circumvented by engaging the community in playing with crayons and drawings – and through that – building a new identification with the "dream toilets." The consequence was reframing the symbolic perception of the toilets into clean, modern social centers associated with the value of cleanliness. Also, it gave the community a feeling of success stemming from cooperation. Taking responsibility triggered a high-potential commitment and energy, which yielded cooperation. As a result, which could be labeled as *consequences of consequences* (see Chapters 2 and 4), people incorporated entrepreneurial attitudes that proved successful; finally, new, enterprising behaviors have emerged.

Manon Barbeau, part 2: Solution

Manon Barbeau's goal was "to fight the isolation, lack of employment, distress and suicidal tendencies of First Nation youth in remote communities, and to address their lack of confidence in themselves, and the ignorance, prejudice and contempt that harm them here and elsewhere in the world."[6] She was convinced that there must be a way to attract and involve youth so that young people will be the ones who initiate the healing process. In so doing, her aim was also to reach and involve the older generations through the activities of the young people.

In the process of making documentary films in northern Quebec, she met a First Nation chief who introduced her to Wapikoni, a young girl at that time. Manon decided to make a movie together with Wapikoni. The script was titled *The End of Humiliation*. The project lasted for two years, during which several times a month Manon Barbeau stayed with the Aboriginal communities for a few days.

The film was important, although quite quickly also became a tool for the real issue: the encounters that arose around the art of filmmaking. These meetings opened up new opportunities to restore dialogue between the young and the elderly. This experience led Manon Barbeau to start the Wapikoni Mobile project.[7]

---

[5] http://www.ecotact.org.   [6] See http://www.ashoka.org/fellow/5696
[7] See http://wapikonimobile.com/.

She trains young Aboriginal people in filmmaking. They choose their own topic, usually rooted in their own communities. Again, filmmaking is only a tool: Through a reflective process involving community members, a dialogue is initiated.

The movies are shown to the entire community. This triggers a new round of dialogue; for example, a father (abuser) and his son (the filmmaker, also an alcoholic) reconciled with one another and hugged in front of the community. Others then stand up in front of the audience and reveal their hidden pains. These community meetings become an enabling environment for a transformative healing process. They also inspire new films, which again involve the community and lead to new community gatherings for presenting the next new film, where again community members tell their stories in front of the audience.

This social transformation around making and showing films is a huge influence on people's lives. For example, a well-known First Nation rapper and alcohol abuser learned about Manon Barbeau's project while in prison and decided to change and incorporate rapping into the ethnic Algonquian language. He says that the Wapikoni project enabled him to change his life. There are also several stories of young people inspired by the project to learn their native language, which opens avenues of communication and restores bonds with the older, non-French-speaking generation.

The Wapikoni project started with two studios on wheels that began visiting Aboriginal communities in Quebec. The crew comprised filmmakers and community organizers, who served as mentors. The principal creators were the young people; they chose the topics and made the films, involving the community members.

For their first movies, the youth often chose to portray painful and hidden social issues. Their films break the silence on difficult issues and encourage dialogue in their own communities and beyond. Later, other topics (for example, the beauty of the region and spirituality) were also chosen. Making, showing, and discussing their films increased young First Nation people's self-esteem, which was previously very low.

The other component of the strategy is to disseminate those films outside the reservation. This not only introduces problems (often totally unknown) of the First Nation to the French-speaking Canadians, it also stimulates multiple bonds and connections between both parts of the society by, for instance, opening new educational avenues for the Aboriginal youth. As of 2009, Wapikoni movies have won twenty-one national and international prizes, and one of the short movies was presented as an introduction to a blockbuster film on eighty-five screens in Quebec.

Dr. Ebrahim "Eboo" Patel, part 2: Solution

Dr. Eboo Patel founded Interfaith Youth Core (IFYC)[8] to bring young people from different faith communities together to work in social action projects. The goal of the project is to foster cooperation (instead of conflict) among youth of diverse religious beliefs and to make interfaith cooperation a social norm. IFYC's program involves thousands of people working on social-action projects, addressing problems ranging from homelessness and hunger to education.

The far-reaching goal is to build a national interfaith youth movement that can transform religious education within faith-based institutions, provide a model for engaging religious diversity in civic institutions, and encourage relationships characterized by understanding and cooperation among different religious communities. Dr. Patel says that his idea is based on the conviction that if you are young and religious in America, part of what you should be about is coming together with people who are from different religious backgrounds to strengthen your own religious identity, build understanding across religious communities, and cooperate to serve others.

One of the Interfaith Youth Core's essential educational components is the methodology of highlighting shared values. Most adult interfaith endeavors start with theological questions such as how Christians, Jews, and Muslims view Abraham. The IFYC begins conversations by asking how our different faith traditions "speak to" shared values such as hospitality, peace, and generosity. The shared-values approach allows people to speak from their experience ("Here's what my Jewish family does to show hospitality . . . ") and highlights what is common whereas also creating room for the articulation of religious particularity. Furthermore, shared values are applied through social-action projects ranging from building houses to cleaning up rivers. Religiously diverse young people build special relationships and powerful understanding when they work side by side for the common good, all acting out of their own religious inspiration and thus recognizing that their religion calls them to live in understanding and cooperative service with and for others.

The approach also includes high-profile programs such as the National Day of Interfaith Youth Service and more intensive programs that focus on

---

[8] See http://www.ifyc.org.

developing faith-based youth leaders skilled in interfaith work. Dr. Eboo Patel wants to build a "field" of interfaith youth work through academic courses and publications. Moreover, he is using a network approach that brings the leaders of local interfaith youth projects together in conferences to discuss theories, methodologies, and best practices in interfaith youth work. This way, local projects retain their own identity, improve their quality by learning from others, and collectively create a movement by cooperating on national projects. One of the very tangible results is building an IFYC model interfaith youth city in Chicago.

When Barack Obama was elected president of the United States, Dr. Eboo Patel became a member of the administration's New Faith Advisory Council.

TRANSFORMING AN INSURMOUNTABLE CONFLICT OR SOCIAL PROBLEM

In the three cases discussed in this chapter, social problems were protracted and intractable; many top-down attempts had already failed, and the situations seemed hopeless. The profiled individuals who were committed to changing the situation faced a choice: to confront the problem head-on (bring educational programs, teach and preach, build new toilets, organize special events for the reserves, etc.) or, instead, find a way to circumvent and transform the social problem. In these instances, the new attractor was built around the strategy of circumvention (implementing such ideas as drawing dream toilets, making films, and creating interfaith understanding through cooperation), and the socio-psychological environment, as a consequence, automatically transformed itself: People became involved and changed their attitudes and mindsets. In David Kuria's case, the community became enthusiastic and took ownership of the new toilets; cleanliness became "trendy." In Manon Barbeau's narrative, through restoring the cross-generational bonds, the society opened its hidden traumas and issues, causing old wounds to heal. Dr. Eboo Patel, instead of preaching or patronizing young people, found attractive ways to foster their dialogue and cooperation through doing something meaningful together, which fostered interfaith understanding and cooperation. In all three cases, circumventing the conflict or insurmountable social situation triggered a durable process, empowering communities and strengthening the social fiber and bolstering self-reliance that, as a consequence, triggered the societies' economic development.

Looking at David Kuria, Manon Barbeau, Dr. Eboo Patel, and other social entrepreneurs' creative approaches to intractable social conflicts or problems leads to reflections on their specific abilities to find methods that circumvent and ultimately transform the seemingly insurmountable situations. These specific abilities were partially addressed in Chapter 9, although they are worth exploring further, with a specific focus on conflict resolution and peace-building.

CHAPTER HIGHLIGHTS

- Social entrepreneurs often address intractable, protracted, and insur-mountable social problems, which are similar to intractable conflict situations.
- Around the protracted conflict (social problem), the situation over time often creates a specific socio-psychological environment, which, in a feedback loop, sustains and augments the conflict (social problem).
- The way to efficiently address intractable conflicts (social problems) is through conflict transformation (changing the social environment, mindsets, providing growth opportunities, etc.) or through circum-venting the conflict (social problem) by building new, compelling attractors, which become the seeds for growing a durable social process.
- Social entrepreneurs have a specific ability for transforming and cir-cumventing intractable conflicts and social problems.

The Past and the Future

We have so far been looking at social entrepreneurship through the lenses of the social processes they facilitate. First, some theories of social change were presented, followed by a discussion of social complexity and how new emerging social qualities become irreversible; we also introduced the concept of social capital as a pivotal mechanism used by social entrepreneurs for empowering groups and societies. Next, we focused on the transformative power of social networks and how they can be fertile ground for building social capital. We also explored how personality traits strengthen the potential for building social capital. In Section 4, we delineated our understanding of the phenomenon of social entrepreneurship and the new kind of leadership it represents. In short, we pointed out that social entrepreneurs initiate and manage the process of emergence. They create an enabling environment for launching one's own bottom-up social networks; they provide the opportunity for social coordination, so that the networks operate in a cohesive way, leading to emergent occurrences. They change the properties of the social system by modifying such parameters as trust and the propensity for cooperation, attributes that build social capital. Finally, we illustrated how social entrepreneurs – in keeping with our definition – address insurmountable, intractable social problems.

This is, of course, far from a definitive exploration of social entrepreneurship – a vast open space still remains to be studied. The following case studies featuring the work of other social entrepreneurs not examined in the body of this text provide an opportunity to suggest possible directions of further study.

SOCIAL ENTREPRENEURSHIP IN THE PAST

One of the prevailing questions is whether the practice of social entrepreneurs is truly a phenomenon of the modern age (mostly based in the nineteenth and twenty-first centuries), or, if we were to look further back into history, would we find an earlier prototype of socially committed, innovative individuals? At the other end of the time line, will there be a need for social entrepreneurship in the future? First, we'll look at a handful of examples from the past, starting with the Victorian era.

Elizabeth Fry

In the Victorian era, Elizabeth Fry (1780–1845), a known social reformer, was changing life in prisons by raising public awareness of inhumane conditions and initiating legislation to humanize the treatment of prisoners. It all started when she visited a prison, where she was horrified by the living conditions. The women's section was overcrowded with women and children, some of whom had been held for years without trial; she returned the next day with food and clothes. Elizabeth Fry, whose parents were from prominent bankers' families, would often stay overnight in some of the prisons in order to experience and understand firsthand the conditions there. She decided to disseminate this knowledge and started inviting influential people to come and stay and see what she saw. She also started a prison school for children who were incarcerated with their parents; moreover, she initiated an education system, which included teaching women to sew and to read the Bible. In 1817, she cofounded the Association for the Reformation of Female Prisoners, which led to the eventual creation of the British Ladies' Society for Promoting the Reformation of Female Prisoners, believed to be the first national women's organization in Britain.

Octavia Hill

Octavia Hill (1838–1912) was a British social worker, particularly concerned with the welfare of the inhabitants of London and other overpopulated cities. An artist and a radical, she was a pioneer of affordable housing and has been seen by some as the founder of modern social work. It was Octavia Hill who initiated the development of housing for the poor, and it was she who campaigned for the availability of open spaces for them. Her methodical approach and her use of trained volunteers (whom she called "fellow workers") laid the foundations of the modern profession of housing management. She was the founding member of the charity Organization Society (currently called Family Action), which organized charitable grants and pioneered the first home-visiting service. Moreover, she was a member of the Royal Commission on the Poor Laws, influencing the legislation around these pressing social issues. Her achievements as an environmental and open-space advocate led to the cofounding of the British National Trust, which until today preserves 250,000 hectares of land open to all.

Thomas John Barnardo

Thomas John Barnardo (1845–1905) was an Irish philanthropist and founder and director of homes for poor children. This endeavor began with his medical work in the East End of London during the cholera epidemic of 1866, which first drew his attention to the great numbers of homeless and destitute children. As a result of his commitment to help them, he established a first-of-its-kind network of a variety of homes aimed at sheltering, caring for, and training homeless, needy, and afflicted children. To do so, he raised the sum of 325 million pounds sterling, which transformed the lives of some 60,000 destitute boys and girls.

The system was comprehensive, addressing the needs of children of various ages. The infants and younger girls and boys were usually sent to schools and prepared for the future; for example, girls were taught useful domestic occupations, and boys were trained for the various trades for which they were deemed to be suited. The variety of institutions included a rescue home for girls in serious danger, a convalescent seaside home, and a hospital for critically ill children.

Montes Pietatis

Looking even further back in history, we find the example of *montes pietatis*, a Middle Ages project. The history of *montes pietatis* represents one of the earliest forms of organized charitable institutions, offering financial loans at low rates of interest or without interest at all. Instead of seeking financial profits, the establishment used all of its profits as payments for employees or in disseminating funds to charities throughout Europe.

The first known true *montes pietatis* was founded in London in 1361 in the form of a bank. However, because the bank did not receive any interest at all, it was not a viable enterprise. Still, there was a clear need for establishing charitable institutions with the idea of lending money at low interest rates, a notion articulated by Doctor Durand de Saint-Pourçain, the French Bishop of Mende. In 1389, Philippe de Maizières published his project for the establishment of an institution that would lend money without interest but would receive provisions on profits made by loans. Doesn't this concept resemble the contemporary microcredit system?

Based on the aforementioned ideas and experiences, the first recorded *monte pietatis* was finally established in Perugia in 1462, almost immediately sparking the establishment of similar institutions throughout Italy. They were either autonomous entities or, as in Perugia, municipal corporations; they had a director, an appraiser, a notary or accountant, salesmen, and other employees. Soon the Franciscan monks took the lead in disseminating *montes pietatis*; starting from 1534, the success of this idea grew in its authenticity and was spread throughout Europe – in Belgium, France, Germany, Austria, Spain, and back in England.

The idea enabled the poor to lend money and invest it in their business, thus combating the extreme poverty prevalent in those days. Successful businesses contributed to the funds for new loans, accelerating the impact immensely.

If there is a track on social commitment and innovations in the Middle Ages, then can we find evidence of these phenomena even earlier, even in the time before Christ? The answer is yes, and following is one example.

Emperor Ashoka

This is about one of the greatest emperors of all time – Emperor Ashoka (born in 265 BC), known as Ashoka the Great, whose empire spread across the Indian subcontinent. His life was and is an inspiration to many, as he excelled in everything that he did. His name, "Ashoka," means "without any sorrow" in Sanskrit.

Shortly after becoming king, Ashoka the Great planned to seize the territory of Kalinga (today known as Orissa). He led a huge army and fought a dreadful and cruel battle; although Ashoka emerged victorious, the sight of the battlefield made his heart break with shame, guilt, and disgust. This made him pledge to never fight a battle ever again.

Ashoka saw his *dharma* (one's righteous duty) as a path showing the utmost respect for all living things. This *dharma* brought harmony and unity to India in the form of much-needed compassion, and it became the link between the king and his subjects, as everyone lived by the same law of moral, religious, and civil obligations toward others.

What Ashoka left behind was the written language, which we know from the edicts inscribed on rocks and pillars, proclaiming Emperor Ashoka's reforms and policies and establishing an empire on the foundation of righteousness, indicating that the primary concern is the moral and spiritual welfare of his subjects and the sanctity of all human life.

Unnecessary slaughter or mutilation of animals was abolished. Wildlife became protected by the king's law against hunting for sport and branding; however, limited hunting was permitted for the purpose of consumption, although the vast majority of the population chose to become vegetarians. Ashoka also showed mercy to those imprisoned, allowing them to leave the prison one day a year. He opened the educational system to the common man by building public universities and invested in water transit and irrigation systems for trade and agriculture. Moreover, he treated his subjects as equals regardless of their religion, political beliefs, or caste.

In some way, we may consider him the original social entrepreneur, whose ideas to this day exert a powerful influence on the culture and mindsets of millions of people. In fact, it is the extraordinary legacy of Emperor Ashoka that led Bill Drayton to name the international association he founded after him – Ashoka: Innovators for the Public.

AND IN THE FUTURE

It is hard to predict, but presumably the world will continue to be full of pressing social issues that will require innovative and passionate responses for as far as we can see. The nature of those social issues (see Chapter 2) may change, but the need for innovative ideas and committed, creative, and entrepreneurial individuals to address them will always be there.

One of the issues that will apparently be with us for a long time to come is the profound concern for our environment and for the production and distribution of energy. Some social entrepreneurs are already "on the case." Following are two inspiring examples.

Ursula Sladek and Brent Kopperson, Germany and Canada, respectively: Citizens producing and distributing "green" energy

The problem of green and clean energy production and distribution is beginning to loom large as a major challenge of this and future centuries. Ursula Sladek's[1] vision is a decentralized form of green energy production, both in terms of increasing the efficiency of energy transmission and of empowering citizens to take charge of their energy consumption. She realized that the best way to save energy is through turning energy consumers into a combination of producers *and* consumers. Her idea was to motivate individuals to produce and save energy and to sell the surpluses back to the grid. This way of thinking led her in 1999 to initiate the process

---

[1] See http://www.ashoka.org/usladek.

of equipping the inhabitants of the German community of Schönau with resources to produce energy and manage it through a citizen-owned social business, Power Supplier of Schönau,[2] which she cofounded. In most of the households of this community, families produce energy by diverse means and then manage the process of its distribution. However, to achieve that, Ursula Sladek had to advocate a change in the law so that the inhabitants could become the owners of their part of the energy grid and the managers of the distribution process. She succeeded in doing so, and this innovation became a model of decentralized energy production and distribution for other communities to replicate.

With an energy-efficiency rate of 90 percent, these independent citizen-producers are three times more efficient than conventional power plants, which waste up to 70 percent of produced energy through heat loss. Ursula Sladek's innovative approach has created a new paradigm that shifts energy production, management, and ownership into the hands of citizens, thereby promoting energy savings and use of renewable energy sources.

Similar ideas are being implemented in other parts of the world. In Canada, for example, Brent Kopperson applies a similar philosophy.[3] He is transforming Canada's electricity production and distribution from highly centralized ones, dominated by nonrenewable resources, to more decentralized, green, and locally owned systems. Brent Kopperson piloted his project in Aboriginal communities, where he saw the greatest need, but also where there existed openness to this approach. The First Nation groups not only can manage wind farms and solar-energy-systems production but in the future will also manage the distribution of energy surpluses. The process starts with education and retrofitting the existing homes so that the loss of energy is minimized. This process brings jobs and education and contributes to the growth of social capital.

Brent Kopperson founded the Windfall Ecology Centre[4] in 1998, pursuing small-scale energy production as a means of community development. He also developed a cooperative model called Community Power, in which a community creates and owns a fund to buy shares in a social enterprise that produces energy. He also created the Ontario Sustainable Energy Association and the Canadian Renewable Energy Alliance to support the development of the green energy sector. Moreover, Brent and his

---

[2] Elektrizitätswerke Schönau, EWS, see http://www.ews-schoenau.de.
[3] See http://www.ashoka.org/fellows/kopperson_brent.
[4] See http://www.windfallcentre.ca.

colleagues were largely involved in, and led the process of conceptualizing and advocating for, the Green Energy Act. This is a pioneering law favorable to green-energy production and distribution policies; it has been passed by the provincial government of Ontario and currently expanded to other Canadian provinces.

Ursula Sladek and Brent Kopperson are probably much ahead of the global trend. We may predict that they are setting model examples for future energy solutions. What is worth highlighting is that their achievements are based on down-to-earth businesslike thinking, and they are successful in providing economic motivations at all stages of the energy chain. This, in effect, empowers communities, builds social capital, and raises their self-reliance and efficacy, contributing – in the long run – to their overall development.

THE INDIVIDUAL

The other avenue still open for further exploration is rooted in one of the crucial sociological dilemmas related to social change (see Chapter 4): It is the question of whether change comes about from the individual or from the society. Our answer is that it comes from both, and both are worth pursuing. Next are some thoughts on possible issues to explore.

The Creative Brain

A creative act involves the discovery of an analogy between ideas or images previously perceived as unrelated (Martindale, 2004). There are several neuronal components of creativity (for example, creative people tend to control automatically the level of cortical arousal; Martindale, 2004).

Creativity is also described as *quantum-leap thinking* (by analogy to the discontinuity jump of an electron from one orbit to another, discharging or absorbing a quantum of energy; Mapes, 2003). It is a trait that is undoubtedly related to the brain's structure and its neuronal connections. In order to find unexpected solutions (enable the quantum leap), one must open the brain up to new neural connections; otherwise, the brain "freezes" and the synapses keep connecting (either directly or through neurotransmitters) according to old, rigid patterns. The term *neuroplasticity* (defined as the ability of the human brain to change as a result of one's experience; in other words, the brain's malleability) reflects the brain's ability to establish new neuronal connections. In infancy, the brain's plasticity is very high;

it is a time when a child's learning activity is operating on all cylinders. However, over time, we increasingly keep drawing from already learned patterns of reacting, which are stored in the brain and ready to serve. In other words, the flexibility of neuronal connections decreases with age, which means a reduced ability for quantum-leap thinking. It takes special abilities to reestablish the lost neuroplasticity, and social entrepreneurs seem to possess an abundance of this capacity.

A compelling avenue of research, then, would clearly be to investigate the rapport between the creative brain and the entrepreneur's innovative ways of thinking and acting, especially in light of the fact that many authors profess that one can control and influence the brain's creativity (e.g., Mapes, 2003; Begley, 2007). The conclusions of such research may help to create a curriculum for encouraging people's level of creative output.

Mary Gordon, Canada: Cultivating the capacity for empathy in children through the Roots of Empathy program

Empathy in relation to social entrepreneurship is by all means worth further exploration. In Chapter 12, we mentioned ethnoempathy as a key driver for finding solutions to insurmountable social problems and conflicts. Ethnoempathy stems from simple empathy, a key factor in understanding others through the ability to share their emotions. Empathy enables the identification of latent tendencies, dreams, and capabilities. On the basis of this special ability, social entrepreneurs are finding solutions that help others realize their latent desires and capacities.

The significance of raising empathetic children was raised by a social entrepreneur, Mary Gordon,[5] who established the growing global organization Roots of Empathy.[6] Elementary- and middle-school students have regular classes on empathy; children are taught how to care for a baby and how to understand its behavior and then become involved in hands-on experiences, such as sitting in a circle around a real baby and its parents (the family usually is from the neighborhood) and trying to discern what the baby wants to "say" through various sounds, expressions, or movements. They interact with the parents and have some practical experience in touching and taking care of the baby. The baby, in this case, is the professor teaching them to understand its needs and emotions and how that relates to the students' own experience (Gordon, 2005; Bornstein & Davis, 2010).

---

[5] See http://www.ashoka.org/fellow/mgordon.
[6] See http://www.rootsofempathy.org.

Longitudinal research (Berkowitz & Bier, 2006) on the impact of the Roots of Empathy as compared to other groups documented the following results:

- Increase in social and emotional knowledge
- Decrease in aggression
- Increase in pro-social behavior (e.g., sharing, helping, and including)
- Increase in perceptions among Roots of Empathy students of the class-room as a caring environment
- Increased understanding of infants and parenting
- Lasting results

Other research supports the hypothesis that empathy augments children's social intelligence and is a significant preventive factor for children's antisocial behaviors (Kaukiainen et al., 1999; Björkqvist, 2007; Blair, 2007; Dolan & Fullam, 2007).

The power of Mary Gordon's Roots of Empathy is probably the reason for this program's rapid spread throughout Canada, Northern Ireland, New Zealand, and Seattle, Washington, with Germany planned for 2011 and Korea in 2012.

Future research on neurological components of social entrepreneurship could definitely go in the direction of studying the conditions of empathy, especially because there is a growing conviction that empathy is based on the relatively recently discovered *mirror neurons*, which reflect the behavior of the others, as though the observer were itself the actor (Bauer, 2005; Ferrari and Gallese, 2007; Iacoboni, 2009).

Karen Worcman, Brazil: Building self-esteem and ethnic pride through the Museum of the Person

The importance and power of the individual is best illustrated by the following account. Karen Worcman[7] created the idea of the Museum of the Person.[8] The premise behind this idea is that human beings wish to immortalize their story. This reflection gave rise to a virtual museum aimed at providing each and every individual with the opportunity to integrate his or her history into a network of social memory. To do so, Karen Wor-cman created a multimedia database of oral reports, videos, photographs, and personal documents. She wants the oral histories to be accessible to

[7] See http://www.ashoka.org/fellow/3336.
[8] See http://www.museudapessoa.net/ingles/.

communities, building self-esteem and ethnic pride, through giving voice to people from disadvantaged or marginalized groups.

She also initiated a traveling museum – a mini mobile studio equipped with digital video and audio recorders – reaching several places such as public squares and subway stations in São Paulo. One of her projects, Local Memory, is aimed at helping schools and communities make their own history. Karen Worcman discovered the real power embedded in the transformative power of individual stories.

LARGE SOCIAL NETWORKS

The impact social entrepreneurs achieve is mainly through the networks they create; we outlined some basic information on networks in Chapter 8. However, this subject opens another avenue for further inquiry on the properties of networks that would make them the most helpful tool for spreading a novel idea; also, what sort of networks would help in building social capital as a desired outcome/feature?

Chapter 8 provides some basic information; a closer look offers several paths for further exploration. For example, one may think that the *density* of the network (the proportion of pairs connected compared to all possible connections) would increase the likelihood of social capital (the more connections the better, one would say). Surprisingly, it is not as simple as that: Borgatti et al. (1998) asserts that if we consider individual networks (links and relations of one individual), then the higher the density, the lower the social capital! Why? Because the multiple connections eventually become redundant, especially given the limited rational energy of network participants – they would need to put too many eggs into too many baskets. Following this path, one may ask where the threshold is, because when starting from zero, an increase in connections would augment the likelihood of social capital up to a certain turning point, after which the density may produce a self-cannibalizing effect (more links would mean dispersing to too many relations, which automatically become redundant formalities).

Looking at *density* from the point of view of the group's properties – density of "positive" relations (friendship, respect, acquaintance, past collaboration, etc.) – it becomes positively correlated with social capital, that is, the probability of the appearance of social capital and its strengths grows with the increase of density. Looking at the density of close relationships from still a different point of view, one may find that if those close and friendly relationships in a given circle last for a certain period of time, they actually become saturated and create the tendency of participants to follow the same friendship-confirming paths and rituals. The group may become reaffirming and supportive (which is definitely an asset), although closed to the external world. That is why Mark Granovetter wrote his famous article, "The Strength of Weak Ties" (1973), indicating that only weak ties assure the connection of close circles that are closed to the external world. A weak tie between an individual and his (even distant) acquaintances becomes a crucial bridge among previously separated, densely knit clumps of close friends (Granovetter, 1983). Individuals with a few weak ties will be deprived of information from distant parts of the social system and will be confined to the provincial news and views of their close friends. This deprivation will not only insulate them from the latest ideas and fashions but may put them in a disadvantaged position in the labor market, where advancement can depend on knowing about appropriate job openings at just the right time (Granovetter, 1983). Weak ties may provide people with access to information and resources beyond those available within their own social circle.

Clearly, these insights provide fertile soil for an exploration of the properties of networks launched by social entrepreneurs.

THE ROLE OF SYMBOLS

The powerful influence of symbolic representations was mentioned in Chapters 4 and 10. Indeed, one of the aspects of social transformation is the change that occurs on the symbolic level. Symbols fortify societal beliefs and add to the existing attractor. Change on a symbolic level causes the emergence of a new attractor. The symbolic transformation could be another path of further research, leading to a better understanding of the permanence of the change process facilitated by social entrepreneurs. One of the best illustrations of the power of symbols is the following account.

Cindy Blackstock, Canada: Empowering Aboriginal communities to develop their own health care system for children

Dr. Cindy Blackstock of Canada[9] is a lecturer, academic researcher, and advocate who focuses on addressing the systemic risks that undermine the success of Aboriginal children and families. This is one side of the coin; the other is that Cindy Blackstock comes from the First Nation community and is fully identified with traditional Aboriginal knowledge and culture. She deliberately merges Western science with the indigenous knowledge and

[9] See http://www.ashoka.org/fellows/cblackstock.

traditions, showing that those two can mesh well if perceived as complementing one another. Dr. Blackstock's primary focus and professional specialty is promoting cultural equity in child care and the health care system, especially in underserved areas. Her approach is to engage mainstream and Aboriginal peoples in an active reconciliation processes to redefine these systems on the basis of community-driven visions of healthy children and families. The process is guided by the Reconciliation in Child Welfare: Touchstones of Hope for Indigenous Children, Youth and Families[10] process, which sets out five constitutional principles (self-determination, holistic response, culture and language, nondiscrimination, and structural interventions) that are meant to be interpreted within the distinct culture and context of a community. Community gatherings are held to create a vision of a healthy child, and families take care to invite people who traditionally have been outside of the child care system in order to ensure the resulting vision is inclusive of all and invites new ideas beyond the child care clique. Symbolism is invoked throughout this process. For example, participants bring chosen stones or other objects appropriate to the culture, which they first touch with spiritual attention then pile up together to build a symbolic community committed to shared well-being. This is why her approach is called Touchstones for Hope and is known as such throughout Canada. The core idea is that through several meetings, each community comes up with its own ideas and is then prompted to take the responsibility for the realization of their dream vision for children in its own hands. At the end of this process, each of the participants takes and keeps a stone chosen from the pile – symbolizing further identification with the gatherings' decisions and serving as a reminder of their personal responsibility for action. Based on the natural cultural context, Dr. Blackstock is triggering the chaos-to-order process, that is, the first meetings are usually spontaneous, with unstructured interactions, just sharing and brainstorming. From this chaos, there appears an emergent higher-level structure. This new structure leads to building the community's child care system. The piled stones serve throughout the entire process as a bonding symbol. This approach and experience remains deeply ingrained in the community, serving as an asset far beyond child care: The newly born social capital together with the emergent social structure also helps to address other problems. As a result of their cooperation, the Touchstone for Hope participants become mutually committed to a vision of child health and create new pathways to achieving this shared goal, fully cognizant of the benefits of working together.

---

[10] See http://www.reconciliationmovement.org.

PICTURE 22. Touchstone for Hope logo: artists Michelle Nahanee and Joey Mallett (2005) show three phases of the relationship between indigenous and nonindigenous peoples in Canada: before colonization (lower left), residential schools (upper right), and the beginning of reconciliation (lower right). The vision of reconciliation painted by two First Nation children, Paisley Nahanee and Chelsey Marie Musqua (upper left)

The conjecture is that the social-change processes initiated by social entrepreneurs are emergent (for emergence, see Chapter 6) because they also influence the societal sphere of symbols, for example, moving from disempowering, dependent symbolism to self-reliant and "yes-we-can" symbolic thinking.

It is also worth mentioning that one of the great German philosophers, Ernst Cassirer, held that the key to human innovation is a symbolic thought; great reformers, through symbolic thinking, are able to look at the impossible and perceive it as possible (Cassirer, 1962). This may be an indication that

PICTURE 23. Dr. Cindy Blackstock

social entrepreneurs may tend to think symbolically about insurmountable problems, which helps in outside-the-box thinking.

BETWEEN THE SOCIAL AND THE BUSINESS ENTREPRENEUR

Most of the social entrepreneurs presented in this book combine social passion with businesslike thinking (see, for example, Steve Bigari, Introduction to Section 1; Kaz Jaworski, Introduction to Section 2; or Megh Ale, Chapter 10). The topic of connections between the worlds of business and social activism is worth a separate book, illustrating both sides of the coin: On one hand, socially committed entrepreneurs use businesslike approaches for building the financial sustainability of their projects; on the other hand, many business leaders and teams often maintain an involvement in the social sector, as attested to by the growing Corporate Social Responsibility

(CSR) movement across the globe. Paul Herman, the founder and CEO of the HIP Investor (Human Impact + Profit) company says that one can make a bigger profit investing in a better world, which means investing in socially responsible companies (Herman, 2010). Social issues are playing an increasing role in potential employees' choices about where to work. For example, taking into account the commitment to social issues of their potential employer was an important factor for 48 percent of respondents in 2001–2004 surveys and has grown to 77 percent in a 2007 survey; a similar trend was documented with regard to making investment decisions, where evidence of the factor of commitment to social issues has grown accordingly – from 40 percent to 66 percent (Herman, 2010, after Cone, Inc.).

One of the many business-social modes of operating worth following is that, with relatively small investments, one can achieve a huge impact while at the same remaining in harmony with the cultural and social context. As shown in this book, social entrepreneurs usually start with nearly nothing and through manipulating smart and novel levers, achieve an immense impact. Moreover, they do not risk shattering the local traditions; on the contrary, they try to draw on the cultural context, finding ways for harmonious growth. The best illustration of this phenomenon is the following story from Mali.

Alou Keita's village banking

When Alou Keita[11] approached the community of a village located in the most disadvantaged part of Mali with the idea of starting up a village bank, everybody laughed at him, saying that they were poor, had no money, no food, roads, wells, and so on. In other words, to them the notion of a bank in the midst of their misery was truly ridiculous.

However, Alou Keita knew about the life and conditions of the villages very well, as he was himself born in that area. He knew that people envisioned banks as something alien and distant – big, scary buildings in the big city, charging unbelievably high interest rates for money transfers. The latter was the main source of distress of the villagers, as their relatives worked hard in France and needed to send their earned money back home. Usually they transported their income in suitcases, as the big banks charged too much for transfers. Besides the fact that this manner of transport was an expensive proposition, those suitcases were often lost or stolen. In addition,

[11] See http://www.ashoka.org/fellow/3876.

the emigrants became totally detached from their native communities, as they rarely could afford a trip home.

Alou Keita kept explaining to the villagers that if each of them would contribute with even a small amount of money, amassing those investments would amount to a sizable amount of start-up capital that, for example, could contribute to some community investments or could be deposited in a bank yielding an interest rate. Finally, the villagers agreed and built a hut in the center where the money was deposited and locked with a few padlocks, each of which was guarded by a chosen key-keeper. Opening up the hut for banking activities required three key-keepers and was always done in the presence of the community. The community as a whole played a crucial role in deciding who was worthy of a loan and which investments were priorities – Alou wanted the new banking system to be embedded in the village's cultural roots, so that it wouldn't shatter the shared traditions and values.

In 1998, Alou Keita set up a microfinance and investment organization, PASECA, a federation of village banks. One of Alou's key innovations was the establishment of a direct and affordable money transfer service for those living abroad. This service reconnects the emigrants directly to village affairs, thus as community members and investors; as such, they are able to participate in the economic decision making.

The program in one village was a success; the bank operated on a micro-credit basis, investing part of the money in supporting family businesses and part in community development, for example, building roads and wells. The extreme poverty of the village has been replaced by growth and economic development. News of the success spread to other neighboring communities, so in addition to the Program for Self-Managed Savings and Credit Systems (PASECA), Alou Keita established a national support Centre for Microfinance and Development (CAMIDE).[12] In 2005, forty-four village banks in the Kayes region had a total of 14,200 account holders with nearly the equivalent of 2 million US$ in deposits and had loaned out around 1,300,000 US$.

As seen in this and many other examples, in the contemporary world social change and social innovations cannot remain isolated from their economic context; otherwise, they would become idealistic utopia, which may backfire destructively because of unfulfilled promises. It seems that the future trend of introducing social change is through a conflation of

---

[12] See http://www.camide.org.

business and social entrepreneurship, which may result in the creation of a new profession.

Social entrepreneurs achieve their goals through virtually no initial investments, with a commitment to preserving the traditional lifestyle. One of many examples is the aforementioned project of Alou Keita, who introduced the new idea of village banking while at the same time preserving traditional ways of decision making through village gatherings and of guarding the centrally located bank through three key-keepers.

Perhaps the biggest and most compelling mystery of social entrepreneurship worth further exploration is how does one build "something out of nothing" when addressing the most pressing and, often believed to be unsolvable, social problems?

CONCLUSION

The challenge for this book was to identify and ascertain some invariable principles in the social entrepreneur's approach to pressing social problems and how they bring innovative and lasting solutions that make an impact on multiple levels. Moreover, we posed the question: How do they facilitate the change process in a way that is empowering and changes "the performance capacity of the society" (from Peter Drucker's quote in the Preface).

The departure point was an overview of existing definitions of social entrepreneurship, which were then structured into a framework with five pivotal dimensions (a syndromatic model). Because the core role of the social entrepreneur is the introduction of social change, an overview of various theories of social change was presented, starting with sociology and four sociological dilemmas, one of which asks if social change is endogenous or exogenous. Social change was also presented through the lenses of psychology, ancient Greek philosophy, and some historical processes.

As social entrepreneurs usually operate in multiagent environments, with multiple feedback loops and mutually reinforcing influences, complexity theory was presented as means for understanding the change processes and the appearance of emergent phenomena, that is, new, durable, and irreversible solutions. The way social entrepreneurs pursue their mission is through facilitating a bottom-up (endogenous) change process by empowering people, groups, communities, and societies to act in their own interest. We showed that they do this by weaving specific social networks, which become the backbone of social capital; one of the hypotheses documented was that social entrepreneurs pursue their mission thorough building social capital. Because building social capital involves specific abilities, the personality traits that enable fostering social capital were identified and analyzed; research comparing seven personality traits among groups of social entrepreneurs, leading social activists, and a random sample of the society was presented. This led to a new, dynamical description of social entrepreneurship: Social entrepreneurs facilitate the process of social emergence. This approach involves and requires a specific kind of leadership, which was termed "an empowering leadership" and compared to the traditional sociological kinds of leadership. Finally, we presented an analysis of how these sorts of leaders address insurmountable and protracted social problems and conflicts: They do this by circumventing the conflict and by building alternative, positive attractors "somewhere else"; those new attractors deepen and, over time, make the negative (conflict) attractor irrelevant.

The following appendices deal with more practical issues; the first addresses young people and all those willing to become involved in social entrepreneurship. The next two provide an account of the process Ashoka uses for selection to its fellowship.

Moreover, the scope of this book covers twenty-two case studies from various continents, representing diverse fields and walks of life.

HOW DO THEY DIFFER?

One of the core questions raised at the beginning of this book was: How do social entrepreneurs differ from other types of leaders and activists? This has been addressed at various levels; for example, in Chapter 2, it was mentioned that they operate at all five dimensions of social entrepreneurship; in Chapter 11, the differences in the kinds of leadership they represent was pointed out: They are catalysts and enablers, attributes that are not necessarily always visible. Finally, the basic dynamical difference, in a nutshell, was captured: Social activists often approach change head-on, whereas social entrepreneurs facilitate the long-term process of emergence (see the last section of Chapter 10).

This insight could inform the development of a different approach to philanthropy: Instead of giving money or bringing top-down solutions, the new, social-entrepreneurial version of philanthropy would facilitate a process of change in the long run, so that it builds social capital, empowers individuals, groups, or communities, and enables their taking into their own hands the creation of emergent social phenomena.

Becoming a Social Entrepreneur

Our considerable experience tells us that the field of social entrepreneurship has been shown to be a highly appealing choice for young people. Since 2000 one of the authors of this book co-initiated and has led a project called Ashoka School for Young Social Entrepreneurs (ASYSE), where the undergraduate and graduate students participate in a series of hands-on experiences with active social entrepreneurs, including workshops, internships, and mentoring. At the end of the project, participants have the opportunity to start a social enterprise of their own. The students' feedback revealed that this encounter made a life-long impact on their lives. Following are some of their comments.

"Enormous experience which will influence my entire life. I want to send my brother for an internship with the social entrepreneur I visited." – Gretchen, MBA student, USA.

"ASYSE showed how to change the reality, having nothing but a vision, strong will, commitment and faith, plus innovative and entrepreneurial ideas; that there exists such a thing as *goodness*, which helps in realizing the dreams. After ASYSE I learned how to fill the gap between the dream and just doing it." – Gabi, MBA student, Poland.

"A lifetime experience. It will not only help me in my professional life but also my personal life. One of the most important things that I learnt from my Fellow mentor is to follow the heart. The tools can be always obtained; support from exceptional individuals is rare." – student from Nepal.

"Thanks to the ASYSE workshops I realized that it is most important to have good ideas. Other things – tools, resources can be then somehow assembled." – Julianna Czyz, student from Poland.

Talking to young people revealed that usually they think that pursuing a career, especially in business, means giving up on their own dreams. They usually think that a real impact can only be made by visionary business

PICTURE 24. A Nepali social entrepreneur, Anil Chitrakar, presenting the course to the Nepali students

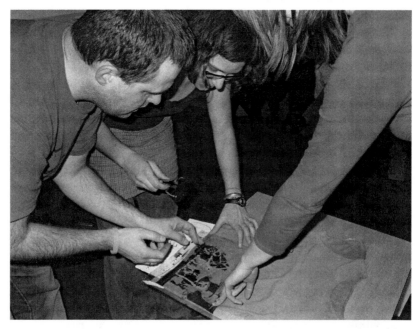

PICTURE 25. Polish students at Ashoka School for Young Social Entrepreneurs working on a project

personalities, such as Lee Iacocca (Ford Motor Company) or Bill Gates (Microsoft Corporation). The encounter with social entrepreneurs, learning about their ideas, visions, and creative approach, opens a new avenue: a conviction that one can do something very big and leave a significant impact on society through revisiting and revitalizing their own childhood dreams. This is an *aha!* experience. Moreover, they suddenly become aware of entrepreneurial approaches blossoming in the social sector, whereas before they thought that entrepreneurship only applied to business enterprises. They are also thrilled by social entrepreneurs' creativity and innovative spirit, belying their previous notions that the social sector is supported uniquely by classical philanthropy. Finally, many of them continue to be involved in social activities; some actually change their career goals. For example, Gabi (who is quoted previously), after earning an MBA, postponed her initial business plans and became a fully committed social entrepreneur.

Because many were interested in learning how one becomes a social entrepreneur, we decided to share our experience with some practical guidelines. They are not meant to be a comprehensive overview nor an official guide, but rather a handful of conclusions drawn from our experience with social entrepreneurship, capturing what was especially enlightening and mind-opening for young people.

First, we will share our recommendations on how to prepare the early phase, prior to taking off. Then, we will discuss what seems important to know after launching a new project.

BEFORE TAKING OFF — THE SOURCES OF POWER

The Power of Your Dreams

Rodrigo Baggio, a social entrepreneur from Brazil,[1] is providing young people in low-income communities (mostly *favelas*) with computer skills. His organization[2] is expanding the idea throughout Latin America and beyond. Rodrigo Baggio is currently featured in many international media, has received various prestigious awards, and is a fellow of several global organizations. His journey to success started with a dream as early as his childhood. In a CNN-featured video,[3] one can hear him saying:

> "Twelve years ago I had a dream. In my dream I saw young poor people using computers, having discussions about their reality and finding solutions to their problems."

[1] See http://www.ashoka.org/node/3396.   [2] See http://www.cdi.org.br.
[3] Available on http://www.ashoka.org/video/4131.

Dreams are critical, as they are the source of personal motivation, energy, commitment, and passion. For example, a young person may dream since early childhood of doing something for kids from families with an addicted parent, on the basis of his or her own childhood experience. At some point, this young person faces a fork in the road – whether to postpone and repress one's own dreams and pursue a personal career elsewhere, or fully accept and capitalize on them, building on this future career.

The Power of Your Passion

Allowing yourself to realize the big dream requires passion and commitment. Passion is one of the critical components of the "magic" of social entrepreneurship; Bill Drayton, the founding CEO of Ashoka, usually says that social entrepreneurs won't sleep until they find solutions.

One important caveat here: Being *possessed* by an idea shouldn't mean being *obsessed*. Passion is defined as a strong inclination toward a self-defining activity that one likes or even loves (Vallerand, 2008). But there are two types of passion: obsessive and harmonious, and only the latter is constructive (Vallerand, 2008).

Passion means not only fun but often also hardship, especially if you can't stop turning over in your mind how to solve the onslaught of problems as they present themselves on a regular basis; this fixation may draw your thoughts away from social or even family life and, as a result, may even endanger your relationships. Being passionate is balancing on the edge of reality and the future (solutions, plans, and innovations). To remain balanced, you should give yourself real breaks and periods of total withdrawal; resetting your mind, even if for a short period of time, helps you come back to planning with more strength.

The Power of Positive Deviance

In the Introduction to Chapter 9, we mentioned that social entrepreneurs are often regarded as "positive deviants" or "unreasonable people." John Elkington and Pamela Hartigan's book, *The Power of Unreasonable People* (2008), tells it all.

Positive deviance is an approach to social change based on the observation that behind the change process there are usually special people – positive deviants – whose uncommon and untypical, although successful, behaviors or strategies enable them to find better solutions than many others, despite having no special resources (Sternin, 2002; Elkington & Hartigan, 2008; Pascale et al., 2010).

Yes, positive deviants bring positive change, even though the choice may mean not fulfilling their family's expectations; this can certainly be problematic. Social entrepreneurs, when taking the big leap into the social universe, often hear: "Why don't you take a real job?" "Come on, you are so smart, you should pursue your career in business." "Think about your future, make some money." They report that the moment of veering off their prescribed path with the new social idea was tough, especially for their personal lives. Seen as "deviants," some are divorced, others are abandoned by friends, and yet others are treated as "strange."

Social entrepreneurship is becoming a new profession, and in the long run you will join this professional assembly of many other similar professionals who are located all around the world. However, at the very beginning, you should be prepared for and immune to the feeling of loneliness when struggling against all odds to pursue your big social dream.

The Power of Your Mind

Big dreams usually relate to big and seemingly unsolvable social problems (see Chapter 12). The more insurmountable the social problem is, the more creative should be the idea on how to address it – as you can assume all the traditional approaches have already failed. The challenge is to set your mind on a creative track so that you are able to see things from outside the box and develop solutions that others haven't thought of.

You may prepare your mind for being creative. One of the games is to imagine some absurd set of objects, for example, an old aquarium, a toy bumper car, and some colored strings. How would you build something out of these three objects? What would it be? You may ask a friend to come up with the most incompatible objects and your task would be to find out how to create something interesting out of them. Then you may shift roles.

Use all possible opportunities to run simulations, trying to conceive creative solutions. The best opportunities are when someone is complaining about something that is hopeless and undoable. You may be inspired to play (not necessarily arguing with this person) with some shocking and unexpected ways of solving this situation.

Be prepared for encountering tough obstacles. Do not grapple with and confront those problems head-on! The more you wrestle with the obstacle, the less creative you will be. What is advised by some business consulting firms is to step back and focus on something completely different. There are many ways you can do this. For example, currently it is trendy to write haiku poems. Haiku is a form of Japanese poetry from the seventeenth century consisting of three lines of five, seven, and five syllables.[4] Here are two examples.[5]

> Falling to the ground,
> I watch a leaf settle down
> In a bed of brown.

> Snow falling slowly
> Blanketing the trees and road
> Silence and beauty.

The haikus you write should refer neither to your work nor to any difficulties – instead think about nature, love, beauty, and so forth. The result is magical: When after writing a few haikus you go back to solving tough problems, your mind is more prone to look at them from outside the box, perceiving the situation from a broader angle. Often the innovative solution appears unexpectedly.

The Power of Future Trends

There is a natural tendency to superimpose the present time onto the future. This especially relates to planning: People usually forget that the future will be different, and solutions that soar now may sink tomorrow. When thinking about implementing your idea, you should try to imagine future developments: what will become pressing and what will be trendy; which current novelties will appear obsolete and what new resources will be available. Actually, this is sort of a sci-fi game – trying to envision the future world and how your idea would fit in it. Consider this quotation from Wayne Gretzky, one of the greatest hockey players of all time, who used to say: "I skate to where the puck is going to be, not where it has been." However, it takes a lot of skills to predict where the puck will be next; and it takes a lot of flexible mind games and simulations to imagine the world of the future.

The Power of Mapping

One of the most important components of your future success is mapping. You must deeply understand the field, tendencies, latent dreams, and dormant conflicts (Kurt Lewin's force-field theory, see Chapter 5); but first

---

[4] Haiku Talks Business has 640,000 hits on Google (as of October 2010).
[5] From http://www.international.ucla.edu/shenzhen/2002ncta/cunningham/Webpage-HaikuPoems.htm.

of all, understand the visible and the hidden capabilities, the below-the-surface strengths of the people, groups, communities, or societies your idea relates to. Your mapping should be theoretical and practical; the first important thing to know is the statistics of the problem – its prevalence now and in the past (what does the curve of the problem's manifestation over time tell you?) – and what it looks like when broken down by age, education, location, or other factors. Also how does it compare with other countries and regions; what attempts were made to solve the problem, and why did they fail?

As for practical mapping – just go out to the field, talk to people, and spend some time listening to their stories, pains, complaints, desires, and ambitions. Ask a lot of questions, especially "How can we do this?"; "How would *you* solve it?"; "Who are the key players?" Soon you will find that under the thin skin of bitter complaints and suffering there are quite sober thoughts and capabilities. This relates to all sorts of problems, for example, the parents of mentally disabled children or a region with high unemployment – go, listen, breathe their air, and get into their shoes. Prior to taking off, all successful social entrepreneurs deeply understood the target population, its structure, and systemic relationships, and their innovations were deeply embedded in this understanding.

The Power of the Bang for the Buck

Very often people think that the bigger their plans and social targets, the more investments they require. Munir Hasan (see Introduction to Section 1) could think that changing Bangladesh into a mathematics paradise would require a lot of investments in marketing, publishing, and organizing events. The way he did it was cost-effective and self-sustaining: Most of the costs of mathematics festivals were covered by the educational system and the local communities; the student volunteer organizations as well as the teachers' association took care of leveraging the standards of education. Moreover, publishing and disseminating the subject of mathematics through media became a revenue-generating business. In sum, the entire change process involved minimal initial investments and yielded a tremendous impact – an unquestionable "bang for the buck."

Think creatively about how to shape your social passion into a businesslike model so that over time it will become a sustainable and revenue-generating proposition. For example, one of the social entrepreneurs from Kenya[6] turned the disaster of depositing used car oil by mechanics directly

---

[6] Collins Apuoyo, see http://www.ashoka.org/capuoyo.

into the soil into a profitable enterprise: He paid them to collect used oil either with small cash or through microcredit and sold the collected oil to producers who use it for lubricating their machines. This process additionally gave jobs to the poor communities, for example, for collecting oil from small receptacles and transporting it to bigger ones. The microcredits leveraged the community's economic development; also, the participants were supplied with protective attire; and on top of that, the system yielded some revenue, which permitted the expansion of the idea to other places. The environmental disaster was solved (dumping used oil by many mechanics over a longer period of time created a real threat) and the system was sustainable, yielding some additional benefits for the society.

AFTER TAKING OFF

Assuming that you have already launched your project, here are some more hints.

The Power of Building a New Program

Creating and gradually building a new program can be great fun: You are giving birth to something new, which has the potential to contribute to changing the world for the better. It is good to keep a record of those days and later – when struggling with unavoidable obstacles – to load your batteries from the documentation you have diligently gathered (photos, stories, videos, etc.).

The personal story of how one of the authors, Ryszard Praszkier, launched the Ashoka program from scratch in the mid-90s in Poland[7] may serve as an example.

> In 1994, I was hired as the director of Ashoka in Poland. At the time, we did not have a formal training program, so I had to learn to identify the characteristics of a social entrepreneur on my own. Quite a challenge in a country where "entrepreneurship" had a negative connotation, especially just after the romantic Solidarity movement – a movement that was driven by passion and heart.
>
> The decade of the Solidarity movement actually fueled entrepreneurship in Poland, as the nation organized itself in supportive networks to publish illegal materials, educate citizens, and boycott official institutions. This

---

[7] Ashoka archives, unpublished.

spontaneous movement arose from a deep national desire for independence and freedom. Many of those involved were social entrepreneurs but would never have identified themselves as such. For most in those days, "entrepreneur" was associated with unethical business people (the fallout from communist brainwashing).

The Solidarity movement united citizens through common goals. For example, people began boycotting the official television evening news because of its manipulative propaganda. All across Poland, families would leave their houses promptly at 7:30 P.M., when the news began, walking in the streets, rather than watching television. These walks facilitated groups of people happily socializing in the streets and strengthened their bonds and their ability to act. Eventually the movement succeeded and civil society peacefully overthrew the regime.

It was following the Solidarity movement that I was chosen by Ashoka to launch the search for social entrepreneurs in Poland. I knew that my country was a hotbed of social entrepreneurship, even if they disliked the terminology. It takes creative, entrepreneurial individuals to launch underground education systems, develop undercover printing methods, and distribute thousands of copies of banned reading materials. It takes entrepreneurs to organize millions and change the course of a country.

But Poland still felt the sharp effects of communist brainwashing, which twisted the minds of many into a zero-sum game: If one person succeeded, it implied that someone else failed. Society was both prejudiced against individual success and skeptical about solutions that supposedly benefited everyone.

Rather than give up, I became more motivated by these challenges. Poland was in genuine need of Ashoka and the belief in the power of social entrepreneurs. I began to build a collaborative network that linked social entrepreneurs in order to increase their social impact by coordinating and organizing common goals.

In our very first year, we elected twelve Ashoka fellows, many more than anyone had anticipated for a country of Poland's population. Fifteen years later, those fellows are still pursuing their ideas, some of whom have brought their work well beyond Poland's borders.

So without training, how was I able to identify so many successful social entrepreneurs? I relied on what I call my "excitement indicators." Much of it was instinctive: I could quickly pick up the spark – the passion, intensity, and commitment – of social entrepreneurs.

Such stories are a source of strength even years after, especially in difficult moments; they also help to uphold the pivotal values of your mission.

The Power of the New Professional Identity

Making the decision, and jumping in at the deep end, to become a social entrepreneur often correlates with cutting loose a previously deeply rooted identity and facing the basic question: Who am I now? If a medical doctor decides to commit totally to developing a new national system for autistic children, at some point he inevitably finds himself deeply involved in many issues that can be perceived as entrepreneurial activities: public education and marketing, lobbying for new laws and procedures, building care centers, training medical professionals, helping adult autistic persons to perform a job and earn some money, developing strategies for early prevention, organizing climbing camps for autistic children, weaving the network of parents, professionals, and volunteers, and many more.[8] Another medical doctor who is deeply involved in fostering Palestinian-Israeli cooperation[9] uses health issues to organize mixed groups of medical students and doctors for improving health in the region. Moreover, he publishes in the prestigious medical journal, *Lancet,* an article relating not to medical issues per se but to Middle East peace-building through medicine.[10]

Clearly, we can see that both of these individuals took on a new identity – that of a professional social entrepreneur. This new identity is perceived as one of the most significant benefits mentioned by the newly elected Ashoka fellows; for example, many of them ordered new business cards advertising their new profession – social entrepreneur.

This new identity includes the additional benefit of the huge support that comes with the membership in a professional society – in this case, the society of social entrepreneurs, which provides a forum for dialogue, mutual education and support, and for developing new global projects together.[11] This means that when taking on this new role, you are not alone!

The Power of Community Building

Social entrepreneurs are not alone because they are also building a strong, supportive community. This is a profession based on collective and cooperative action; a lone ranger would never be capable of accomplishing the life-changing effects that social entrepreneurs are known for.

---

[8] Based on the case of Dr. Michal Wroniszewski; see http://www.ashoka.org/fellows/michal_ wroniszewski.

[9] Dr. Arnold Noyek; see http://www.ashoka.org/fellow/anoyek, also http://www.cisepo.ca.

[10] See http://www.cisepo.ca/pdf/publications/Lancet%20article.pdf.

[11] That is, Ashoka global fellowship program.

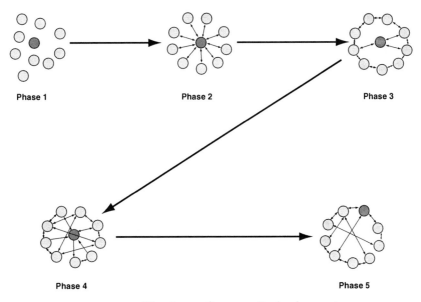

Phase 1   Phase 2   Phase 3

Phase 4   Phase 5

FIGURE 17. The phases of community development

We define community building as facilitating a long-term and continuous process, which is aimed at strengthening the feeling of a shared identity
of belonging, co-ownership, willingness to connect and cooperate, resilience
in response, and eagerness to contribute. You start simply with a group of
people well known to you but usually not known to one another. They are
not yet defined as a regular group, as there are no bonds, no common goals,
and no group structure. See phase 1 of Figure 17.

You are in the center, fostering communication; participants gradually
understand and share the mission and the goals, so they form a circle
around you. Communication still takes place through you; in other words,
there is no communication yet among the participants (phase 2). This is
the beginning of a subtle decision-making momentum, as you control the
communication flow and everybody is relying on you, waiting for your
initiatives, and not reaching out to others (this is called star-style communication). For some managers (not social entrepreneurs), preserving this as
a status quo may be a temptation, as it allows them to maintain control and
power. The downside is that participants are depending on you, not taking
their own initiatives nor providing mutual support. You are then forced
into the position of a lone ranger! However, if you initiate communication
links among participants, you will gain the power of joined, supportive
heads. You would enable some peer-to-peer communication without your

participation (phase 3). The amorphous gathering turns into a definite group and there appear some bonds and rules; however, you are still in the center, channeling most of the communication (this is called mixed-style communication).

The real threshold is when the group moves to phase 4: You no longer need to orchestrate the communication among participants; it takes on a life of its own. You are still unquestionably the leader (maintaining the central position), although there is a strong likelihood that the participants will take responsibility and become supportive. This also provides an enabling environment for the creation of value-added ideas, as participants themselves may come up with some new solutions; hence, a strong social capital will be built (for a discussion of social capital, see Chapter 7). At this point, we may consider the emergent phenomena (for the concept of emergence, see Chapter 6) and see the appearance of a self-driven and productive group.

At some point, you may want to move ahead, expand the program (see next section), and launch other similar groups elsewhere. You want the group to remain cohesive, cooperative, and productive while you move on to other challenges. The best way is to be considered as a senior partner, although no longer in the central position – just communicating with one another on a partnership basis (phase 5). This is once again a delicate balance, as on the one hand, you want the group to realize your mission, vision, and values while at the same time keeping the standards high. On the other hand, you want them to be independent, no longer needing you to invest your time except for providing constructive support. Getting to this phase is usually possible when the group has really internalized the basic values and the mission itself and when they accept your seniority as a *person*, not necessarily as a *manager*. Moreover, there should be someone in the group who will become your representative when the program spreads beyond the possibility of your communicating directly with every single participant. Getting to that stage makes you free to generate new groups.

Finally, you get to the stage of weaving a large network. Chapter 8 could be a resource at this point, as it provides some hints on building vibrant networks (especially recommended are the stages of developing networks that produce social capital).

To recap this process: The initial gathering turns into a productive group, creating a supportive community; many such communities transform themselves into a vibrant network, which becomes an enabling environment for delivering emergent ideas and projects. A network structured as such (hubs linked with one another) turns into the most resilient kind of network – the scale-free network (see Chapter 8).

The Power of Augmentation

Social entrepreneurship usually start out small and local. The first step is piloting the new idea and the initial implementation strategy. Be it a new innovative school or care center, a local community, or marginalized minority, the first step is to test, verify, and, accordingly, modify the innovation and its implementation. The leader at this phase usually strongly identifies with the people and local context, meaning with everybody and everything within reach.

If the pilot is successful, there appears a temptation to remain in this familiar, caring, safe, and friendly "nest." This happens to many social activists or innovators: They remain identified with the first and local endeavor, which we evaluate neither as good nor as bad. The advantage of remaining at the local level is that many excellent community projects operate for the public good, with the founding leader being continuously fully involved.

A true social entrepreneur, however, is not satisfied with such a situation: If her or his ideas worked locally, why shouldn't others benefit as well? The drive is the passion to replicate what has worked and proved efficient. And yes, moving forward means leaving the warm nest and taking risks (the propensity for risk taking is an outstanding personality trait of a social entrepreneur; see Chapter 9). In this next phase, a social entrepreneur pilots, tests, and verifies how the local idea can be applied to other places or groups, raising the following questions: Is the project context-proof? Will it work in new places without all the extraordinary resources (including the leader's time) invested in the initial endeavor? Is it easily adaptable? Does it attract key players? This new situation requires splitting the leader's own time into pursuing various replications and overseeing the developments from a more distant position.

From this phase (piloting the spread), conclusions are drawn as to how to develop and refine a broader strategy. The existing implementations usually serve as showcases and as a basis for training new leaders. At this stage, and at a distance, the social entrepreneur usually trains, cultivates, and facilitates a group of master trainers who will carry the idea to other places, presumably identifying more trainers or leaders to move the idea forward. As said in Chapter 8, the most vibrant and robust networks are of the scale-free type, which means many smaller hubs driven by a hub leader (who is strongly related with the social entrepreneur, drawing inspiration and positive energy from the very source); the hubs are interconnected (for example, participating in training retreats and sharing an intranet forums), so that the network looks like Figure 12, although much larger.

There is a next stage, which is influencing national and regional policies and drafting laws, structures, and procedures so that the legal and structural issues turn into an enabling environment instead of posing obstacles (which usually happens at the beginning). This requires another step in expanding the role of the social entrepreneur as he/she advances the sphere of influence to the development of national policy, wider outreach, and public education through various media.

Role-shifting (for example from the old profession to the profession of social entrepreneurship) is arguably the most challenging part of the social entrepreneur's work, although the most rewarding one. It takes a special personality to be able to enjoy such major professional and life changes.

The issues associated with the professional cycle of a social entrepreneur are not limited to the ones explored in this appendix; however, we wanted to pinpoint here some of the pivotal characteristics of the practice of social entrepreneurship, so that those who want to pursue this kind of work would be prepared for what to expect.

The Process of Assessing Candidates for a Fellowship

To illustrate the process of candidates' assessment, two narratives will be presented. In the interest of maintaining the confidentiality of the individuals involved, the context is an amalgam of data from several cases and the names have been altered (only the names of the elected candidates are being released).

SOCIAL ACTIVIST OR SOCIAL ENTREPRENEUR?

Hans Jürgen of Germany was deeply concerned about the quality of tap water in Dresden and the purity of the Elbe River. While at the university in Dresden, he joined an environmental organization that was mobilizing against factories responsible for causing industrial pollution. They were especially concerned with the chlorostyrenes, copper, and zinc found in fish and sediment samples from the Elbe River. They organized huge rallies forming blockades of the factories and placing posters with an image of a fish swallowing all the toxic and nontoxic substances.

Realizing that these tactics did not result in discernible change, Hans decided to organize a symposium on the nature–economy dialectic at the Dresden University of Technology. Many of his friends characterized this as "collaborating with the enemy" and boycotted Hans's symposium, some holding banners in front of the conference hall's entrance. Finally, the organization split and Hans became a leader of a new social entity known as Functional Reality Balance (FRB), whose mission was to establish platforms for dialogue and debate embracing the arguments from both sides. After graduating, Hans devoted full time to running his organization, which expanded all along the Elbe River, with chapters in Torgau, Magdeburg, and Hamburg. FRB also gradually widened the pool of key players involved in the dialogue, inviting architects and city authorities. The organization's name evolved into the Nature–Economy–Culture Thrualism (playing on words "three" and "true") and became quite popular, as heated discussions were frequently aired on TV; those TV shows were also used as springboards for initiating discussions in schools.

Gradually, the Elbe River had become much cleaner and the salmon had returned. Using the Elbe success as a model, he and his fellow activists were planning to move the focus of the forums to other German rivers.

Hans's candidacy was impressive. His application included photographic documentation and press clippings, and he was supported by many recommendations and endorsements. The selection team did due diligence, including Internet searches and checking references from experts and authorities.

There was no doubt that Hans was pursuing a social mission, demonstrating "an inner calling for which a person is evidently destined in life to pursue an activity leading to solving one or more of the existing social problems" (see Chapter 2). In addition, the social issue addressed "directly affected many or all members of a society and was considered to be a problem."

The social innovation was also evident, as illustrated by replacing a confrontational approach with discussion and debate – a new approach embedded in the way the discussion forums were shaped, searching for balanced solutions and optimizing the three key elements: nature, economy, and culture. Nature–Economy–Culture Thrualism was considered "a new idea that worked in meeting social goals."

Doubts arose, however, around the element of social change. On one hand, the impact of Functional Reality Balance and other environmental organizations was self-evident: cleaner rivers and the reappearance of salmon. Furthermore, the three-sided discussions transmitted through the media fostered the understanding that multiple factors contribute to the achievement of environmental goals, and that the only way to reach them is to search for a balance among the multiplicity of viewpoints.

On the other hand, no chain of far-reaching change was discernible, and the selection team deduced that the idea worked only as long as Hans's organization, FRB, continued its involvement in running the discussion forums. Moreover, there was no program in place that would create a "ripple effect"; on the contrary, without hands-on support, the organization's influence faded over time. The selection staff considered some hypothetical solutions that might enhance the impact of Hans's approach: He could, for example, launch an Eco-Forum Day in schools, with the goal of involving students in discussions, some of which might be covered by the media. Another solution that was suggested was to establish local Nature–Economy–Culture Thru-alism clubs in the hopes that the approach to solving common problems would be adopted by local communities and applied to such problems as the impact of urbanization, creating public spaces, and combating air pollution.

The entrepreneurial dimension of the endeavor also caused some doubt, despite the fact that this was a low-cost project – the participants were volunteers and the venue was donated by the university. However, there was no evidence that Hans was "always searching for change, responding to it, and exploiting it as an opportunity"; instead, he continued to replicate the initial formula, even when the situation changed: The Elbe River became cleaner and environmental awareness was increasing. Also he didn't seem to have a strategy for creating a mechanism that would enable the idea to become more self-sustaining and less of an ongoing dependence on hands-on management.

When considering the subject of personality, questions arose with regard to the applicant's creativity as well as his entrepreneurial qualities. It is true that Hans took a creative approach when he made the decision to break away from the initial militant ecological organization and launched the alternative group. The two groups shared similar goals, but Hans's offshoot group held different ideas about how to achieve them. For example, they initiated discussion forums, searching for a balance among the three elements (nature, economics, and culture). However, the selection staff considered this episode of creativity to be just that – an episode, rather than an indication of a constant creative attitude. As for doubts as to his entrepreneurial skills, the judges felt that Hans did not demonstrate an inner drive to constantly search for and find new solutions that would lead the organization to ratchet up (intensify) its efforts and become a major force in effecting societal change.

AN INNOVATIVE PROFESSIONAL OR A SOCIAL ENTREPRENEUR?

Identifying social entrepreneurs in practice is always a challenge, especially when candidates are already well-known leaders and experts in their fields.

Toronto native Dr. Rebecca Fallard was a well-known specialist in pediatric neurology and autism. She developed several new methods for treating autistic children, such as combining a special diet, including micronutrients, with physical exercise, in an effort to create new neuronal connections, which, thanks to what we now know about the plasticity of the brain, could lead to the creation of new psycho-neurological patterns. She involved family members who were trained to be experts in home-based treatment and techniques designed for children at various stages of development.

Dr. Fallard opened the Autism Spectrum Disorders Center at the University of Toronto's Faculty of Medicine, department of pediatric neurology. Besides treating autistic children and their families, the center also provides training and houses a scientific research department. Her center became a focal point for developing new methods of treating autism and was especially well known for its family outreach program. Dr. Fallard is convinced that autism is a complex chronic disease and that it is therefore critical to provide ongoing support to families as they cope with the many challenges of autism: educational, rehabilitative, nutritional, and with a particular focus on continuous brain-plasticity stimulation.

Dr. Fallard has published numerous articles and participated in professional forums and conferences, frequently serving as a keynote speaker. Her approach has been recognized by the administration at other clinics and has been disseminated throughout Canada. She was nominated to one of the social entrepreneurship' organizations because of the innovations she brought to the field and the wide impact of her approach. One recommendation for her candidacy highlighted the fact that she not only influenced the medical system but also engendered a shift of cognition among the professionals, who came to understand that autism had to be seen as more than a medical impairment requiring professional medical treatment. Rather, she believed that treating the syndrome should involve the active cooperation and participation of families, who should be empowered and quasi-professionalized.

For the selection team, this recommendation posed a difficult challenge: Dr. Fallard was a well-known figure who garnered high praise from her peers for her role in changing the field from the inside, starting with a model in her own center and gradually bringing change to professional and nonprofessional networks alike. She was unquestionably a professional innovator. Was she, however, a social entrepreneur?

The selection staff's heated discussion opened with the concept of mission, questioning whether it was social or professional. On one hand, one can say that expanding the focus to include patients' families has a social component, especially having organized the parents' support group. On the other hand, one could say that her solution was a natural consequence of her understanding that gradual and continuous stimulation of the brain leads to increasing the propensity of the neurons to fire new neuronal connections and thus develop new and more adaptive paths of cognition and behavior. Dr. Fallard saw that the only way to provide treatment on a daily basis, ad infinitum, is to motivate and involve families so that they become an ongoing extension of the treatment in the clinic. Finally, considering the way she identified herself as a medical doctor and as a member of the medical community, the selection staff became convinced that her mission was medical – not social – despite the fact that within her field she is recognized as an exemplar of commitment and creativity.

Also the social innovation component revealed some ambiguity: The innovation was unquestionable yet fully professional. She consequently leveraged her professional knowledge of how to overcome the brain's so-called limitations. The staff agreed that social innovation (professionalizing parents, creating parents' clubs, etc.) was a logical consequence but in a way also a by-product of her professional mindset.

The categories of social change were considered on various levels: The parents of autistic children felt more empowered instead of chronic hopelessness. They became responsible partners with the medical team and equipped with a concrete rehab toolkit, and the act of sharing mutual experiences with other parents enhanced their range of possible methods. Moreover, parents of autistic children often drop out of their professional careers and lose their professional identity, and the support groups provided a new identity and new connections. The second layer of impact was on the medical professionals and their perceptions of the parents, who became allies and colleagues in the process of providing treatment. Finally, the third layer of social impact was on the general population's perceptions and understanding of autism. Once the subject of autism was an unknown quantity, but through TV and other media, the public has become more familiar with the complexity of this disease.

However, there was a lingering doubt as to whether the change process would continue to exist without Dr. Fallard's initiatives and hands-on management, as the whole system was based on her professional and personal input and leadership. The entrepreneurship dimension was thoroughly analyzed, and there was no doubt about the presence of Schumpeter's notion of "creative destruction," as Dr. Fallard shattered the field, shifting the focus from patients to families. Some questions appeared around Drucker's criterion of "always searching for change, responding to it, and exploiting it as an opportunity." In that respect, the staff thought that she could do more: For instance, she could have turned the family group into a separate legal entity, which would officially delegate more power and responsibility to the families. The new entity could have provided a platform for launching a national network, which would conceivably gain clout as a special-interest/lobby. Other opportunities to explore could include elevating the status of quasi-professional families. This is especially critical as families usually lose their benefits when they leave their jobs, and a new status could help maintain continuation of their benefits. Thus, the aspect of entrepreneurship that encompasses the act of creating and acting through organizations seemed weak.

Also, there were doubts related to the business component of the project, which was totally dependent on medical grants and support from the University of Toronto's Faculty of Medicine. This might have been acceptable as a starting point if Dr. Fallard had treated this stage as a pilot and planned to build a more sustainable system in the future; however, she did not appear to be thinking along those lines. There were also doubts around her entrepreneurial qualities, especially considering that being entrepreneurial means constantly looking for new ways to add value to existing solutions or weighing the social and financial returns on each investment.

The personality dimension: Dr. Fallard seemed to possess a kind of problem-solving creativity, which helped her set new paths in treating autism and to disseminate her ideas. She also demonstrated the kind of creativity that was both far-reaching and visionary, but to a lesser extent.

Hans Jürgen and Dr. Rebecca Fallard are fictional cases. The reader is encouraged to develop her or his own opinion with regard to each candidate's capacity to meet the criteria as a practitioner of social entrepreneurship. In reality, not all candidates are elected into the fellowship. However, in most of those cases, candidates report that the selection process was a "win" in itself, as the questions asked opened new ways of thinking. Moreover, many of those who were not elected remain long-term strategic partners and experts.

APPENDIX 3

Excerpts from Interviews

WHERE DOES THE SOCIAL PASSION COME FROM?

The following fragment is a part of a dialogue with Munir Hasan (presented at the beginning of Section 1) and illustrates how the seed of the social entrepreneurial spirit was planted (original language is kept unchanged).

> Q: *From whom did you inherit this social passion?*
> A: *From my grandfather, Late Ahmed Chowdhury. He was very keen to work for the education of the suppressed – women and others. He usually spent his earnings for this cause (he was only a school teacher and earned very little money). He identified several issues in our education system, wrote textbooks and other materials. For his long career and after the retirement, he became involved with different schools as well. When he was in his late sixties, he led an initiative for funding a school for the girls in an area where the moneyed men didn't show any educational interest for their daughters. The school is now one of the best in that community. From 2004, I am also associated with this school as a volunteer. My grandfather is my role model.*

This response shows that Munir Hasan has been inspired with social sensitivity from early childhood, inheriting from his grandfather the commitment to helping people by launching durable institutions.

EMPATHY AND PLANNING

A fragment of the interview with Dorota Komornicka (who is presented in Chapter 8) on the strategy for motivating those who are unmotivated follows:

> Q: *You mentioned that working with the rural community you often encounter people who are initially reluctant to join your initiatives. How do you cope with that situation?*

A: *This is a question of understanding people, getting into their shoes. They are sometimes very specific. For example, I learned that open question sessions do not make sense at the beginning, as some farmers never will ask a question they don't know the answer to. So then I must start with feeding them with well-formulated questions I am sure they know how to answer. Then they warm up and start dialoguing. And this I always feel as a success: when people start talking with each other, without me orchestrating the discussion.*

Another example: Women would join a meeting if there is time to work and time to sing. So then I am organizing the most important meetings with a regional singing and dancing session at the end.

Finally, when they get the sense of all that, they take it in their own hands and boy, they become awesome leaders!

This dialogue illustrates social empathy at work, as well as the strategic "how-to" type of thinking.

BUILDING A NEW ATTRACTOR

The following quote is from the interview with Ursula Sladek (mentioned in the Epilogue):

Q: *You said that it takes a mindset and paradigm shift to change the energy-consumer attitude to energy-saver and energy-producer approach. How did you initiate this process of change?*

A: *I started in a small group, just saving, without a major change in the lifestyle. I wanted the whole town to see and accept it. Everybody said yes, though quickly they started giving arguments why not to do it. So then I launched an energy saving competition, with prizes to win. It was in the Schonau area, lasted for eight years. Then the competition spread to other places in Germany. So then we introduced the first component: energy-saving agenda.*

Then I asked: Okay, do you think saving is enough? Maybe you can earn more through producing energy, not solely saving. So they started to think how to produce. The first success with saving encouraged them to take a bold step into the next phase, of producing. Yes, it was sort of scary at the beginning, but it clicked and worked! We all understood that in Germany over 80 percent was produced in large power plants, very inefficient. Thirty-five percent of electricity and 65 percent goes into heating, and the latter is wasted. Coal, gas, oil are not infinite and can go extinct. So you shouldn't waste two-thirds of the resources! Home producing, especially from renewable sources, is the response to this challenge.

Soon the Schonau community turned into a model example for other regions of how to save and produce energy, also how to take ownership of their part of the energy grid – which was a total novelty, probably in Europe. However, without the initial small saving competitions people wouldn't feel strong nor motivated enough to set all those new paths.

This is an illustration of finding ways to build on something easy that, through its success, becomes a new attractor, enabling the next and much more challenging steps. The community was empowered and became self-reliant after mastering the process of energy saving and thus was ready to take on the enterprise of production.

REFERENCES

Adler, P. S., & Kwon, S.-W. (2002). Social capital: Prospects for a new concept. *The Academy of Management Review*, *27*(1): 17–40.

Aldrich, H., & Zimmer, C. (1986). Entrepreneurship through social networks. In Sexton, D., & Smilor, R. (Eds.), *The Art and Science of Entrepreneurship* (pp. 3–23). Cambridge, Massachusetts: Ballinger Publishing Company.

Alvord, S. H., Brown, L. D., & Alvord, S. H. (2003). Social entrepreneurship: Leadership that facilitates societal transformation – An exploratory study. *Center for Public Leadership*, Retrieved November 11, 2010, from http://dspace.mit.edu/bitstream/handle/1721.1/55803/CPL_WP_03_5_AlvordBrownLetts.pdf?sequence=1.

Alvord, S. H., Brown, L. D., & Letts, C. W. (2004). Social entrepreneurship and societal transformation: An exploratory study. *The Journal of Applied Behavioral Science*, *40*(3): 260–282.

Amabile, T. M. (1996). *Creativity in context: Update to the social psychology of creativity.* Boulder: Westview Press.

Amit, D. (1989). *Modeling brain function: The word of attractor neural networks.* Cambridge, UK: Cambridge University Press.

Arthur, W. B. (1999). Complexity and the Economy. *Science*, *284*(5411): 107–109.

Ashoka: Innovators for the Public (2000). *Selecting leading social entrepreneurs.* Arlington: Ashoka.

Austin, J., Stevenson, H., & Wei-Skillern, J. (2006). Social and commercial entrepreneurship: Same, different, or both? *Entrepreneurship Theory and Practice*, *30*(1): 1–22.

Bandura, A. (1976). *Social learning theory.* Englewood Cliffs, NJ: Prentice Hall.

Bar-Tal, D. (2007). Sociopsychological foundations of intractable conflicts. *American Behavioral Scientist*, *50*(11): 1430–1453.

Bar-Tal, D., & Rosen, Y. (2009). Peace education in societies involved in intractable conflicts: Direct and indirect models. *Review of Educational Research*, *79*(2): 557–575.

Barabási, A. L. (2003). *Linked.* Cambridge, Massachusetts: A Plume Book.

Bass, B. M. (1985). *Leadership and performance beyond expectations.* New York: Free Press.

Bass, B. M., & Riggio, R. E. (2006). *Transformational leadership.* Mahwah, New Jersey: Lawrence Erlbaum Associates, Publishers.

Bauer, J. (2005). *Warum ish fühle, was du fühlst. Intuitive Kommunikation und das Geheimnis der Spiegelneurone.* Hamburg: Hoffmann und Campe Verlag.

Bedau, M. A., & Humphreys, P. (2008). Introduction. In Bedau, M. A., & Humphreys, P. (Eds.), *Emergence: Contemporary Readings in Philosophy and Science* (pp. 1–6). Cambridge, Massachusetts: A Bradford Book.

Begley, S. (2007). *Train Your Mind, Change Your Brain: How a New Science Reveals Our Extraordinary Potential to Transform.* New York: Ballantine Books.

Bem, D. J. (1967). Self-perception: An alternative interpretation of cognitive dissonance phenomena. *Psychological Review, 74*(3): 183–200.

Berkowitz, M., & Bier, M. (2006, February). What works in character education. *A Report for Policy Makers and Opinion Leaders.* Character Education Partnership & Center for Character & Citizenship, University of Missouri – St. Louis. Retrieved November 11, 2010, from http://www.characterandcitizenship .org/research/WWCEforpolicymakers.pdf.

Björkqvist, K. (2007). Empathy, social intelligence and aggression in adolescent boys and girls. In Farrow, T. F. D., & Woodruff, P. W. R. (Eds.), *Empathy in Mental Illness* (pp. 76–88). New York: Cambridge University Press.

Blair, H. (2005). Civil society and pro-poor initiatives in rural Bangladesh: Finding a workable strategy. *World Development, 33*(6): 921–936.

Blair, R. J. R. (2007). Empathic dysfunction in psychopathic individuals. In Farrow, T. F. D., & Woodruff, P. W. R. (Eds.). *Empathy in Mental Illness* (pp. 3–16). New York: Cambridge University Press.

Bonabeau, E. (2001). Agent-based modeling: Methods and techniques for simulating human systems. Paper presented at the Arthur M. Sackler Colloquium of the National Academy of Sciences, *Adaptive Agents, Intelligence, and Emergent Human Organization: Capturing Complexity through Agent-Based Modeling, October 4–6, 2001,* at the Arnold and Mabel Beckman Center of the National Academies of Science and Engineering in Irvine, California. Retrieved November 11, 2010, from http://www.pnas.org/content/99/suppl.3/7280.full.pdf.

Bonabeau, E. (2002). Predicting the unpredictable. *Harvard Business Review, 80*(3): 109–116. Retrieved November 11, 2010, from http://www.psych.lse.ac.uk/ complexity/PDFiles/publication/hbr_unpredictable.pdf.

Bono, J. E. & Judge, T. A (2003). Self-concordance at work: Toward understanding the motivational effects of transformational leaders. *Academy of Management Journal, 46*(5): 554–571.

Borgatti, S. P., Jones, C., & Everett, M. G. (1998). Network measures of social capital. *Connections, 21*(2): 27–36.

Bornstein, D. (1998, January). Changing the world on a shoestring. *The Atlantic Monthly, 281*: 34–39.

Bornstein, D. (2004). *How to change the world: Social entrepreneurship and the power of new ideas.* New York: Oxford University Press.

Bornstein, D., & Davis, S. (2010). *Social entrepreneurship: What everyone needs to know?* New York: Oxford University Press.

Bourdieu, P. (2003). The forms of capital. In Halsey, A. H., Lauder, H., Brown, P., & Wells, A. S. (Eds.), *Education: Culture, Economy, Society* (pp. 46–58). Oxford: Oxford University Press.

Boyle, M. E., & Ottensmeyer, E. (2005). Solving business problems through the creative power of the arts: Catalyzing change at Unilever. *Journal of Business Strategy*, 26(5): 14–21.

Brehm, J. & Rahn, W. (1997). Individual-level evidence for the causes and consequences of social capital. *American Journal of Political Science*, 41(3): 999–1023.

Brinckerhoff, P. C. (2000). *Social entrepreneurship. The art of mission-based venture development*. New York: John Wiley & Sons, Inc.

Brockhaus, R., & Horwitz, P. (1986). The psychology of the entrepreneur. In Sexton, D., & Smilor, R. (Eds.), *The Art and Science of Entrepreneurship* (pp. 25–48). Cambridge, Massachusetts: Ballinger Publishing Company.

Burns, J. M. (1978). *Leadership*. New York: Harper & Row, Publishers, Inc.

Burns, J. M. (2003). *Transforming leadership*. New York: Grove Press.

Burt, R. S. (1997). The contingent value of social capital. *Administrative Science Quarterly*, 42(2): 339–365.

Burt, R. S. (2001). Structural holes versus network closure as social capital. In Lin, N., Cook, K. S., & Burt, R. S. (Eds.), *Social Capital: Theory and Research* (pp. 31–56). New York: Aldine de Gruyter.

Business Wire. (2002, June 27). Hill and Knowlton and Ashoka form precedent-setting global partnership. *Business Wire*. Retrieved November 11, 2010, from http://findarticles.com/p/articles/mi_m0EIN/is_2002_June_27/ai_87867887.

Carey, P. (2000). Community health promotion and empowerment. In Kerr, J. (Ed.), *Community Health Promotion: Challenges for Practice* (pp. 27–50). Oxford: Bailliere Tindall.

Cassirer, E. (1962). *An essay on man: An introduction to a philosophy of human culture*. London: Yale University Press.

Casson, M. (2005). Entrepreneurship, business culture and the theory of the firm. In Acs, Z. J., & Audretsch, D. B. (Eds.), *Handbook of Entrepreneurship Research* (pp. 223–246). New York: Springer.

Castells, M. (2009). *The rise of the network society: The information age: Economy, society, and culture*. Chichester, UK: Wiley-Blackwell.

Chell, E. (1985). The entrepreneurial personality: A few ghosts laid to rest? *International Small Business Journal*, 3(3): 43–54.

Chemers, M. M. (2000). Leadership research and theory: A functional integration. *Group Dynamics: Theory, Research, and Practice*, 4(1): 27–43.

Chemers, M. M. (2002). Integrating models of leadership and intelligence: Efficacy and effectiveness. In R. E. Riggio, R. E., Murphy, S. E., & Pirozzolo, F. J. (Eds.), *Multiple Intelligences and Leadership* (pp. 223–246). Mahwah, New Jersey: Lawrence Erlbaum Associates, Publishers.

Coleman, J. S. (1988). Social capital in the creation of human capital. *The American Journal of Sociology*, 94: 95–120.

Coleman, J. S. (1990). *The foundations of social theory*. Cambridge: The Belknap Press of Harvard University Press.

Coleman, J. S. (2000). *Foundations of social theory*. Cambridge, Massachusetts: Belknap Press.

Coleman, J. S. (2003). Social capital in the creation of human capital. In Halsey A., Lauder H., Brown P., & Wells A. S. (Eds.), *Education: Culture, Economy, Society* (pp. 80–95). Oxford: Oxford University Press.

Coleman, P. T. (2003). Characteristics of protracted, intractable conflict: Toward the development of a metaframework. *Peace and Conflict: Journal of Peace Psychology, 9*(1): 1–37.

Cooper, J. R. (1998). A multidimensional approach to the adoption of innovation. *Management Decision, 36*(8): 493–502.

Corning, P. A. (2002). The re-emergence of "emergence": A venerable concept in search of a theory. *Complexity, 7*(6): 18–30.

Csikszentmihalyi, M. (1997): Creativity. *Flow and the psychology of discovery and intention.* New York: Harper Perennial.

Davis, G. A. (1993, April). Personalities of creative people. *R&D Innovator, 2*(4). Retrieved November 11, 2010, from http://www.winstonbrill.com/bril001/html/article_index/articles/1–50/article34_body.html.

De Bono, E. (1990). *Lateral thinking: Creativity step by step.* New York: Harper & Row.

Dees, J. G. (1998, October 31). The meaning of social entrepreneurship. *Kauffman Center for Entrepreneurial Leadership.* Retrieved November 11, 2010, from http://www.fntc.info/files/documents/The%20meaning%20of%20Social%20Entreneurship.pdf.

Degenne, A., & Forsé, M. (1999). *Introducing social networks.* London: Sage Publications.

De Rosnay, J. (1997, February 17). Homeostasis. *Principia Cybernetica Web.* Retrieved November 11, 2010, from http://pespmc1.vub.ac.be/HOMEOSTA.html.

De Tocqueville, A. (2003). *Democracy in America and two essays on America.* New York: Penguin Books.

Deutsch, M. (1973). *The resolution of conflict: Constructive and destructive processes.* New Haven, Connecticut: Yale University Press.

Dolan, M., & Fullam, R. (2007). Empathy, antisocial behaviour and personality pathology. In Farrow, T. F. D., & Woodruff, P.W.R. (Eds.), *Empathy in Mental Illness* (pp. 33–48). New York: Cambridge University Press.

Drayton, W. (2002). The citizen sector: Becoming as entrepreneurial and competitive as business. *California Management Review, 44*(3): 120–132.

Drayton, W. (2004). Needed: A new social financial services industry. *Alliance,* March 2004. Available at http://www.alliancemagazine.org/en/content/needed-a-new-social-financial-services-industry.

Drayton, W. (2005). Where the real power lies. *Alliance, 10*(1): 29–30.

Drayton, W. (2009). Social entrepreneurs don't want to help. They want to change the world. Interview. *Focus, 12*(2): 53–57.

Drayton, W., & Budinich, V. (2010, February 2). Get ready to be a changemaker. *Harvard Business Review, The Conversation Blogs.* Retrieved November 11, 2010, from http://blogs.hbr.org/cs/2010/02/are_you_ready_to_be_a_changema.html.

Drucker, P. F. (1985). *Innovation and entrepreneurship.* New York: Harper Business.

Drucker, P. F. (2001). *Management challenges for the 21st century.* New York: Harper Business.

Dubakov, M. (2009, March 23). Simple rules, complex systems and software development. *Edge of Chaos.* Retrieved November 11, 2010, from http://www.targetprocess.com/blog/2009/03/simple-rules-complex-systems-and.html.

Duncan, J. W. (1999). *Small worlds: The dynamic of networks between order and randomness.* Princeton: Princeton University Press.

Duncan, J. W. (2003). *Six degrees: The science of a connected age.* New York: W. W. Norton & Co.

Durkheim, E. (1984). *The division of labor in the society.* New York: The Free Press.

Dweck, C. S. (2000). *Self-Theories: Their role in motivation, personality, and development.* Philadelphia: Psychology Press.

Dweck, C. S. (2006). *Mindset: The new psychology of success.* New York: Random House.

Eck, D. L. (2001). *A New Religious America: How a Christian Country Has Now Become the World's Most Religiously Diverse Nation.* San Francisco: Harper Collins Publishers.

Edwards, J., Cheers, B., & Graham. L. (2003). Social change and social capital in Australia: A solution for contemporary problems? *Health Sociology Review, 12*(1): 68–85.

Elkington, J., & Hartigan, P. (2008). *The power of unreasonable people.* Boston: Harvard Business Press.

Ellison, N. B., Steinfield, C., & Lampe, C. (2007). The benefits of Facebook "friends:" Social capital and college students' use of online social network sites. *Journal of Computer-Mediated Communication, 12*(4): article 1. Retrieved November 11, 2010, from http://jcmc.indiana.edu/vol12/issue4/ellison.html.

Érdi, P. (2008). *Complexity explained.* Berlin: Springer.

Farley, J. E. (2002). *Sociology.* Englewood Cliffs: Prentice Hall.

Ferrari, F. P., & Gallese, V. (2007). Mirror neurons and intersubjectivity. In Braten, S. (Ed.), *On being moved: From mirror neurons to empathy* (pp. 73–88). Philadelphia, Pennsylvania: John Benjamins Publishing Co.

Festinger, L. (1957). *A theory of cognitive dissonance.* Stanford, California: Stanford University Press.

Festinger, L., Riecken, H. W., & Schachter, S. (2009). *When prophecy fails.* London: Pinter & Martin.

Fiedler, E. E. (1964). A contingency model of leadership effectiveness. In: L. Berkowitz (Ed.), *Advances in experimental social psychology, vi*: 149–190. New York: Academic Press.

Field, J. (2008). *Social capital.* London: Routledge.

Fisher, L. (2009). *The perfect swarm: The science of complexity in everyday life.* New York: Basic Books.

Florida, R. (2002). *The rise of the creative class.* New York: Basic Books.

Fukuyama, F. (1996). *Trust: The social virtues and the creation of prosperity.* New York: A Free Press Paperbacks.

Garnier, S., Tâche, F., Combe, M., Grimal, A., & Theraulaz, G. (2007). Alice in pheromone land: An experimental setup for the study of ant-like robots. Proceedings of the 2007 IEEE Swarm Intelligence Symposium held on 1–5 April 2007 (pp. 37–44). Retrieved November 11, 2010, from http://138.100.21.254/lari/apuntes/papers/garnier07.pdf.

Gartner, W. B. (1998). Who is an entrepreneur? is the wrong question. *Entrepreneurship Theory Practice, 13*(4): 47–68.

Gendron, G. (1996). Flashes of genius. Interview with Peter Drucker. *Inc. Magazine, 18*(7): 30–39.

Gentile, M. C. (2002). *Social impact management and social enterprise: Two sides of the same coin or totally different currency.* New York: Aspen Institute for Social Innovation in Business. Retrieved November 11, 2010, from www.aspeninstitute.org/sites/default/files/content/docs/business%20and%20society%20program/SOCIMPACTSOCENT.PDF.

Gifford, S. (2005). Risk and uncertainty. In Acs, Z. J., & Audretsch, D. B. (Eds.), *Handbook of Entrepreneurship Research* (pp. 37–54). New York: Springer.

Gladwell, M. (2002). *The tipping point: How little things can make a big difference.* Boston: Back Bay Books.

Goldstein, J. (1999). Emergence as a construct: History and issues. *Emergence. A Journal of Complexity Issues in Organizations and Management, 1*(1): 49–72.

Gordon, M. (2005). *Roots of empathy: Changing the world child by child.* Toronto: Thomas Allen Publishers.

Granovetter, M. S. (1973). The strength of weak ties. *The American Journal of Sociology, 78*(6): 1360–1380.

Granovetter, M. S. (1983). The strength of weak ties: A network theory revisited. *Sociological Theory, 1*(1): 201–233.

Granovetter, M. S. (1985). Economic Action and Social Structure: The Problem of Embeddedness. *The American Journal of Sociology, 91*(3): 481–510.

Granovetter, M. S. (1995). *Getting a job: A study of contacts and careers.* Chicago: University of Chicago Press.

Grootaert, C., Narayan, D., Jones, V. N., & Woolcock, M. (2004). *Measuring social capital: An integrated questionnaire.* Washington, D.C.: World Bank Publications.

Hammonds, K. H. (2005, January 1). A lever long enough to move the world. *Fast Company, 90.* Retrieved November 11, 2010, from http://www.fastcompany.com/magazine/90/open_ashoka.html.

Hardt, M., & Negri, A. (2004). *Multitude: War and democracy in the age of empire.* New York: The Penguin Press.

Henton, D., Melville, J., & Walesh, K. (1997). The age of the civic entrepreneur: Restoring civil society and building economic community. *National Civic Review, 86*(2): 149–156.

Herman, R. P. (2010). *The HIP, human impact + profit investor.* Hoboken, New Jersey: John Wiley & Sons, Inc.

Hersey, P. H, Blanchard, K. H., & Johnson, D. E. (2001). *Management of organizational behavior.* Upper Saddle River, New Jersey: Prentice Hall.

Hock, D. W. (2000). *Birth of the chaordic age.* San Francisco: Berrett-Koehler Publishers.

Holland, J. H. (1999). *Emergence: From chaos to order.* Cambridge, Massachusetts: Perseus Books.

Hsu, C. (2005, October 31). Entrepreneur for social change. *US News & World report.* Retrieved November 11, 2010, from http://www.usnews.com/usnews/news/articles/051031/31drayton.htm.

Iacoboni, M. (2009). Imitation, empathy, and mirror neurons. *Annual Review of Psychology, 60*: 653–670.

Jervis, R. (1998). *System effects: Complexity in political and social life.* Princeton, New Jersey: Princeton University Press.

Johnson, N. (2009). *Simply complexity: A clear guide to complexity theory.* Oxford: One World.

Johnson, S. (2001). *Emergence: The connected lives of ants, brains, cities and software.* New York: Simon & Schuster.

Jordan, K., Hauser, J., & Foster, S. (2003, August 4). The augmented social network: Building identity and trust into the next-generation Internet. *First Monday, Peer-reviewed Journal of the Internet, 8*(8). Retrieved November 11, 2010, from http://pear.accc.uic.edu/htbin/cgiwrap/bin/ojs/index.php/fm/article/viewArticle/1068.

Judge, T. A., & Piccolo, R. F. (2004). Transformational and transactional leadership: A meta-analytic test of their relative validity. *Journal of Applied Psychology, 89*(5): 755–768.

Kao, R. W. Y. (2006). Defining entrepreneurship: Past, present and ?. *Creativity and Innovation Management, 2*(1): 69–70.

Kauffman, S. (1995). *At home in the universe: The search for laws of the self-organization and complexity.* Oxford: Oxford University Press.

Kaukiainen, A., Björkqvist, K., Lagerspetz, K., Österman, K., Salmivalli, C., Rothberg, S., et al. (1999). The relationships between social intelligence, empathy, and three types of aggression. *Aggressive Behavior, 25*(2): 81–89.

Kenney, P. (2001). Framing, political opportunities, and civic mobilization in the eastern European revolutions: A case study of Poland's freedom and peace movement. *Mobilization, The International Journal of Research and Theory about Social Movements, Protest, and Contentious Politics, 6*(2): 193–210.

Kenney, P. (2002). *A carnival of revolution: Central Europe 1989.* Princeton, New Jersey: Princeton University Press.

Kotter, J. (1995). Leading change: Why transformation efforts fail. *Harvard Business Review, March-April:* 59–67. Retrieved November 11, 2010, from http://lighthouseconsultants.co.uk/wp-content/uploads/2010/08/Kotter-Leading-Change-Why-transformation-efforts-fail.pdf.

Kouzes, J., & Posner, B. (2008). *The leadership challenge.* San Francisco: Jossey Bass.

Kuper, L. (2006). *Ethics – The Leadership Edge.* Cape Town: Zebra Press.

Kramer, M. R. (2005). *Measuring innovation: Evaluation in the field of social entrepreneurship.* The Skoll Foundation. Retrieved November 11, 2010, from http://www.foundationstrategy.com/documents/Measuring%20Innovation.pdf.

Kriesberg, L. (1998). Intractable conflicts. In E. Weiner, (Ed.), *The handbook of interethnic coexistence* (pp. 332–342). New York: Continuum International Publishing Group.

Krueger, N. F., Jr. (2005). The cognitive psychology of entrepreneurship. In Acs, Z. J., & Audretsch, D. B. (Eds.), *Handbook of Entrepreneurship Research* (pp. 105–140). New York: Springer.

Lederach, J. P. (1996). *Preparing for peace: Conflict transformation across cultures.* Syracuse, New York: Syracuse University Press.

Lederach, J. P. (2003). *The little book of conflict transformation.* Intercourse, Pennsylvania: Good Books.

Locke, E. A., & Baum, J. R. (2007). *Entrepreneurial motivation.* In Baum, J. R., Frese, M., & Baron, R. A. (Eds.), *The Psychology of Entrepreneurship* (pp. 93–111). New York: Psychology Press.

Latané, B. (1981). The psychology of social impact. *American Psychologist,* 36(4): 343–356.

Latané, B., Liu, J., Nowak, A., Bonevento, M., & Zheng, L. (1995). Distance matters: Physical space and social influence. *Personality and Social Psychology Bulletin,* 21(8): 795–805.

Leadbeater, C. (1997). *The rise of the social entrepreneur.* London: Demos.

Lewenstein, M., Nowak, A., & Latané, B. (1993). Statistical mechanics of social impact. *Physical Review,* A, 45(2): 763–776.

Lewin, K. (2004). *Resolving social conflicts: Field theory in social science.* Washington D.C.: American Psychological Association.

Lewin, K., Lippitt, R., & White, R. K. (1939). Patterns of aggressive behavior in experimentally created "social climates." *Journal of Social Psychology,* 10: 271–299.

Light, P. C. (2006). Reshaping social entrepreneurship. *Stanford Social Innovation Review,* 4: 47–51. Retrieved November 11, 2010, from http://wagner.nyu.edu// performance/files/ReshapingSE.pdf.

Light, P. C. (2008). *The search for social entrepreneurship.* Washington D.C.: Brookings Institution Press.

Lin, N. (2001). Building a network theory of social capital. In Lin, N., Cook, K., & Burt, R. S. (Eds.), *Social capital: Theory and Research* (pp. 3–29). New York: Aldine de Gruyter.

Livesay, H. C. (1982). Entrepreneurial history. In Kent, C. A, Sexton, D. L., & Vesper, K. H. (Eds.), *Encyclopedia of Entrepreneurship* (pp. 7–19). Englewood Cliffs: Prentice Hall, Inc.

Lozano, M., Morillo, P., Lewis, D., Reiners, D., & Cruz-Neira, C. (2007). A distributed framework for scalable large-scale crowd simulation. *Lecture Notes in Computer Science* (LNCS), 4563/2007: 111–121.

Lumpkin, G. T. (2007). Intrapreneurship and innovation. In Baum, J. R., Frese, M., & Baron, R. A. (Eds.), *The psychology of entrepreneurship* (pp. 237–263). New York: Psychology Press.

Macionis, J. J. (2010). *Sociology.* Upper Saddle River, New Jersey: Prentice Hall.

Mapes, J. J. (2003). *Quantum leap thinking.* Naperville, Illinois: Sourcebooks, Inc.

Martin, M. (2007). Intervening at the inflection point. UBS Philanthropy Services Viewpoints, Retrieved November 11, 2010, from http://www.acumenfund.org/ uploads/assets/documents/Viewpoints%202007%20-%20UBS_3GnYUiZ5.pdf.

Martin, R. L., & Osberg, S. (2007). Social entrepreneurship: The case for definition. *Stanford Social Innovation Review, Spring 2007:* 29–39.

Martindale, C. (2004). Biological bases of creativity. In Sternberg, R. J. (Ed.), *Handbook of Creativity* (pp. 137–152). Cambridge, UK: Cambridge University Press.

Maskell, P. (2000). Social capital, innovation, and competitiveness. In Baron S., Field J., & Schuller, T. (Eds.)*Social Capital: Critical Perspective* (pp. 111–123). New York: Oxford University Press.

McClelland, D. C. (1967). *The achieving society.* New York: The Free Press.

McLaughlin, B. (2008). Emergence and supervenience. In Bedau, M. A. & Humphreys, P. (Eds.), *Emergence: Contemporary Readings in Philosophy and Science* (2008) (pp. 81–97). Cambridge, Massachusetts: A Bradford Book.

McNamara, C. (2010). *Field guide to leadership and supervision in business.* Minneapolis: Authenticity Consulting, LLC.

Mair, J., & Martí, I. (2006). Social entrepreneurship research: A source of explanation, prediction, and delight. *Journal of World Business, 41:* 36–44.

Mair, J., Robinson, J., & Hockerts, K. (2006). Introduction. In J. Mair, J. Robinson, & K. Hockerts (Eds.), *Social Entrepreneurship* (pp. 1–13). New York: Palgrave MacMillan.

Martin, R. L., & Osberg, S. (2007). Social entrepreneurship: The case for definition. *Stanford Social Innovation Review, Spring 2007:* 29–39.

McGoldrick, M., & Gerson, R. (1985). *Genograms in family assessment.* New York: W.W. Norton & Co.

Meinhardt, H. (2003). *The algorithmic beauty in sea shells.* Berlin, Germany: Springer Verlag.

Miall, H. (2004). *Conflict transformation: A multi-dimensional task.* Berghof Handbook for Conflict Transformation. Retrieved November 11, 2010, from http://kar.kent.ac.uk/289/1/miall_handbook.pdf.

Milgram, S. (1967). The small world problem. *Psychology Today, 2:* 60–67.

Milloy, J. S. (2006). *A national crime.* Winnipeg: The University of Manitoba Press.

Mischel, W. (1969). Continuity and change in personality. *American Psychologist, 24*(11): 1012–1018.

Mischel, W. (1973). Toward a cognitive social learning reconceptualization of personality. *Psychological Review, 80*(4): 252–283.

Mischel, W., & Shoda, Y. (1995). A cognitive-affective system theory of personality: Reconceptualizing situations, dispositions, dynamics, and invariance in personality structure. *Psychological Review, 102*(2): 246–268.

Mulgan, G., Tucker, S., Ali R., & Sanders B. (2008). Social innovation: What it is, why it matters and how it can be accelerated. *Skoll Center for Social Entrepreneurship working paper.* Retrieved November 11, 2010, from http://www.youngfoundation.org/files/images/03_07_What_it_is__SAID_.pdf.

Mumford, M. D. (2002). Social innovation: Ten cases from Benjamin Franklin. *Creativity Research Journal, 14*(2): 253–266.

Nakagaki, T., Yamada, H., & Toth, A. (2000). Intelligence: Maze-solving by an amoeboid organism. *Nature, 407*(6803): 470–470.

Neace, M. B. (1999). Entrepreneurs in emerging economies: Creating trust, social capital, and civil society. *The ANNALS of the American Academy of Political and Social Science, 565*(1): 148–161.

Nicholls, A. Introduction. In Nicholls, A. (Ed), *Social Entrepreneurship: New Models of Sustainable Change* (pp. 1–35). New York: Oxford University Press.

Nicholls, A., & Cho, A. (2008). Social entrepreneurship: The structuration of the field. In Nicholls, A. (Ed), *Social Entrepreneurship: New Models of Sustainable Change* (pp. 99–118). New York: Oxford University Press.

Noble, T. (2000). *Social theory and social change.* New York: Palgrave.

Northouse, P. G. (2010). *Leadership: Theory and practice.* Los Angeles: Sage.

Nowak A. (2004). Dynamical minimalism: Why less is more in psychology. *Personality and Social Psychology Review, 8*(2): 183–193.

Nowak, A., Deutsch, M., Bartkowski, W., & Solomon, S. (2010). From crude law to civil relations: The dynamics and potential resolution of intractable conflict. *Peace and Conflict, 16*: 189–209.

Nowak A., & Lewenstein, M. (1994). Dynamical systems: A tool for social psychology? In Vallacher, R., & Nowak, A. (Eds.), *Dynamical Systems in Social Psychology* (pp. 17–53). Burlington, Massachusetts: Academic Press.

Nowak, A., Szamrej, J., & Latané, B. (1990). From private attitude to public opinion: A dynamic theory of social impact. *Psychological Review, 97*(3): 362–376.

Nowak, A., & Vallacher, R. R. (1998a). *Dynamical Social Psychology.* New York: The Guildford Press.

Nowak, A., & Vallacher, R. R. (1998b). Toward computational social psychology: Cellular automata and neural network models of interpersonal dynamics. In S. J. Read & L. C. Miller (Eds.), *Connectionist models of social reasoning and social behavior*, Mahwah, NJ: (pp. 277–311) Erlbaum.

Nowak, A., & Vallacher, R. R. (2000). Societal transition: Toward a dynamical model of social change. In Wosinska, W., Cialdini, R. B., Barrett, D. W., & Reykowski, J. (Eds.), *The Practice of Social Influence in Multiple Cultures* (pp. 130–149). Mahwah, New Jersey: Lawrence Erlbaum Associates.

Nowak, A., & Vallacher, R. R. (2005). Information and influence in the construction of shared reality. *IEEE: Intelligent Systems, 1*: 90–93.

Parsons, T. (1972). Research with human subjects and the "professional complex." In Freund, P. A. (Ed.), *Experimentation with Human Subjects* (pp. 116–151).

Pascale, R., Sternin, J., & Sternin, M. (2010). *The power of positive deviance: How unlikely innovators solve the world's toughest problems.* Boston: Harvard Business Press.

Perroux, F. (1950). Economic space: Theory and application. *Quarterly Journal of Economics, 64*(1): 89–104.

Petro, N. N. (2001). Creating social capital in Russia: The Novgorod model. *World Development, 29*(2): 229–244.

Piven, F. F. (2008). Can power from below change the world? *American Sociological Review, 73*(1): 1–14.

Port, R., & van Gelder, T. J. (1995). It's About Time: An Overview of the Dynamical Approach to Cognition. In Port, R., & van Gelder, T. J. (Eds.), *Mind as Motion: Explorations in the Dynamics of Cognition.* Cambridge MA: MIT Press.

Praszkier, R, Nowak, A., & Zablocka-Bursa, A. (2009). Social capital built by social entrepreneurship and the specific personality traits that facilitate the process. *Psychologia Spoleczna, 4*(10–12): 42–54.

Praszkier, R., Nowak, A., & Coleman, P. (2010). Social entrepreneurship and constructive change: The wisdom of circumventing conflict. *Peace and Conflict: Journal of Peace Psychology, 16*(2): 153–174.

Putnam, R. D. (1993). The prosperous community: Social capital and public life. *The American Prospect, 13*: 35–42.

Putnam, R. D. (1996). Who killed civic America? *Prospect, 6*: 66–72.

Putnam, R. D. (2000). *Bowling alone: The collapse and revival of American community.* New York: Simon and Shuster.

Putnam, R. D., & Gross, K. A. (2002). Introduction. In Putnam, R. D. (Ed.), *Democracies in Flux* (pp. 3–19). New York: Oxford University Press.

Rauch, A., & Frese, M. (2007). Born to be an entrepreneur? Revisiting the personality approach to entrepreneurship. In Baum, J. R., Frese, M., & Baron, R. A. (Eds.), *The Psychology of Entrepreneurship* (pp. 41–65). New York: Psychology Press.

Reynolds, C. W. (1987). Flocks, herds, and schools: A distributed behavioral model. *Computer Graphics*, 21(4): 25–34.

Roberts, D., & Woods, C. (2005). Changing the world on a shoestring: The concept of social entrepreneurship. *Business Review, Autumn 2005*: 45–51. Retrieved November 11, 2010, from http://www.uabr.auckland.ac.nz/files/articles/Volume11/v11i1-asd.pdf.

Rogers, E. M. (2003). *Diffusion of innovations.* New York: The Free Press.

Roper, J., & Cheney, G. (2005). Leadership, learning and human resource management: The meanings of social entrepreneurship today. *Corporate Governance*, 5(3): 95–104.

Rotter, J. B. (1996). Generalized expectancies for internal versus external control of reinforcement. *Psychological Monographs*, 80(1): 1–28.

Runco, M. A. (2007). *Creativity. Theories and themes: Research, development and practice.* Burlington: Elsevier Academic Press.

Sakurai, M. (2008, July). Social entrepreneurs and resource mobilization: The role of social capital. Paper presented at The Third Sector and Sustainable Social Change: New Frontiers for Research held 9 July – 12 July 2008 in Barcelona.

Sawyer, R. K. (2007). *Social emergence: Societies as complex systems.* Cambridge: Cambridge University Press.

Schumpeter, J. A. (1994). *Capitalism, socialism and democracy.* New York: Routledge.

Schuster, H. G. (1995). *Deterministic chaos.* Weinheim, Germany: Wiley-VCH.

Sen, P. (2007). Ashoka's big idea: Transforming the world through social entrepreneurship. *Futures*, 39(5): 534–553.

Selecting Leading Social Entrepreneurs. (2007). Arlington: Ashoka.

Senge, P. M. (1999). *The dance of change: The challenges to sustaining momentum in learning organizations.* New York: Doubleday.

Senge, P., Kleiner, A., Roberts, C., Ross, R., Roth, G., & Smith, B. (1999). *The dance of change.* New York: Currency Doubleday.

Shane, S., & Venkataraman, S. (2000). The promise of entrepreneurship as a field of research. *Academy of Management Review*, 25(1): 217–226.

Smith, A., James, C., Jones, R., Langston, P., Lester, E., & Drury, J. (2009). Modelling contra-flow in crowd dynamics DEM simulation. *Safety Science*, 47(3), 385–404.

Smith, E. R., & Mackie, D. M. (1995). *Social psychology.* New York: Worth Publishers.

Sternberg, R. J., & Lubart, T. I. (2004). The concept of creativity: Prospects and paradigms. In Sternberg, R. J. (Ed.), *Handbook of Creativity* (pp. 3–15). Cambridge, UK: Cambridge University Press.

Sternin, J. (2002). Positive deviance: A new paradigm for addressing today's problems today. *The Journal of Corporate Citizenship*, 5: 57–62.

Steyaert, C., & Hjorth, D. (2006). Introduction: What is social entrepreneurship? In Steyaert, C., & D. Hjorth (Eds.), *Entrepreneurship as Social Change* (pp. 1–18). Cheltenham: Edward Elgar Publishing Ltd.

Strogatz, S. (2003). *Sync: How order emerges from chaos in the universe, nature, and daily life*. New York: Hyperion.

Sztompka, P. (1993). *The sociology of social change*. Oxford: Blackwell Publishers.

Thornton, P. (1999). The sociology of entrepreneurship. *Annual Review of Sociology*, 25: 19–46.

Vago, S. (2004). *Social change*. New Jersey: Pearson Prentice Hall.

Vallacher, R. R., Coleman, P. T., Nowak, A., & Bui-Wrzosinska, L. (2010). Rethinking intractable conflict: The perspective of dynamical systems. *American Psychologist*, 65(4): 262–278.

Vallacher, R. R., & Nowak, A. (2007). Dynamical social psychology: Finding order in the flow of human experience. In Kruglanski, A. W., & Higgins, E. T. (Eds.), *Social Psychology: Handbook of Basic Principles* (pp. 734–758). New York: Guildford Publications.

Vallacher, R. R., Read, S. J., & Nowak, A. (2002). The dynamical perspective in personality and social psychology. *Personality and Social Psychology Review*, 6(4): 264–273.

Vallerand, R. J. (2008). On the psychology of passion: In search of what makes people's lives most worth living. *Canadian Psychology*, 49: 1–13.

Villani, A. (2010). Romanticizing social entrepreneurship. *Beyond Profit*, Retrieved November 11, 2010, from http://beyondprofit.com/romanticizing-social-entrepreneurship/.

Vittori, K, Talbot, G., Gautrais, J., Fourcassié, V., Araújo A. F. R., & Theraulaz, G. (2006). Path efficiency of ant foraging trails in an artificial network. *Journal of Theoretical Biology*, 239(4): 507–515.

Uslaner, E. (1998). Social capital, television, and the "mean world": Trust, optimism, and civic participation. *Political Psychology, Special Issue: Psychological Approaches to Social Capital*, 19(3): 441–467.

Waddock, S. A., & Post, J. E. (1991). Social entrepreneurship and catalytic change. *Public Administration Review*, 51(5): 393–401.

Waldrop, M. M. (1992). *Complexity: The emerging science at the edge of order and chaos*. New York: Simon & Schuster.

Wasserman, S., & Faust, K. (1994). *Social network analysis: Methods and applications*. Cambridge: Cambridge University Press.

Watts, D. J. (2003). *Six degrees: The science of a connected age*. New York: W. W. Norton & Company.

Watts, D. J., Dodds, P. S., & Newman, M. E. J. (2002). Identity and search in social networks. *Science*, 296(5571): 1302–1305.

Wolfram S. (2002). *A new kind of science*. Champlain, Illinois: Wolfram Media, Inc.

Woolcock, M., & Narayan, D. (2000). Social capital: Implications for development: Theory, research, and policy. *The World Bank Research Observer*, 15(2): 225–249.

Woolcock, M. (1998). Social capital and economic development: Toward a theoretical synthesis and policy framework. *Theory and Society*, 27(2): 151–208.

INDEX

225